Threats to Our Liberty & Survival

William James Moore

"Knowledge will forever govern ignorance, and a people who mean to be their own Governors, must arm themselves with the power knowledge gives." — James Madison (1751 – 1836)

"To sit back hoping that someday, someway, someone will make things right is to go on feeding the crocodile, hoping he will eat you last — but eat you he will." — Ronald Reagan (1911-2004)

"In the End, we will remember not the words of our enemies, but the silence of our friends." — Martin Luther King, Jr. (1929-1968)

"Victory at all costs, victory in spite of all terror, victory however long and hard the road may be; for without victory, there is no survival." — Winston Churchill (1874-1965)

"A free people ought not only to be armed and disciplined, but they should have sufficient arms and ammunition to maintain a status of independence from any who might attempt to abuse them, which would include their own government." — George Washington (1732-1799)

= = =

Dedication

To Ann, my wife; Jamie, our daughter; Ryan, our son; and Matthew, our grandson. My most treasured blessings.

With special gratefulness that Ryan and Stanna blessed our families with Matthew . . . and in the hope that his unalienable rights, and those of other present and future generations of Americans, are forever secured . . . and that among these being . . . *Life, Liberty and the Pursuit of Happiness.*

"In the beginning God created the heaven and the earth."
— Genesis 1:1

"God grant me the . . .
Serenity to accept the things I cannot change;
Courage to change the things I can; and
Wisdom to know the difference."

— Reinhold Niebuhr (1892–1971)

= = =

"Extremes to the right and to the left of any political dispute are always wrong." — Dwight D. Eisenhower (1890-1969)

"Let us not seek the Republican answer or the Democratic answer, but the right answer. Let us not seek to fix the blame for the past. Let us accept our own responsibility for the future." — John F. Kennedy

"Learn from yesterday, live for today, hope for tomorrow. The important thing is not to stop questioning." — Albert Einstein

"Our lives begin to end the day we become silent about things that matter." — Plato

"Those who stand for nothing fall for anything."
— Alexander Hamilton

Contents

Contents – *(Continued)*

Contents – *(Continued)*

Contents – *(Continued)*

= = =

"I am only one, but still I am one. I cannot do everything, but still I can do something; and because I cannot do everything, I will not refuse to do something that I can do." –Helen Keller

"Memories of our lives, of our works and our deeds will continue in others." – Rosa Parks

Threats to Our Liberty & Survival

Fear ~ Ignorance ~ Apathy ~ Complacency ~ Denial ~ Greed
IRS ~ Uncontrolled Immigration ~ Pandemics ~ CFPB
Unprotected U.S. English Language ~ Terrorism
National Debt ~ Dependency ~ Dictatorship
Racism ~ Political Correctness ~ War
Uncontrolled Fed Gov't Agencies
Radical/Militant Islam
Lost U.S. Culture ~ Cyber-Attacks
Radical Liberalism ~ Radical Conservatism
Deserve & Entitled vs Opportunity ~ Unions
Biased News Media ~ Nuclear Disaster ~ Tyranny
Unsecured U.S. Borders ~ Military Industrial Complex
Expanding/Over-reaching/Intrusive Federal Government

William James Moore

"There's no way to be a perfect mother and a million ways to be a good one." – Jill Churchill

"Biology is the least of what makes someone a mother."
                                                    –Oprah Winfrey

"In a child's eyes, a mother is a goddess. She can be glorious or terrible, benevolent or filled with wrath, but she commands love either way. I am convinced that this is the greatest power in the universe." – N.K. Jemisin

"A mom forgives us all our faults, not to mention one or two we don't even have." –Robert Brault

"The best years of your life are the ones in which you decide your problems are your own. You do not blame them on your mother, the ecology, or the president. You realize that you control your own destiny." –Albert Ellis

In Remembrance of Our Mothers

To my mother, Hazel; and Ann's mother, Lillie. Tremendously proud and family-dedicated daughters, sisters, wives, mothers, grandmothers, and great-grandmothers. True friends to a countless and very fortunate many. Wanting so much for their children; expecting of them no more than their very best. Never-failing sources of unconditional love. Exceptionally-special ladies; worthy of much more honor and respect than expected, or received. Once young girls with the worries and aspirations of their respective youth. Both, born into terribly tough economic circumstances; tragically widowed as young mothers; beautiful and highly principled women of great courage, inner-strength, gratitude, and self-sacrifice. Each, a survivor of the Great Depression (the deepest, longest-lasting, and most wide-spread economic depression of the 20th Century). Always quick to extend respect, consideration, and a helping-hand to others in need. While never applying to themselves, attitudes of deserve, entitled, and victim. Freely giving so very much of themselves—too often taken for granted—and owed so much by so many. Both, while humbly in touch with their own human-shortcomings, deeply spiritual and life-long examples of unfailing faith and trust in the God of their personal understanding. Each—beyond description—so very dearly loved, cherished, and now so terribly missed—always.

= = =

"This is what we do, my mother's life said. We find ourselves in the sacrifices we make."
                                                    – Cammie McGovern

"There's no better cure for the fear of taking after one's father, than not to know who he is." — Andre Gide

"I never had a speech from my father 'this is what you must do or shouldn't do' but I just learned to be led by example. My father wasn't perfect." — Adam Sandler

"Letting go means to come to the realization that some people are a part of your history, but not a part of your destiny."
— Steve Maraboli

"Any man can be a father. It takes someone special to be a dad."
— Author Unknown

"We never get over our fathers, and we're not required to."
—Martin Sheen

In Remembrance of Our Fathers

To my natural father, James; and Ann's natural father, Robert. Both tragically losing their lives while relatively young men — before their children gaining memory of them. To Ann's stepfather, George, and my stepfather, Ernest. To my later stepfather, Marvin, joining our family at a time when our children were especially in need of another grandpa. Each, a once young boy with curiosity and awe, born into daunting economic circumstances of the Great Depression — beyond true understanding of later generations. Like so many others of that time, each, along with their families, often faced with unrelenting and life-consuming focus on basic survival. Challenged by limited education and scarce, often extremely-hazardous and physically-demanding job opportunities. The how-to as husbands, fathers, and grandfathers, coming from learn-as-you-go — with strengths, weaknesses, failures, and successes, not always equally experienced within family. Men whose legacies may, for some, continue for a time to be a work-in-progress, and include a mix of earned and unearned respect, credit, blame, and scorn. For others, a memory limited only to that passed on by others. To yet others, they were once, and will remain, regardless of their respective often-challenging ways — loved, longed-for, and now missed, always.

= = =

"There is wisdom in every man, in every father, in your father. And that's true whether you love him or despise him." — Joe Kita

"I know why families were created with all their imperfections. They humanize you. They are made to make you forget yourself occasionally, so that the beautiful balance of life is not destroyed."

— Anais Nin

"We all have our strengths and our failings. *— Hannah Simone*

"Enjoy the little things, for one day you may look back and realize they were the big things." *— Robert Brault*

"Sometimes you will never know the value of a moment until it becomes a memory." *— Dr. Seuss*

"God gave us memory so that we might have roses in December."

— J.M. Barrie

Special Appreciation

To Bill L. and Bob L., my Brothers. Sources of special love, bonds, experiences, and memories—shared only by brothers.

To Mike H. A most special, loving, gifted, hardworking, devoted, and honorable man—who will always be, "Family."

To *(in last-name alphabetical order)* my sisters-in-law and brothers-in-law: Theresa D., Kay F., David F., Jim G., Jeani G., Beverly L., Jewel L., Linda L., Mary R., and John R.

To our Grandparents, Aunts, Uncles, Cousins, Nieces, and Nephews. To all "Family"—mentioned and not mentioned herein—with whom my Wife Ann and I have been, or may yet be, privileged to share treasured relationships and priceless memories.

= = =

"A family is a bunch of people who keep confusing you with someone you were as a kid." — Robert Brault

"Remember, we all stumble, every one of us. That's why it's a comfort to go hand in hand." — Emily Kimbrough

"Children begin by loving their parents; as they grow older they judge them; sometimes they forgive them." –Oscar Wilde

"Other things may change us, but we start and end with family."
— Anthony Brandt

Recognition

I have at times expressed to others my doubts of ever having an "original thought." While said in humor — such is possibly a bit closer to reality. On same note, it is also most doubtful that any book has ever been written "totally alone." Certainly, this one was not. For the content of this book was not only drawn from my personal life experiences, but also from that of countless known and unknown others. To whom I wish to express my sincere appreciation for the enlightenment shared and for the access to much worthwhile information.

= = =

"As we express our gratitude, we must never forget that the highest appreciation is not to utter words, but to live by them."
— John F. Kennedy

"Those who expect to reap the blessings of freedom, must, like men, undergo the fatigue of supporting it." —Thomas Paine

"Government exists to protect us from each other. Where government has gone beyond its limits is in deciding to protect us from ourselves." — Ronald Reagan

"The welfare of our country is the great object to which our cares and efforts ought to be directed." — George Washington, 01/09/1790

"Ask not what your country can do for you; ask what you can do for your country." — John F. Kennedy

Introduction

"... that this nation, under God, shall have a new birth of freedom — and that government of the people, by the people, and for the people, shall not perish from the earth." — Abraham Lincoln

Dear Reader,

Throughout our world, rapidly growing numbers of us now have virtually "anytime and anywhere" access to an absolutely overwhelming vastness of information and reading options. But, regardless of how compelling our seemingly unlimited choices may be, even the longest human-lifespan can accommodate exploration of only a very minuscule fraction thereof. For example, in addition to the nearly 130 million books Google estimates to have been published in all of modern history, millions of new titles and editions are being created each year.

And, while the availability of books and many other things can often appear boundless, our "time" is of course unquestionably not. Which makes how we use ours — and that of others — truly important beyond words. Among many realities a number of us unfortunately don't get in touch with until late in life — if ever. With such in mind, it seems fitting and proper that this *Introduction* begin with a few upfront words about "why this book." And, about what it *does* and *does not* include—in exchange for a priceless portion of one's truly limited . . . "blessing of time."

Why this book? Like countless others, my wife Ann and I are deeply concerned, frustrated, angry, and ashamed that our generation is not passing on to our descendants the same great country of liberty and opportunity that was left to us. And, it is our sincere wish, therefore, that *Threats to Our Liberty & Survival* in some positive manner, encourages and supports other nation-wide constructive efforts aimed at righting this terrible wrong. Through lawful (U.S. Constitution-supported) efforts, unrelentingly pursued with proactive focus on:

- Refreshed awareness of, justified pride in, and sincere appreciation for—the many "envy-of-the-world" blessings of our constitutional republic, and the precious liberty/freedom we are so fortunate to enjoy;

- The more-pressing critical threats to—not only our liberty/freedom—but to our ultimate survival as well;

- Our ultimately-inescapable citizen-obligation to present and future generations of Americans, to protect, defend, and preserve this great nation and the unique liberty/freedom it, and only it, provides—so far, that is.

"NOT" Included: (1.) **Information** void of political bias and controversy; (2.) **Content** symbolizing proper sentence structure, punctuation, or other grammar etiquette; and absent of wordiness and repetition; (3.) **Any aim** to compete with or otherwise measure-up to countless other writers and information-sources, past and present; (4.) **Any effort or intent** to abide by or otherwise support the growing expectations (often demands) for political-correctness; and (5.) **Any commitment** not to offend someone. For, countless other available sources address these five wants and needs; and many if not most, do so well beyond my aims and aspirations.

Included: An assortment of facts and opinions, presented in-good-faith through articles and letters by this author on a wide range of topics. Supplemented by letters, quotations, references, and other writings, from other sources. Mostly politically-conservative; some otherwise. Where at times a bit of satire is used to highlight a meant-to-be serious point. Where names and actual experiences have been adjusted, as appropriate and in respect of privacy considerations. Presented with no claim or inference of special knowledge, experience, or insight on any subject, or access to privileged information of any nature. Other than that gained so far from the "university of life."

= = =

A Preview: That we live in an increasingly-dangerous world should certainly not be a news-flash to any of us. Wars, terrorism, tyranny, mass-murder, religious/ethnic persecution, mob-violence, economic chaos, disease, famine, earthquakes, devastating wildfires, volcanism, nuclear reactor accidents, weather disasters, etc. — are but a few examples.

With our high-tech global/mobile communications, ever-expanding internet access, sky-rocketing social-media frenzy, and "constantly-connected" mindset, one would think that a highly-visible and wide-spread **"threat-awareness"** would be a given. Likewise, common sense would suggest that a "threat-awareness" and basic "survival instincts" would in turn result in "widespread alarm" and "unified defensive-actions." At least in response to our nation's more serious and immediate threats. Indisputable threats, such as: the methodical destruction of our United States <u>borders</u>, <u>common language-English</u>, <u>culture</u>, <u>economic system</u>, and <u>middle-class</u>! While our <u>U.S. Constitution</u>, the root guarantee of our liberty/freedom, also undergoes unrelenting assault!

But, unfortunately, common sense does not always exist or prevail. And, the above-cited and other truly serious threats to our liberty and survival are too often overlooked and left unchecked! Ironically, too often the result of our very own self-defeating *ignorance, apathy, complacency, denial, greed,* and *counter-productive fears*! Six potentially self-destructive human characteristics repeated many times throughout this book. Aspects of human behavior that are also magnified and exploited by a constant flow of agenda-driven news headlines, political spin, and propaganda. By the purveyors of "division" and "diversion." Seeking to focus our attention on emotional and fear-promoting phrases and subjects, such as: *inequality, unfairness, discrimination, racism, political-correctness, class-warfare, gun-control, climate-change, the war on women, Black lives matter, the 99 percent versus the 1 percent,* and *various other* distractions and diversions.

All with the aim of dividing us, pitting one group of Americans against another, and otherwise taking our focus and energies away from other much more pressing matters, such as:

- The growing threat of Radical/militant Islam.
- An ever-growing, over-reaching, and continually intrusive federal government.
- Failure to secure our country's borders.
- Failure to protect our common U.S. Language— English.
- Failure to protect and promote our U.S. culture.
- Irresponsible tax and spend policies.
- A rapidly growing and out of control national debt.
- Programs turning the United States into a country of dependents, entitled, and victims.
- Propaganda from the radical political-left, radical political-right, special interest groups, and profit- driven and politically-biased new media.
- Politicians and bureaucracies that put keeping their job, staying in power, and promoting their personal ideologies— all above the best interests of our Country.
- Political-Correctness gone mad.
- Countless other liberty-destroying policies, agendas, practices.

Often we might wish to just "tune it all out!" But, it is to the peril of present and future generations of Americans that we continue to let ourselves be *distracted, misguided,* or *neglectful,* about the above-listed and other very real and present threats to our nation . . . to our liberty and survival. No single story, one book, or lone effort, could ever begin to address them all. And while none should be ignored, it is only common sense that our limited energies and other resources be priority-focused. Directed at those dangers responsibly determined and soundly judged to be the more serious and immediately pressing. It is from such a growing mix that many of the topics in this book were chosen. Selections based solely on the author's personal judgement, and suggestions from family and other concerned individuals. Guided primarily by judgement honed from the "journey and blessings of life."

It is sincerely wished that this book's overall message receive very diverse and wide-spread interest; with truly reader-rewarding and nation-constructive results. And, while applying and crucially important to "all," it is recognized that the politically-conservative nature of much of the information herein may be a speed-bump for some. Especially for those hell-bent to pursue, support, or otherwise be identified with "progressive transformation" of America; the politically-radical left; politically-radical right, or other liberty-destroying agendas. Likewise, this material may be of little to no interest to the terminally closed-minded among us—those intolerant of any view other than their own. As well as to those who—through choice or unpreventable circumstance—fall among the many uninformed, misinformed, or just seemingly unconcerned.

Nevertheless, and regardless of one's background, political persuasion, or other life-circumstances, it is truly hoped that something within these pages helps to encourage, support, and demand much more responsible government from—not only our political leaders—but from ourselves as well.

Resulting in a government much more focused on what is best for our country—on unapologetic patriotism, liberty/freedom, and opportunity. And less on "self-serving," "deserve," "entitled," and "dependency." A unified country unrelentingly dedicated to protecting and preserving our U.S. borders, common language-English, culture, and constitution!

However, in expressing the above, I am reminded that—while *hopes* and *wishes* are crucially important, they are but feelings of expectation and *desire* for a certain thing to happen. And, in order to achieve our goals, we must also have *plans, methods, and means*—and the *ability, willingness*, and *courage* to carry them out. Furthermore, achieving goals under "conditions of uncertainty" also requires *strategies* (hi-level plans). Conditions of uncertainty, such as, the growing foreign and domestic threat of radical/militant Islam; our out-of-control $18 trillion national debt; and the unrelenting destruction of our U.S. borders, English language, culture, middle-class, and economic system—to again cite a few of the growing many.

And of **"special importance"**—if the need, urgency, encouragement, and support for constructive efforts against the many threats to our nation, liberty, and survival, are not found within this particular book . . . then the reader is encouraged to aggressively search for such enlightenment elsewhere. For, at the end of the day, **what** prompts each of us to be more responsible custodians of our country's affairs is of little measure. Compared to the awesome responsibility that—as individuals and together—we unrelentingly and unfailingly **do so**! —William James Moore

"It does not require a majority to prevail, but rather an irate, tireless minority keen to set brush fires in people's minds."
— Samuel Adams (1722-1803)

"The only sure bulwark (defense) of continuing liberty is a government strong enough to protect the interests of the people, and a people strong enough and well enough informed to maintain its sovereign control over the government." — Franklin D. Roosevelt

"The accumulation of all powers, legislative, executive, and judiciary, in the same hands, whether of one, a few, or many, and whether hereditary, self-appointed, or elective, may justly be pronounced the very definition of tyranny."
— James Madison, Federalist 47, 1778

"We the people are the rightful masters of both Congress and the courts, not to overthrow the Constitution but to overthrow the men who pervert the Constitution." — Abraham Lincoln

"All that is necessary for the triumph of evil is for good men to do nothing." — Edmund Burke (1729-1797)

"Behold the turtle. He makes progress only when he sticks his neck out." — James Conant

"How you spend your time is more important than how you spend your money. Money mistakes can be corrected, but time is gone forever." — David B. Norris

Our
Constitutional Republic

There is sound reason why our United States Pledge of Allegiance refers to our country as a *Republic* and why our Declaration of Independence and Constitution do not mention the word *democracy*.

Our country's founders were very aware of the failures of prior democracies, such as ancient Athens and Rome. They feared creating a government having too many similarities to a pure democracy. They especially recognized the importance of ensuring the right of political dissent and protecting minority groups and individuals from the *tyranny of the majority*. They knew that a *pure democracy* could result in *mob rule*, where fifty-one percent of the people could take away the rights of the other forty-nine. Through their experience, insight, and great wisdom, they put in place a one-of-its-kind *constitutional republic* — **not** a *pure democracy*.

In so doing they passed to us a very special form of government where sovereignty deliberately rests with *we the people.* Where we may act on our own or through our elected representatives to deal with issues, where our government is a servant of its people — *where our government's power comes from and is limited by its citizens.* That is, until we further screw-it-up by irresponsibly continuing to give up our U.S. citizens' Constitution-guaranteed power to an ever-growing government loaded with self-serving, self-perpetuating, power and influence craving officials!

Our *Constitutional Republic* does include some likeness to a *democracy,* such as our use of democratic processes to elect our representatives, pass new laws, etc. But, as opposed to a democracy, our U.S. Constitution *limits* our government's power and spells out how our government is to be structured. As a result, our Constitutional Republic is divided into three separate but equal branches of government. The <u>Executive</u> (*Presidency*), <u>Legislative</u> (*Congress*), and <u>Judicial</u> (*Courts*). Our Constitution establishes that no branch has absolute power, therefore providing special checks and balances on our government system and protection for the rule of law.

Our Constitution is the life-blood of our Constitutional Republic. The foundation of this land of unequaled opportunity; best hope for mankind; and envy of countless peoples deprived of and seeking liberty. A liberty for which much sacrifice has been made by so many, and for which limitless measures must always be taken to defend, protect, and preserve!

We the people must forever be most watchful and have zero-tolerance for . . . any political leader or branch of government that demonstrates lack of respect for our U.S. Constitution or the government-system of checks and balances and rule of law it establishes! Should we fail to do so, world-history shows that certain to follow will be tyranny and dictatorship, soon accompanied by loss of liberty/freedom and risk to survival! These are of course not words of exaggeration, nor of unjustified concern. But, rather, are a sincere expression of historically demonstrated facts-of-life.

= = =

"A [pure] democracy is nothing more than mob rule, where fifty-one percent of the people may take away the rights of the other forty-nine." *– Thomas Jefferson*

"By ensuring that no one in government has too much power, the Constitution helps protect ordinary Americans every day against abuse of power by those in authority." *– John Roberts*

"What the Founding Fathers created in the Constitution is the most magnificent government on the face of the Earth, and the reason is this: because it was intended to preserve the American society and the American spirit, not to transform it or destroy it." *– Mark Levin*

"I have no fear that the result of our experiment will be that men may be trusted to govern themselves without a master."
– Thomas Jefferson, Letter to David Hartley, 1787

"Every government degenerates when trusted to the rulers of the people alone. The people themselves, therefore, are its only safe depositories." – Thomas Jefferson

"As good government is an empire of laws, how shall your laws be made? In a large society, inhabiting an extensive country, it is impossible that the whole should assemble to make laws. The first necessary step, then, is to depute power from the many to a few of the most wise and good."
– John Adams, Thoughts on Government, 1776

"We may define a republic to be . . . a government which derives all its powers directly or indirectly from the great body of the people, and is administered by persons holding offices during pleasure for a limited period, or during good behavior."
– James Madison, Federalist 39, 1788

"A wise and frugal government, which shall leave men free to regulate their own pursuits of industry and improvement, and shall not take from the mouth of labor the bread it has earned – this is the sum of good government."
– Thomas Jefferson, First Inaugural Address, 1801

"Pure democracies have ever been spectacles of turbulence and contention; have ever been found incompatible with personal security, or the rights of property; and have, in general, been as short in their lives as they have been violent in their deaths."
– James Madison, Federalist 10, 1787

"The mob is the mother of tyrants." – Diogenes

Liberty & Freedom

*"It is easy to take **liberty** for granted, when you have never had it taken from you." —Dick Cheney*

*"The price of **freedom** is eternal vigilance." — Thomas Jefferson*

Liberty and *freedom* — two words:

- Representing crucially-essential aspects of life that countless are yet deprived of and seek; fortunate others have been blessed with and appreciate; some take for granted and abuse; and haunting numbers have fought and often died for;

- Commonly used; often interchangeably. Much researched, analyzed, and written about. Yet their roots and distinctions often unclear to many if not most of us — to even our government representatives and leaders.

- Their meanings, interpretations, connotations, and differences, often as confusing and numerous as those who write, speak, or otherwise use them. Or, as abundant as those who seek, or feel they know, what they stand for.

Getting "into the weeds a bit," some popular views hold that *liberty* is in regard to a "right" — whereas, *freedom* refers to "independence." Among various formal definitions, the Oxford Dictionary presents freedom as *"the power or right to act speak, or think as one wants"*; whereas, **liberty** is *"the state of being free within society from oppressive restrictions imposed by authority on one's behavior or political views"* – in this case, obviously a rather complicated definition of *liberty,* as compared to that applied to the word *freedom.*

One take-away so far from all this chatter about definitions, etc., is that **liberty** can be viewed as **paving the way for freedom**. That is, freedom results from the demands of people seeking liberty. [In likeness to the "chicken before the egg – egg before chicken" dilemma.] But, again, these are only *interpretations,* of which there are many.

From a historical perspective, the word *freedom* appears to have roots to old-English language and *liberty* to old-French language. Likely a primary reason for their often interchangeable use today, both share the common-definition of "unconstrained" – which simply means *"having no constraints."* This shared definition and often interchangeable use are also the basis for use of the combined words "liberty/freedom" at times throughout this book.

However, that the words *liberty* and *freedom* share "unconstrained" as a common-definition, does not change the reality that our world and lives do in fact involve many *limitations* and *restrictions* – or, in other words, many *constraints.* None the least, our *time.*

Likewise—weather, gravity, and other aspects of nature certainly "constrain" us. But, when encountering these types of limitations and restrictions, we don't typically feel all that personally offended, imposed upon, or taken advantage of. Nor, do we usually march in protest, revolt, etc., as a result of such.

The real rub comes from <u>constraints imposed by other people</u>. When, for example, we are seriously intimidated, forced to obey, abused, over-taxed, or over-regulated. And/or, when our freedom of speech, freedom of religion, right to privacy, right to property, right to bear arms, and right to pursue happiness, etc., are jeopardized.

Given the many intolerable constraints suffered at the hands of the British, our country's founders had a very clear, up close, and personal, understanding of what *liberty* meant—and what the *"absence of liberty"* entailed! A very experienced grasp of the fact that—without liberty—freedom cannot exist.

In 1776 our country's Declaration of Independence from Britain stated in part: *"We hold these truths to be self-Evident, that all men are created equal, that they are endowed by their Creator with certain unalienable Rights that among these are Life, Liberty and the pursuit of Happiness. ---That to secure these rights, Governments are instituted among Men, deriving their just powers from the consent of the governed . . ."*

By 1789 our U.S. Constitution was ratified, but many of the founding fathers still had a very fresh memory of the tyranny and violations of human and civil rights earlier imposed by Britain. They also had very deep concerns about the potential tyranny that can result from a <u>strong central government</u>. As a result they worked hard for a <u>bill of rights</u> specifically aimed at protecting the liberty/freedom of <u>we the people</u>. From their efforts and wisdom the first ten amendments to our Constitution — known as the <u>Bill of Rights</u> — were ratified on 15 December 1791.

Ever since our country's hard-fought-for beginning, countless people from near and far have continued to seek the special liberty/freedom offered by this great nation — this first and one-of-its-kind Constitutional Republic!

Regardless of how defined or interpreted, etc., on a daily basis we deal with the results of differing "attitudes" about what *liberty/freedom* stand for. For example, some seem to believe they mean *"freedom to do whatever we want."* While, thankfully, most of the more considerate among us seem to understand, and generally demonstrate, that the meaning and application of liberty/freedom must always be more in likeness to *"unopposed to do whatever we want, but within limits that protect the equal liberty/freedom of others."*

Arriving at universally accepted definitions is difficult enough. However, for those blessed with liberty/freedom, the challenge of much greater importance and difficulty is their "proper use." That is, having **due respect** for the **rights of others** as we go about exercising **our rights** — and **vice versa**! For it seems there will never be a shortage of those who abuse liberty/freedom, and use such as an opportunity to live their lives in disregard of the rights of others.

Fortunately, throughout the world's civilized societies, the majority of us usually (but, certainly not always) seem to find some way to go about life with a workable-level of mutual respect for one another. That is, "so far" that seems to be the case! And common sense alone dictates that in the interest of civil order and survival we must continue to do so. Regardless of our individual political persuasion, religious preference, national origin, race, economic status, sexual orientation, ethnicity, etc. — **we must continue to do so**!

Of course this is not pie-in-the-sky hype or BS! Whether viewed as an individual citizen or from a nation-perspective — consider the alternatives to mutual respect for one another. Alternatives ranging from a bit unsettling to absolutely unthinkable. Especially with the growing incidence of mob-violence, foreign and domestic terrorism, atrocities at the hands of radical/militant Islamists, and the proliferation of nuclear weapons capable of destroying the human race!

We must open our eyes and ears and take much more serious note of what is taking place around us! Of the many places throughout the world where mutual respect for one another and liberty/freedom have been lost! We are becoming dangerously desensitized to the pain, suffering, and atrocities of others. We are not talking about "virtual reality" or "video games," etc., here — but about real-world human suffering! And of real-world threats to liberty and survival! To mention but a few of the more recent examples—the ongoing tragedies regarding Iraq, Iran, Lebanon, North Africa, and Syria! As well as the growing incidence of violence within our borders! We must take to heart the resulting tyranny, civil disobedience, property damage/loss, carnage, government collapse, disease, famine, religious persecution, and other chaos, suffered by so many—past and present! And **never** be so foolish and irresponsible to ever assume—or be led to believe—that *we* and *this great nation* are somehow immune to such tragic outcomes!

We must not be ignorant of the lessons of history or inattentive of current events. The liberty/freedom we enjoy today are not gifts from the *tooth fairy*, or a *virtual-reality* from a popular *"App,"* or the result of a meager *"tap or swipe"* on our smartphone, e-tablet, PC monitor, or other e-device. Rather, our priceless liberty/freedom are the result of much wisdom, planning, effort, and great sacrifice by countless past and present. A fragile gift *we* now have the responsibility to protect, defend, and preserve. For not only "our" sake, but also that of future generations of Americans!

= = =

"We hold these truths to be self-evident: that all men are created equal; that they are endowed by their Creator with certain unalienable rights; that among these are life, liberty, and the pursuit of happiness." – *Thomas Jefferson*

"Freedom is never more than one generation away from extinction."
– *Ronald Reagan*

The "Lifespan" of Our Constitutional Republic

> *"America will never be destroyed from the outside. If we falter and lose our freedoms, it will be because we destroyed ourselves."*
>
> —*Abraham Lincoln*

To many of us, our local, state, and federal government election campaigns represent an unwanted distraction from daily life; being engulfed by annoying commercials; endless hassle for contributions; mixed emotions about the candidates; and often doubts and confusion regarding who we should vote for (or against).   Each campaign also involving considerable time, effort, and money spent trying to influence our votes. The overall extent being proportional to the power and influence of the political position being sought.   In presidential election campaigns the money alone entails ever-growing millions upon millions of dollars—from sources ever more difficult to identify—especially for the average voter.

Through it all, some of us do our best to cast informed and otherwise responsible votes; sadly, a larger number do otherwise. More tragically, untold millions never bother to participate at all in this hard-fought-for special *right* and citizen *responsibility*. Elections and voting—expressions of citizen-sovereignty and right of representation denied to countless millions of others worldwide. As millions of Americans continue a most dangerous assumption—that the liberties, freedoms, and opportunities we enjoy are forever-secured givens. Losing touch that such blessings originate from and rely upon a truly special form of government established long ago—<u>our constitutional republic</u>.

As mentioned in prior sections of this book, being very aware of the failures of prior *democracies* such as ancient Athens and Rome, our country's founding fathers feared creating a government too similar to a *pure democracy*—which can result in mob-rule and tyranny-of-the-majority; where fifty-one percent could take away the rights of the other forty-nine. Through experience, insight, and great wisdom, they instead established a first and to date one-of-its-kind *constitutional republic*—where sovereignty deliberately rests with *we the people*. Where we can act lawfully on our own and through elected representatives to deal with issues; where our government's power comes from and is limited by its citizens. Thus establishing our nation of unequaled liberty, freedom, and opportunity—governed by its citizens through three separate but equal branches of government: the legislative, executive, and judicial.

Nevertheless, years of ignorance, apathy, complacency, denial, greed, and fear—on the part of too many eligible voters and elected representatives—have taken our country down a most dangerous path. One possibly best symbolized by the following "life-cycle of a democracy" scenario (an assertion of questionable origin, for years quoted, referenced, and accessible in many forms through an array of internet sources and other media):

The Life Cycle of a Democracy

"A democracy cannot exist as a permanent form of government. It will continue until the voters discover they can vote themselves generous gifts from the public treasury. From that point on, the majority will always vote for the candidates who promise the most benefits from the public treasury. Eventually every democracy will collapse, due to loose fiscal policy, and be followed by a dictatorship. From the beginning, the greatest civilizations of the world have only lasted about 200 years, and have always progressed through the following sequence:

1. *From bondage to **spiritual faith**;*
2. *From spiritual faith to **great courage**;*
3. *From courage to **liberty**;*
4. *From liberty to **abundance**;*
5. *From abundance to **complacency**;*
6. *From complacency to **apathy**;*
7. *From apathy to **dependence**;*
8. *From dependence back to **bondage**."*

Regardless of above scenario's origin, little open-minded consideration is required to note some very unsettling similarities, between it and the dangerous path our country is on. And any realistic comparison would find us very disturbingly somewhere around mid-point between Sequence 6 and 7! That is, a nation heavily consumed with *apathy* and dangerously deep into the even more self-destructive phase of *dependence*. Leaving *bondage* the next step in this scenario — towards loss of the liberty/freedom we now enjoy; thereafter facing a path of serious threat to our survival!

The remainder of this section includes and makes reference to information that should be an aid to getting a constructive grasp of how *apathy* and *dependence* apply to our country's current status and direction. Some facts-of-life our mainstream media and political leaders don't spend much, if any, time and effort talking about.

Such as, the following partial-snapshot taken from information presented in more detail in later Sections herein, titled, *"Our National Debt & Unfunded Liabilities"* and *"The Bottomless Pit of Our Federal Government"*:

According to September 2015 U.S. Census data, we are a nation of about 321.7 million. However, only 122.1 million (37.9%) are full-time workers; 26.9 million (8.3%) are part-time workers; 8.07 million (2.5%) are "officially" unemployed; 16.1 million (5%) are "actually" unemployed; 94.0 million (29.2%) are not in labor force; and only 118.9 million (37%) are income taxpayers. Furthermore, 57.0 million (17.7%) are Medicare enrollees; 76.4 million (23.7%) Medicaid recipients; 40.7 million (12.6%) are without health insurance; 10.8 million (3.3%) are disabled; 47.6 million (14.8%) live in poverty; 45.3 million (14.0%) are Food Stamp recipients; 1.7 million (0.05%)

are homeless; 122 thousand are unaccompanied-minors; 1 in 6 live on incomes at risk for hunger; 14 million American children rely on food banks; food insecurity exists in every county in the U.S.; and about **157 million (49%)** of us are presently receiving some type of "benefits" from the public treasury.

And, for a little *icing on the cake* — "we the people" are also strapped with a rapidly growing national debt of over $18 trillion — that's about $57 thousand per citizen; or $154 thousand per taxpayer! And, for U.S. Unfunded Liabilities totaling some $97.5 trillion — that's over $820,000 for every man, woman, and child in the U.S.

Again, the above information being but a snapshot of our growing *dependency* status — the result of years of agendas taking us down the path of becoming reliant upon the government for our every want and need. A liberty and survival threatening path accommodated by government representatives and bureaucrats more focused on keeping their jobs, staying in power, and promoting their personal interests and ideologies, than addressing the best interests of our country. And driven by our ignorance, apathy, complacency, denial, greed, and fear.

We must not continue to tolerate an ever-growing government; vote ourselves generous benefits from our public treasury; and be a nation of more and more takers and less and less contributors! We must timely wake-up to reality!

A constitutional republic that protects its citizens' rights to life, liberty, and the *pursuit* of happiness, is realistic and sustainable. One that promotes and accommodates irresponsible and ever-growing *dependency-upon* and *entitlement-to* the public treasury is not!

Until replaced by dictatorship, tyranny, and bondage — the sovereignty (supreme power and authority) and lifespan of our constitutional-republic form of government rests with *we the people*. As does, our liberty and ultimate survival — and that of future generations of Americans. "We" must step up, speak up, and do the right thing!

= = =

"The tyranny of a prince in an oligarchy is not so dangerous to the public welfare as the apathy of a citizen in a democracy."
— Charles de Montesquieu

The strength of the Constitution lies entirely in the determination of each citizen to defend it. Only if every single citizen feels duty bound to do his share in this defense are the constitutional rights secure."
— Albert Einstein

"The death of democracy is not likely to be an assassination from ambush. It will be a slow extinction from apathy, indifference, and undernourishment." — Robert M. Hutchins

"It has been said that democracy is the worst form of government except all the others that have been tried." — Winston Churchill

Survival

"Safety from external danger is the most powerful director of national conduct. Even the ardent love of liberty will, after a time, give way to its dictates. The violent destruction of life and property incident to war, the continual effort and alarm attendant on a state of continual danger, will compel nations the most attached to liberty to resort for repose and security to institutions which have a tendency to destroy their civil and political rights. To be more safe, they at length become willing to run the risk of being less free."

— Alexander Hamilton, 1787

"Willingness to Risk our Liberty/Freedom"

As so clearly expressed by the above quotation, Alexander Hamilton long ago warned that so powerful is our drive to seek safety from external danger — so strong is our instinct to survive — that to be more safe we can become willing to even risk our liberty/freedom. To better appreciate the credibility of the wisdom shared in this particular quotation, it is important to consider that: Alexander Hamilton (1755-1804) served in the American Revolutionary War; was Chief of Staff to General George Washington; one of our country's Founding Fathers; among the most influential interpreters and promoters of our U.S. Constitution; our first U.S. Secretary of the Treasury; founder of our country's financial system; and founder of the first American political party.

These very real world, insightful, and cautionary words from Hamilton draw attention to an aspect of our human nature we must never lose sight of . . . and never lessen our guard against! For, we can be assured, that our **enemies** — both foreign and domestic — are very much aware of these and other vulnerable sides of human nature. As are many others who — in order to fulfill self-serving political aims and/or liberty-threatening agendas — strive to control, distract, and manipulate us. *The message contained in the three immediately prior sentences, should alone be an ample discouragement to any temptation to skip the remainder of this particular section.*

For, if there ever was a time that modern-day Americans should (must) be especially mindful of Hamilton's warning, that time is now! In the U.S. and elsewhere we are increasingly surrounded by those who are apathetic and complacent about our precious liberty/freedom. While, at the same time, we are becoming more and more "personally touched" by the rapid spread of foreign and domestic terrorism. By horrific acts of unspeakable atrocities, that are now and will continue to be "selectively used" to fuel agendas aimed at **"offering us the illusion of safety"** in exchange for **"our precious liberty/freedom."** Agendas promoted by some of the most self-serving and untrustworthy among us. Such as, many of our political leaders and representatives, and a majority of our news media, etc. The very same individuals and groups that never caution us or publically acknowledge that — without our liberty/freedom — there can be no true and lasting "safety." No protection against tyranny or other threats to our survival!

With Hamilton's powerful warning fresh in mind, this seems to be a fitting point to get into the weeds a bit on the subject of "survival." Starting with some "survival basics" that apply to "all" threats. Whether the aim is to survive the threats of, for instance, flu viruses, computer viruses, incompetent political representatives or leaders, winter storms, nuclear attacks, or foreign and domestic terrorist acts, etc. Life-critical a "basics" which, as indicated below, are certainly not rocket-science.

Survival Basics

To survive, we and other live forms simply need to: **(1.)** timely recognize threats, and **(2.)** have and execute effective responses (defenses) against them.

But, of course the simplicity ends there! As we strive to *recognize* and *effectively respond to* the dangers around us, there are many obstacles. None the least being those same six potentially self-destructive aspects of human nature, fittingly repeated on purpose throughout this book: *ignorance, apathy, complacency, denial, greed, and counter-productive fear.* Then there are the countless *distractions* and *diversions*. Especially those from biased and agenda-driven media, the entertainment industry, and from political propaganda, etc. Further complicating our survival efforts are harmful events with *little-to-no warning*, such as vehicle accidents, earthquakes, tsunamis, terrorist attacks, and nuclear disasters, etc. Any of which can happen so fast there may be little if any opportunity to realistically avoid or protect against.

Furthermore, *even the thoughts* of the ever-growing number and types of threats involved in our world of likewise rapidly-growing complexity can seem overwhelming. Leaving some to argue that time spent thinking or worrying about such matters is a waste of time. But, any such thinking is not only a self-destructive barrier to our **human instinct of survival** . . . such is also most disrespectful of the precious gift of life!

Our Most Powerful Instinct — "Survival/Self-Preservation"

"Survival/Self-Preservation" can be defined as *"continuing to live after or in spite of some life-threatening event or after another's death."* It is said to be our most powerful drive. We and most, if not all, life forms seem to be hard-wired with such behavior. That is, **"when"** we actually **recognize** and **acknowledge** the **existence** of a threat. To draw attention to just how powerful the instinct to survive can truly be, summarized below are but a random few real-world examples. And, as you read the following, please give some serious thought to the **"in contrast"** level of ignorance, apathy, complacency, denial, greed, and counter-productive fear, we too often apply to very real and serious threats to our ultimately life-sustaining liberty and freedom. Such as those discussed throughout this book.

The Donner Party: In 1846, the Donner Party, a group of settlers headed to California, got trapped by snow in the Sierra Nevada Mountains. Out of food, they survived as best they could — including by eating the bodies of those who had died.

Outdoorsman Aron Ralston: While hiking through the canyons in south-eastern Utah in 2003, outdoorsman Aron Lee Ralston became trapped by a dislodged bolder. After being trapped for five days, he survived this accident by amputating his own right forearm with a dull knife in order to free himself. He then rappelled down a 65 foot cliff to reach safety.

Andes Flight Disaster: On 13 October 1972 Uruguayan Air Force Flight 571 crashed in the Andes Mountains at an altitude of 11,800 feet. It was a chartered flight carrying 45 people, including a rugby team, their family, friends, and colleagues. Over a fourth of the plane's occupants died during the crash, and many others soon gave in to the severe cold and their serious injuries. Although 27 were still alive a few days after the crash, eight more were killed by an avalanche that hit their shelter in the plane's wreckage. On 23 December 1972—more than 2 months after the crash—16 survivors were rescued. Facing starvation, no source of heat, and radio reports that search and rescue efforts had been abandoned—to stay alive the survivors had fed on the dead passengers whose bodies had been preserved by the snow and extreme cold.

Mountain Climber Joe Simpson: In 1985, climber Joe Simpson broke his leg while he and his climbing mate Simon Yates were descending from a record climb of the west face of Siula Grande in the Peruvian Andes. As Yates was lowering Simpson down the mountain, a rope knot connecting the two men snagged. Unable to see Simpson and to prevent being pulled off the face of the cliff himself, Yates decided to cut the rope connecting the two men. Unknown to Yates, this let Simpson fall some 150 feet into a crevasse. Miraculously Simpson survived this fall. Yates not being able to find Simpson, eventually made his way back to their base camp. In spite of his broken leg and other injuries, Simpson rappelled himself deeper into a crevice in the glacier where he was eventually able to find an exit. Then, for the next three and a half days, he crawled and hopped an agonizing five miles to their base camp, where Yates was preparing to depart to seek search and rescue help.

Torture: As evidenced by the experiences of many prisoners of war and victims of domestic violence, etc., in trying to survive we will at times also withstand torture or obey a murderer.

Our Self-preservation Responses (Defenses) "Must Fit the Threats"

Our survival depends upon how we use our self-preservation responses, such as, *fear, pain, fight, and flight, etc.* The emotion *fear* can help us seek safety from recognized threats. The stimulus *pain* can help us withdraw from harmful situations, provide a chance for a wound to heal, and avoid similar injuries in the future. And, the behaviors of fight or flight can help us mitigate, eliminate, or escape, recognized dangers. Clearly, **"how"** we respond to threats is critical to our survival. And, as Alexander Hamilton long ago warned . . . critical also to the survival of our liberty and freedom as well.

Whether dealing with dangers to our life, liberty, pursuit of happiness, or other unalienable rights . . . our self-preservation response (our defense) must fit the nature of the threat. However, this critical need can often be especially complicated by new, strange, or otherwise unfamiliar, threats. Resulting in a survival-response that might not fit the nature of a particular danger — or may not exist at all. For example:

(1.) <u>A Developed-Response Ineffective against Threat</u>: A deer fawn's *freeze-response* to fear can be deadly if there is no cover to hide in while *staying perfectly still* in an effort to be unnoticed. Likewise, a "freeze-response" by us should be recognized as no protection against, for instance, foreign and domestic terrorism, nuclear attacks, etc. The deer fawn's *freeze-response*, when there is no protective cover, could also be compared to our years-ago government-planned citizens'-response to nuclear attack. Which was for school children and others to *duck-and-cover*. A response that obviously offered little to nothing to our chance for survival. Fast-forwarding to the present . . . even greater nuclear threats exist, but who among us understands what true protection we have against such? This being a very real-world "now existing" example of not having an effective survival response to a potentially-devastating threat. One we clearly should <u>recognize</u> and prepare for — but, how? Just one of the many truly meaningful questions never dealt with during our "dog and pony show" State of the Union Addresses, presidential debates, press briefings, social media posts, daily news broadcasts, etc.

(2.) <u>Failure to Recognize an Existing Threat</u>: The Dodo, a flightless bird, extinct within a century of discovery, evolved in a habitat with plenty of food and without natural predators. When eventually faced with human involvement it lacked necessary self-preservation responses, and to its peril did not recognize and lacked fear of dangers from humans, rats, etc. A likewise potential fate to be suffered as the result of our failure to recognize, be fearful of, and apply effective self-preservation responses against, for instance . . . predictions that by about YR 2025, approximately one-half of the World's population will **not** have access to safe drinking water; agendas aimed at disarming law-abiding U.S. citizens; failed immigration policies; the ongoing destruction of our U.S. borders, common-language English, and culture; and the worldwide spread of radical/militant Islam; etc.

(3.) <u>Failure to timely Develop/Execute Effective Response</u>: The Holocaust was an extremely horrendous genocide carried out between 1941 and 1945 by the German military and its collaborators, under the command of Adolf Hitler. This unspeakable atrocity resulted in the horrible deaths of approximately 11 million people, including some 6 million Jews and more than 1 million children. In addition to not early-on recognizing the potential threat posed by this dark-side of mankind—these millions of victims likewise had no effective *self-preservation response*—no defense—against the man-made hell reaped upon them.

But, still today, even with the reality of the Holocaust in the not too distant past, who among us wants to really believe that any political leader, friend, neighbor, fellow citizen, or other human being, could under any circumstances carryout or condone such unspeakable acts! Yet, the Holocaust **"did"** happen—and the barbaric atrocities of radical/militant Islam **"are"** happening. A very real and growing threat that the U.S. and other nations have yet to develop and implement an effective survival/self-preservation response against!

Special "Take-aways" from this Section: As the overall content of this book is considered, hopefully the take-aways from this section on "Survival" include, as a minimum, some *thought-provoking and constructive perspectives*, as well as, *special emphasis on the following*:

For the sake of nothing less than the liberty and survival of present and future generations of Americans, "we the people" must . . .

- Timely recognize and acknowledge our nation's foreign and domestic threats, and successfully develop and execute effective responses (defenses) against each.

- Never relinquish or compromise our precious "liberty/freedom" as we rightfully seek safety through our natural instinct to "survive."

While we remain especially mindful always, that these truly awesome responsibilities are not "the government's." But, rather . . . "ours." For, in this great nation "we" are ultimately the government . . . that is, so far we still are!

"When you examine the lives of the most influential people who have ever walked among us, you discover one thread that winds through them all. They have been aligned first with their spiritual nature and only then by their physical selves." — Albert Einstein

"Our very survival depends on our ability to stay awake, to adjust to new ideas, to remain vigilant and to face the challenge of change."
— Martin Luther King Jr.

"To survive it is often necessary to fight and to fight you have to dirty yourself." — George Orwell

"It is not the strongest or the most intelligent who will survive but those who can best manage change." — Charles Darwin

"Hunger, love, pain, fear are some of those inner forces which rule the individual's instinct for self-preservation." — Albert Einstein

"Fear is a part of life. It's a warning mechanism. That's all. It tells you when there's danger around. Its job is to help you survive. Not cripple you into being unable to do it." — Jim Butcher

"Nature is based on harmony. So it says if we want to survive and become more like nature, then we actually have to understand that it's cooperation versus competition." — Bruce Lipton

"Racism is a refuge for the ignorant. It seeks to divide and to destroy. It is the enemy of freedom, and deserves to be met head-on and stamped out." — Pierre Berton

Our Biggest Threat

> *"I am concerned for the security of our great Nation; not so much because of any threat from without, but because of the insidious forces working from within."* — *Douglas MacArthur*

Among the many threats to our liberty and survival—"We" stand front and center!

For, it is *we the people* who tolerate irresponsible government; have the capacity to murder or otherwise bring physical or mental harm to one another; rob and steal from one another; lack compassion; misuse our planet's resources; contaminate our environment; wage war with one another; and otherwise deny or restrict one another's rights to life, liberty, and the pursuit of happiness.

It is also *we the people* who can (and too often do) treat existing threats with self-destructive ignorance, apathy, complacency, denial, greed, and counter-productive fear. Threats such as the rapidly growing, world-wide spread of radical/militant Islam; and the terrorist state of Iran's aggressive pursuit of nuclear weapons capability, while at the same time openly chanting "death to America" and declaring the intent to destroy Israel and others!

However, it is in turn *we the people* who can choose to be responsible voters; demonstrate compassion and sharing; protect each other from physical or mental harm; conserve and otherwise responsibly use our planet's resources; respect and protect one another's property; not contaminate our environment; peacefully resolve our disputes and differences; and otherwise acknowledge, respect, and defend, one another's rights to life, liberty, and the pursuit of happiness.

And, it is *we the people* who have demonstrated time and again the capability and willingness to sacrifice our country's blood and treasure to protect our liberty/freedom and that of others. The "choices" and their "consequences" are inescapably ours — and that of future generations.

Nevertheless, regardless of even the best of intentions, many obstacles can and do get in the way of making *good choices*. Choices not only in our own personal best interests, but also in consideration of the welfare of others. And, obstacles such as the human-nature aspects reviewed below. Little imagination is needed to grasp how these and similar *potential dark sides* of human nature can, and do, complicate our choices and actions in daily living and efforts to responsibly govern.

Whether in a pure democracy (mob rule) or our constitutional republic, responsible government depends on its citizens *being able to recognize*, and *willing to support*, the best political candidates, policies, and agendas. Our ability to recognize what is best for our country as a whole can be road-blocked by *ignorance*. And in addition to *ignorance*, our willingness to do the right thing can also be critically hindered by *apathy, complacency, denial, greed,* and *fear.* And, in spite of how much we may at times act and want to believe otherwise — these potential barriers to responsible choices and behavior do not just apply to those in "the government." For, ultimately, "they" are "us"!

As if things were not already complicated enough, various "research findings" suggest that most (if not all) of us often do not have the mental tools needed to make good decisions. This being another way of saying that we are not always smart enough to make meaningful judgments. For example, research led by David Dunning, a psychologist at Cornell University, reportedly shows that *incompetent people* are by nature unable to judge the *competence* of other people, or the *quality* of those people's ideas.

For instance, unless we have expertise about *tax reform,* we naturally face great difficulty in determining what political candidates are true experts on that particular subject. Always mindful, of course, that *incompetent* <u>does not</u> mean one is *stupid* — it just basically means one is lacking some particular necessary skill. So, in many ways and on various subjects, we are "all" incompetent!

And, as a result, some research also suggests that no amount of information or facts can make up for many of us being (by nature) unable to accurately evaluate political candidates, government policies, etc. Many of us may simply not have the background, education, or experience needed to recognize good ideas from the bad, and the best political candidate from the otherwise.

And adding to our "good-citizen" dilemma — to further complicate our efforts to responsibly govern — there is also "Illusory superiority" to deal with.   That basically being "pattern of judgment," where we <u>over-estimate</u> our positive qualities and abilities, and <u>under-estimate</u> our negative qualities, in comparison to the qualities of other people. And, it seems we also tend to make judgments of others that reflect favorably back on ourselves.   The result being that our <u>perception</u> of ourselves and of our surroundings can often be far from <u>actual reality</u>.   And, of course, to each of us, our perception is in fact our reality! Or, just another way of saying that our sense of reality is not always accurate — that our outlook on things is not always "the way things truly are."

Then, we also have our <u>emotional ties</u> to political party allegiance and <u>voting practices</u> to contend with. This being further complicated by politicians often more dedicated to seeking or retaining power and personal benefit, than fulfilling their constitutional obligations and abiding by the rule of law.

Adding to our up-hill struggle for responsible government is a politically-biased and agenda-driven mass-media. One that can overwhelm us with emotional-focused messages designed to prohibit rational thinking and good judgment.

Separately, or all together — human nature and/or our lack of personal expertise can (and too often do) result in our being terribly poor judges of political candidates and governing ideas.

It should be noted that this section merely touches-upon but a few aspects of human nature that can (and do) roadblock good judgment in our daily lives and governing efforts. But, this brief *snapshot* on the subject is not intended to suggest or imply that all is hopeless and that our constitutional republic cannot long survive. Much to the contrary — and as is often repeated throughout this book — the information shared herein aims to promote and support positive and otherwise lawfully-constructive efforts to protect, preserve, and defend our nation from threats foreign and domestic. By each of us, individually and jointly, becoming more responsible citizen-custodians of our country's affairs. The information shared herein just highlights that — in order for us to do so — we must unrelentingly put forth the required measure of special-effort!

We must understand and responsibly respond to the fact that "freedom is not free"! We cannot — we must not — sit on our hands with our heads in the sand. And just hope, wish, and assume that all is or will somehow be OK.

For — rest assured — those determined to destroy this great nation and our liberty/freedom are not only aware of our human weaknesses — including those touched upon herein — they are also most certainly working hard and skillfully to use such knowledge against us!

And, to dispel any claim that our form of government is "destined" to fail, and that we as free-people lack the capacity and willingness to responsibly govern and defeat recognized threats—we need (we must) faithfully do two things:

(1.) Truly understand, appreciate, and learn from the wisdom and sacrifices of our nation's founders and other patriots before us. Whereas, almost 240 years ago, in the absence of all the technology and other resources we now take for granted, they established a first and one-of-its-kind form of government (our constitutional republic). Providing a nature of liberty/freedom that brought about the most powerful country on the face of this earth; a haven of unequaled opportunity—enjoyed, envied and still sought after by countless millions—our United States of America; and,

(2.) Have and unrelentingly exercise the same level of wisdom, courage, and sacrifice—focused not only on self-interests, but overwhelmingly on what is best for our country and future generations of Americans! Our inescapable responsibility—as are the consequences of our failing to do so!

= = =

"Let us never forget that government is ourselves and not an alien power over us. The ultimate rulers of our democracy are not a President and senators and congressmen and government officials, but the voters of this country." – Franklin D. Roosevelt

"The people made the Constitution, and the people can unmake it. It is the creature of their will, and lives only by their will."

– John Marshall

"Our"
National Debt
&
Unfunded Liabilities

> *"I place economy among the first and most important virtues, and public debt as the greatest of dangers to be feared...To preserve our independence, we must not let our rulers load us with perpetual debt...We must make our choice between economy and liberty or profusion and servitude..."* — *Thomas Jefferson (1743–1826)*
>
> *"It is incumbent on every generation to pay its own debts as it goes. A principle if acted on would save one-half the wars of the world."*
> — *Thomas Jefferson (1743-1826)*

As shown above, Thomas Jefferson (1743–1826) considered the "public debt" to be the "greatest danger to our independence."

A highly-qualified and not-to-taken-lightly view, considering that Jefferson was one of our country's Founding Fathers; the principal author of our Declaration of Independence in 1776; our third U.S. President; a passionate spokesman for democracy; our first U.S. Secretary of State under President Washington; organizer of the Democratic-Republican Party; and with worldwide influence supported the rights of the individual.

Jefferson's concerns about the dangers of public debt were without doubt founded in much wisdom, experience, and insight—as evidenced by our present-day out-of-control and rapidly-growing **$18 trillion national debt**!

Yes, as of 2015, **every U.S. citizen** (every man, woman and child) currently **owes** over **$56,000** for their share of our $18 trillion national debt (assuming a total citizen-population of about 321.7 million). That amounts to more than **$150,000 per** each of the some 119 million U.S. **taxpayers** that are still left.

A truly inconceivable and irresponsible debt that, as long ago warned by Thomas Jefferson, represents a very real and present danger to our independence—to our liberty/freedom—to our ultimate survival!

The earliest record of our U.S. national debt was prepared by Alexander Hamilton, the first U.S. Treasury Secretary—a self-taught economist. His 1790 analysis showed our national debt to be about $75 million.

In 1906, around the time my dad was born, our national debt was a little more than $2 billion. Around the time my wife and I entered the world it had increased to $201 billion. And, by arrival of our two children it was around $427 billion.

By 1981 our national debt had reached $1 trillion. The year we were blessed with our grandson it had jumped to $6.7 trillion, and by 2008 was more than $10 trillion. As earlier stated, it now exceeds $18 trillion, and by 2018 is projected to be more than $20 trillion!

Yes, empowered by our ignorance, apathy, complacency, denial, greed, and fear—and led by self-serving, irresponsible political leaders, our federal government has put us more than **$18 trillion** in the hole! Or, more appropriately described—**"a bottomless pit."**

It is highly unlikely that anyone can even begin to grasp the real nature and significance of even **"1 trillion"**—let alone, **"18"** of them! Even after considering the many professionally graphic examples available at a growing number of web-sites. However, until you do a highly encouraged search and review of such material, the few relatively simplified rough-examples below should serve as sufficiently-unnerving eye-openers.

And, since our government's "irresponsible spending" has not yet notably kept the perfectionists and otherwise detailed-inclined among us up nights and engaged in public protests—the possibility that some of the "rough-information" presented below might by chance be "off" by a dollar, inch, mile, year, second, cubic foot, etc., or so, shouldn't be all that grievous and unaccepting. Nor, should such potential numbers-glitches detract from this truly serious message:

18 trillion dollars = **$18,000,000,000,000.**

The circumference of the Earth is about 24,901 miles. Lining up 18 trillion one-dollar bills lengthways would circle the Earth **70,050 times**.

A round-trip from the Earth to Saturn and back would be about 1.66 billion miles. A one-dollar bill is 6.14 inches long. 18 trillion of them lined up lengthways could reach more than **1.74 billion miles**!

The largest building in the world is reportedly the Boeing Everett Factory in the state of Washington — 472 million cubic feet in size. About **749.6 million cubic feet of space** would be needed to store $18 trillion — or a building about **1.6 times** the size of Boeing's huge facility.

To pay back $18 trillion, at a rate of one dollar per second, would take about **570,386 years**.

Our federal government *overspends* at least $1 trillion in *new debt* each year. If a *very generous* taxpayer earning about $50,000 per year decided to use "all" of his or her income — to pay-off just the principal of one year of *new debt* — it would take **20 million years** to do so. Paying-off just the principal of our *total debt* of $18 trillion would take **360 million years**.

However, if we were to divide our rapidly growing national debt between the estimated **119 million or so U.S. tax-payers** "that are still left," $18 trillion of the principal of this burden could be wiped out in just a little over **3 years**. But, again, this assumes each taxpayer earned about $50,000 per year and would use **"all"** of their income for payment of this debt, and spend nothing on food, shelter, transportation, healthcare, or entertainment, etc.!

And what makes up this outrageous "national debt"? According to the U.S. Treasury Department, our national debt is the face amount (principal) of *marketable* and *non-marketable* securities currently outstanding. With *marketable* securities consisting of bills, notes, bonds, and TIPS. *Marketable* securities also being negotiable and transferable and able to be sold on the secondary market. On the other hand, *non-marketable* securities consist of Domestic, Foreign, REA, SLGS, US Savings, Gov't Acct. Series (GAS) Securities, etc. But, such detail and "Treasury Department speak" can detract our needed focus away from what must be our bottom-line attention and concern—our "$18 trillion and growing debt!

Our national debt is basically made up of two parts:

(1.) *Intra-governmental debt*—money our government owes itself, such as the Social Security and Medicare trust funds, Federal Reserve Banks, etc.

(2.) *Public debt*—money our government borrows from its citizens through the sale of treasury bonds, pension funds, mutual funds, etc., **and from *foreign investors*** such as China, Japan, etc.

That's right—in addition to being heavily in debt to ourselves—**we are also deeply in debt to other countries.**

While we have had our heads buried in our desktop PC's, laptops, smart-phones, e-tablets, and social-media trivia . . . and distracted by government propaganda, biased news reporting, etc. — our federal government has also put us and our descendants into critically deep debt to other nations!

As we and our main-stream media have been focused on racism, gay rights, gun control, income-inequality, "free" birth-control, bridge-gate, Britain's royal-couple, climate change, air-pressure in NFL footballs, and someone being "offended," etc. — our federal government has put us in debt to China for about $1.2 trillion, Japan for another $1.2 trillion, as well as another total $1.8 trillion to a mix of other nations!

Our national debt has also grown significantly in recent years due to rising annual deficits (government spending exceeding tax revenues). During the eight-year administration of George W. Bush our national debt almost doubled — to $5.7 trillion.

However, despite this massive increase over Bush's eight years, Obama amassed more national debt in his first five years than all previous presidents combined.

Between Bush and Obama our national debt has so far been almost *quadrupled* in size! And, under existing policies it is projected to increase another 50 percent over the next 10 years — then rapidly rise thereafter!

And then there's the "interest" on our national debt, which is becoming a bigger and bigger portion of federal government spending. Federal government interest charges in 2014 reportedly being about $221 billion, rising to more than $876 billion by 2024. Soon afterward it is projected that we will be paying a trillion dollars every year just for the interest on our National Debt. As devastating as this sounds, history tells us that—like most if not all government forecasts—these and other government debt statistics will no doubt turn out to be overly optimistic!

But, wait—there is more!

We have not yet mentioned the real butt-kicker—the 500-pound gorilla—another elephant in the room! That being our **U.S. "Unfunded Liabilities."**

Most clear-thinking persons would acknowledge that "18 trillion" of anything is a number beyond human comprehension, and that our above-reviewed and rapidly growing **$18 trillion national debt** is absolutely unsustainable!

But, what we should be even more alarmed about is something that really keeps being "swept deep under the rug"—our **U.S. unfunded liabilities**. Which, basically, are the amounts of money our U.S. government has "promised" to pay its citizens, but does not yet have. Such as, "promises" to Social Security and Medicare recipients; Federal employee and Veteran benefits; and Federal debt held by the public; etc. Reportedly, those "promises" now add up to over **$97.5**

trillion—that's more than **$820,000** for every man, woman, and child in the U.S.!

Yes, **"in addition to"** an unsustainable **$18 trillion national debt**, we (and future generations of Americans) are also on the hook for a likewise unsustainable **$97.5 trillion of unfunded liabilities**—"promises" which are now on the record as lawful entitled-benefits.

For the most part, this totally absurd, irresponsible, and clearly unsustainable debt is the result of many years of politicians in both major political parties (democrat and republican) "buying votes" with "promises" for benefits from the public treasury. A treasury not yet having the funds to cover such benefits. Votes bought by self-serving politicians from self-serving voters. With all concerned being grossly out-of-touch with economic-reality, and absent of concern for future generations of Americans. Presently, there are about 4 paying into the benefits pot for every 1 drawing out of the pot. Some estimates indicate that by year 2030 only 2 will be paying into the benefits pool for every 1 dipping out of it.

To any right-minded person, it should be clear that we have dug ourselves into a bottomless-pit of unsustainable, unpayable debt. And have put our country on a dangerous path that undoubtedly threatens our liberty/freedom and ultimate survival. For which there are now but the following options: increase income taxes and payroll taxes; decrease federal government spending; and reduce Social Security and Medicare benefits, etc. Corrective measures unlikely to happen until "we the people" and "our government" find and exercise the courage to do right by our country and our descendants—until we choose to no longer enslave future generations of Americans with our irresponsible debt.

Of course there is another option—do nothing—and continue on with our apathy, complacency, denial, greed, and counter-productive fears. Until the wheels come off of our nation's wagon, and through mob-violence and civil war we self-destruct. Unfortunately, these words may be a bit too much reality for some to absorb and responsibly get in touch with.

Nevertheless, just as in our personal lives, we understand that we go in debt anytime our spending exceeds our income . . . we must likewise get a responsible grasp on the fact that a deficit (debt) occurs anytime our government spends more money than it takes in. And that "government-borrowing" to make up the difference is then added to "our" national debt. And that any and all "government-promises to pay," actually represent debt-obligations for "us."

In the end, "debt" is purely and simply "debt"—regardless of how diced, sliced, camouflaged, or downplayed. And, denying that it exists will not make it go away! If in doubt—try some "apathy," "complacency," or "denial" on your home mortgage, auto loan, other financial loans, or credit card accounts—and good luck with that!

At some point in time our national debt will have to be paid—or *otherwise resolved*. At this point there is no intent to "get into the weeds" on what an *otherwise resolved* national debt could involve. But, just some good old real-world common-sense says that when debts are not ultimately "paid" — for example in "bankruptcy" — there are few (if any) true winners and often many, many losers! And, it should not take a lot of imagination to grasp who the "losers" will be, who will pay the consequences — given a default on "our" national debt!

Yes, at some point in time our upward spiraling national debt and reckless tax and spend policies must be brought under control. It is irresponsibly-defiant of any resemblance of clear-thinking for a truly-sane people to believe or act otherwise!

In wrapping-up this section, it seems fitting to include a few words about "the canary in a coal mine."

Legend (more likely, reality) has it, that prior to modern-day ventilation systems being used, miners working in early coal mines would bring along a caged canary, especially when working in new mine-tunnels. Canaries, being real sensitive to methane and carbon monoxide, made them ideal alarms for dangerous, life-threatening gases. A bird that kept singing indicated a safe air supply; whereas a dead canary called for swift evacuation!

There are "Canaries in the coal mines" all around us — warning that our liberty and survival are at great risk. A couple are briefly mentioned below; and should require no assist in seeing a relationship to "our out of control national debt":

Greece: Located in southeastern Europe, Greece, with a population of about 10.8 million, is a democratic and developed country, sporting a high-income advanced economy, and exceptionally-high standard of living. Greece is also "broke" — "essentially bankrupt." In June 2015 it became the first developed-country to fail to make an International Monetary Fund (IMF) loan payment.

And, as these words are being written in August 2015, Greece's financial crisis is nearing its sixth year! As it struggles with a debt of about $353 billion, representing more than 175% of its Gross Domestic Product (GDP). And as the Greek government works exhaustingly to conclude negotiations with international creditors, in hopes to arrange yet another multibillion-euro bailout — the third bailout in the past five years. And as public opposition to the truly-necessary economic reforms (inevitable and painful sacrifices) continue to mount.

And a little geographically-closer to home . . .

The U.S. Territory of Puerto Rico: Although Puerto Rico's population is only about that of the state of Connecticut, as of August 2015, it is reportedly in hopeless-debt to lenders for about $72 billion. More than the total debt of every state in the U.S., other than California and New York. Puerto Rico's governor has stated that *debt restructuring* is now the only way to prevent an economic *death spiral*. Of course, *"debt restructuring"* is *code* and *political-correctness* for saying that a bunch of folks are going to lose lots of money and property;

not get paid; pay more taxes; receive less or no benefits; and otherwise have to do much more with much less, etc.

But, nothing similar to the economic disasters of Greece, Puerto Rico, or elsewhere can ever happen to "us" — here in the continental United States! Because our political leaders have long ago discovered a *magic pill* — a way to endlessly over-spend, over-tax, over-borrow, over-promise, over-control, over-regulate, and otherwise "over-everything" — with no negative consequences!

Sure, they have! And, thus far, *we the people* continue to irresponsibly buy-into, tolerate, and even contribute to such nation-destroying "BS." Through (once again) our ignorance, apathy, complacency, denial, greed, and fear. And our unwillingness and lack of courage to unrelentingly pressure our political leaders — and ourselves — to do otherwise.

As we continue to pass-on to future generations of Americans an unsustainable debt that will — if not checked in time — continue this nation down an unrecoverable economic *death spiral*. Towards an end void of liberty, freedom, opportunity — and ultimately — survival.

As Thomas Jefferson so wisely warned so many years ago — we must choose between economy and liberty or profusion and servitude!

History will record — and future generations will reap — the consequences of our choices. We must do the right thing — we must make the responsible choices and as-required sacrifices to get our country's economic house in order. We must no longer tolerate political leaders and government policies and agendas that fail to unrelentingly pursue this critical aim!

= = =

"The American Republic will endure until the day Congress discovers that it can bribe the public with the public's money."

–Alexis De Tocqueville

"Republicans and Democrats are obsessed with making sure that illegal aliens are granted citizenship. The American people are not. They're concerned about jobs, the economy, debt. They're concerned about a plundering country. They're concerned about a decaying, dying country." – Rush Limbaugh

"Washington's insatiable desire to spend our children's inheritance on failed stimulus plans and other misguided economic theories have given record debt and left us with far too many unemployed."

– Rick Perry

"Blessed are the young for they shall inherit the national debt."

– Herbert Hoover

"If you think health care is expensive now, wait until you see what it costs when it's free!" – P.J. O'Rourke

"Man is not, by nature, deserving of all that he wants. When we think that we are automatically entitled to something, that is when we start walking all over others to get it." — Criss Jami

"We pay too little attention to the reserve power of the people to take care of themselves. We are too solicitous for government intervention, on the theory, first, that the people themselves are helpless, and second, that the government has superior capacity for action. Often times both of these conclusions are wrong."
— Calvin Coolidge

"Since taking office, President Obama has signed into law spending increases of nearly 25 percent for domestic government agencies — and 84 percent increase when you include the failed stimulus. All of this new government spending was sold as 'investment.'
— Paul Ryan

"I want anyone who believes in life, liberty, and pursuit of happiness, to succeed. And I want any force, any person, any element of an overarching Big Government that would stop your success, I want that organization, that element or that person to fail. I want you to succeed." — Rush Limbaugh

"A man in debt is so far a slave." — Ralph Waldo Emerson

Nuclear Energy —
A "Double-Edged Sword"

> "The way to win an atomic war is to make certain it never starts."
> — General Omar N. Bradley
>
> "Although September 11 was horrible, it didn't threaten the survival of the human race, like nuclear weapons do." — Stephen Hawking

The expression "a double-edged sword" is often understood to be in reference to "*something having both good and bad parts or results,*" or "*a situation or event that has negative as well as positive consequences.*"

Nuclear energy is one such "double-edged sword."

As an "energy source" it can light our homes, streets, schools, and businesses; power our home appliances and business equipment; and charge our smartphone batteries, etc. We need little to no convincing of such benefits.

On the other hand, as a "weapon," or an "improperly-maintained nuclear reactor," etc., this awesome and often mysterious power can — in the blink of an eye — kill, injure, or put at health risk, countless thousands of us (in some circumstances – millions). And also render large areas of our environment contaminated and uninhabitable for thousands of years. As such, we must never relax our awareness of, or defense against, this potentially devastating and unimaginable threat! But, to our potential destruction, we often do!

What follows in this section are a few reminders – not only of a truly awesome threat, but also of our related responsibilities.

Nuclear Weapons

Hiroshima & Nagasaki – 1945: _In August 1945, during the final stages of World War II, the United States dropped atomic bombs on the Japanese cities of Hiroshima and Nagasaki. Hiroshima on August 6. Nagasaki on August 9. These two bombings being – so far – the first and only use of nuclear weapons in wartime.

Together they killed an estimated 150,000 to 250,000 people, mostly civilians. About half of the deaths in each city occurred on the day of bombing. The other half, some 75,000 to 125,000 deaths, occurred over the following months, as a result of burns, radiation sickness, and related injuries and illness.

About 132 pounds of highly-enriched uranium was used in the bomb released over Hiroshima, Japan's seventh largest city at that time. It destroyed about 90 percent of the city.

About 17 pounds of plutonium-239 was used in the explosive charge of the bomb dropped 3 days later on Nagasaki.

Within about 6 years after these devastating bombings, atomic weapon devices were being tested which had explosive forces about <u>a thousand times greater</u>.

Both cities have since been rebuilt and include various important industries. Ironically, with Nagasaki being a major <u>nuclear reactor supplier</u>, and both cities highly dependent upon <u>nuclear power</u> for electricity.

In 1945 the U.S. was "the" sole nuclear power on this planet.

But <u>not</u> so today! For, according to the Federation of American Scientists and other sources, our world's nuclear powers now include the United States, Russia, Britain, France, China, India, Pakistan, Israel, and North Korea. And, although, according to some sources, the number of operational nuclear warheads has been reduced from the 1986 total of more than 64,000 to a present "estimate" of 10,000. This remaining arsenal-of-death is still enough to destroy our world many times over!

Furthermore, long-range ballistic missiles such as possessed by the U.S., Russia, and China are capable of delivering "multiple" nuclear warheads, programed to simultaneously strike different targets. And, regardless of where they are launched from, the time required to reach a target (such as the U.S.) on the opposite side of the earth, would typically be about "30 minutes." Hardly enough warning-time to do much more than the futile exercise of "duck and cover." Just a few of today's truly sobering nuclear weapons realities! As the U.S. and various other nations continue futile efforts to—through "deals" and "negotiations"—prevent Iran from joining the "nuclear weapons club." Iran, a terrorist state that continues to publically chant "death to America" and vow to "wipe Israel off the map"! And, not to overlook the radical dictatorship of North Korea—continuing an unabated fast-track agenda to gain the capability of long-range delivery of their nuclear warhead arsenal to distant targets. Including our reportedly "thus far" out of reach United States.

Nuclear Reactors

Worldwide, millions of us live but a few miles from a nuclear reactor. In the United States alone there are more than 100. Man-made nuclear facilities providing us great benefits, along with a potentially devastating threat—double-edged swords.

The loss of both primary and backup power for just a few hours at any of these facilities could lead to a meltdown resulting in the release of a deadly radioactive plume into the atmosphere.

In the event of a major disaster at one or more of these facilities, countless people could be killed, injured, or contaminated with life-threatening radiation. Parts of our environment could be contaminated and rendered uninhabitable for years to come. Survivors could be displaced permanently from their homes and property and lose everything. Likewise, our food supply, utilities, police and medical support, communications systems, and government functions could be critically disrupted or destroyed.

The above scenarios are not fiction-based. They are realistic generalizations of the types of tragedies our world has experienced in the past, and can again in the future. What follows in this section are but three of many examples. Although much summarized, they nonetheless are indicators of our awesome duty to "responsibly" deal with nuclear energy — and of the consequences, should we fail to do so!

1979--Three Mile Island Nuclear Accident in the U.S.: On March 28, 1979 the Three Mile Island nuclear power plant near Harrisburg, Pennsylvania experienced what was reported to be a partial meltdown of the nuclear reactor core. Resulting in the release of radioactive gases into the atmosphere, and prompting the Pennsylvania governor to evacuate pregnant women from the area.

This nuclear accident was reported to be the result of a combination of faulty equipment, misread instruments, and poor decisions on the part of operating personnel and management. An accident that had a profound effect upon public, government, and industry-attention to the risks of nuclear energy and how it would be thereafter pursued in the U.S.

While the Nuclear Regulatory Commission (NRC) reported that the limited amount of radioactive material released did not constitute a health hazard, the crippled reactor itself was deemed unusable and unapproachable for years to come.

This 1979 *partial meltdown* at the Three Mile Island nuclear power plant was a *wake-up call* incident. Rated five on the International Nuclear Event Seven-Point Scale, it resulted in a clean-up effort not ending until 1993, and reportedly to have cost a billion dollars or more.

1986--Chernobyl Nuclear Power Plant Disaster in Ukraine:
It was a little after 1 A.M., April 26, 1986, that one of our world's nightmare scenarios unfolded. Reactor 4 in the huge Chernobyl nuclear power facility experience a fire and explosion.

A devastation that initially claimed the lives of more than 30 people, and resulted in long-term effects involving cancers and other health issues that are the subject of study to this day.

The causes are still the subject of debate. But commonly reported to be some combination of a design flaw involving the control rods that regulate reactor power levels, a poorly trained engineering crew, a test that required a power-down of the reactor, and an old-style Soviet boss who refused to believe anything major could be wrong at what was—at the time—considered a high-tech nuclear power plant.

At any rate, the explosion was spectacular. Eight-hundred-pound cubes of lead were tossed around like a child's toy. The reactor's 1,000-ton sealing cap was blown off, releasing large amounts of life-threatening radioactive particles into the atmosphere, which then spread over large portions of western USSR, Europe, and elsewhere.

A radioactive release reportedly estimated to be ten times that of the 1945 atomic bombing of Hiroshima, Japan.

A disaster that involved a struggle to contain and control a nuclear reactor meltdown in order to prevent **an even greater catastrophe**. A struggle for survival supported at the time by more than a half-million workers, at a cost of billions of Russian rubles.

A disaster involving a costly *contamination containment effort* that continues to this day – at a site that will be uninhabitable for thousands of years!

2011--Fukushima Nuclear Power Plant Disaster in Japan: On March 11, 2011, Japan was hit by its worst crisis in the 65 or so years since the end of World War II.

About 40 some miles off the east coast of Japan a powerful magnitude 9 undersea earthquake took place – the most powerful ever recorded to hit Japan – the fifth most powerful in the world since 1900, the beginning of modern-day record-keeping of earthquakes.

This super earthquake triggered a powerful tsunami with waves that reached a height of 130 feet or more and swept approximately 6 miles inland of Japan. A catastrophic earthquake that reportedly relocated Japan's main island about 8 feet to the east and is estimated to have shifted our Earth on its axis up to about 10 inches.

Early reports confirmed some 16,000 deaths, 6,000 injured, and 2,600 or more missing. As well as, over a million households left without water, and more than four million without electricity. Other early reporting included a collapsed dam, and thousands of buildings collapsed or otherwise seriously damaged.

But, this was not the end of the devastation.

This super tsunami also caused catastrophic nuclear accidents at Japan's Fukushima Nuclear Power Plant complex. Meltdowns and explosions due to cooling systems failures at three of this plant's nuclear reactors forced the evacuation of residents within up to about 12 miles of the damaged plant.

With early-on losses related to this earthquake alone estimated early-on to be as much as $35 billion, this natural disaster so far stands as the costliest in world history.

After more than 4 years since the Fukushima nuclear power plant explosions and meltdowns, Japan continues to struggle with how to deal with the growing hazards associated with this crippled Facility.

None the least being the increasingly urgent and complex task of handling the huge—ever accumulating—amounts of hazardous radioactive water.   Resulting from the critical process of keeping nuclear fuel in the crippled reactors cool— in order to prevent occurrence of **an even greater catastrophe**.

As Japan's nearby forests are being destroyed to make room for more and more storage containers of contaminated radioactive water.   And as Japan and others continue thus far unsuccessful, and seemingly hopeless, efforts to prevent this nuclear nightmare from further contaminating our oceans waters—and the human and other life forms depending upon such.

"Our" Spent (Used) Nuclear Fuel: Although after about three or so years a nuclear reactor's fuel is no longer efficient and must be removed, it is still highly radioactive and thermally hot and therefore must be handled remotely and shielded. As of 2015, our U.S. national inventory of commercial spent nuclear fuel reportedly totals about 70,000 metric tons, and is stored at some 75 urban, suburban, and rural locations throughout 33 states. Some nuclear waste, such as high-level waste from defense nuclear activities, will remain radioactive and hazardous for hundreds of thousands of years. And we have no guarantee that our human-designed waste packages and storage methods can safely and otherwise effectively contain such material for that long. Just another liberty and survival threatening matter consuming untold billions of taxpayer dollars, and getting little to no attention by those pushing "climate change," "racial-unrest" "political correctness," and other designed to distract-and-divide agendas. As mainstream media, our political leaders, and "we the people" continue to treat the dark-side of nuclear energy with ignorance, apathy, complacency, denial, greed, counter-productive fear. Not to mention – irresponsible neglect!

= = =

"For 50 years, nuclear power stations have produced three products which only a lunatic could want: bomb-explosive plutonium, lethal radioactive waste and electricity so dear it has to be heavily subsidized. They leave to future generations the task, and most of the cost, of making safe sites that have been polluted half-way to eternity." – James Buchan

"Nuclear power plants must be prepared to withstand everything from earthquakes to tsunamis, from fires to floods to acts of terrorism." – Ban Ki-moon

"We shall require a substantially new manner of thinking if mankind is to survive." – Albert Einstein

"Peace is the one condition of survival in this nuclear age."
– Adlai Stevenson

"The use of military force against Iran would be very dangerous. It would be very provocative. The only thing worse would be Iran being a nuclear power." – Rudy Giuliani

"The most spectacular event of the past half century, did not occur. We have enjoyed sixty years without nuclear weapons exploded in anger." – Thomas Schelling

Migration, Immigration, & Emigration

> *"Remember, remember always, that all of us, and you and I especially, are descended from immigrants and revolutionists."*
> — *Franklin D. Roosevelt*

Not so long ago a most special, loving, hard-working, insightful, and dedicated young American patriot, shared with her parents some justifiably deep-concerns about one of the more serious threats to our nation.

In doing so, our daughter Jamie was appropriately referring to the federal government's on-going failure to secure our nation's borders. And, likewise failure to responsibly control legal (and prevent illegal) **migration, emigration** and **immigration**. Nation-destroying threats that, now approaching YR 2016, continue unabated!

Threats created and progressively worsened, predominantly over the past thirty-years or so, by government policies and political agendas aimed at <u>obtaining cheap labor</u>, <u>securing votes</u>, <u>changing our nation's demographics</u>, and <u>transforming America</u>. Driven by self-serving and special-interest elements in <u>both</u> the Democrat and Republican Parties! Led by individuals who have sold their political-souls to big-business interests, and to other middle-class destroying agendas of the radical-left and radical-right. Leaving us with a level of damage to our U.S. economy, common-language English, and culture, that may have already passed beyond any realistic near-term recovery — nor without unthinkable chaos and cost!

The result of "liberty and survival threatening" agendas that are progressively "blurring the lines" between **"legal"** and **"illegal"** migration, immigration, an emigration. But, each do exist, and **there is a never-to-be-forgotten**, or overlooked, nor ignored, **difference**! A crucial distinction that growing numbers of the seekers of "cheap labor" and "manipulated votes" keep trying to convince us otherwise! Through intentional distractions such as using the words "undocumented immigrants," etc., when in reality actually referring to "illegal aliens."

Also **never-to-be-forgotten** — we are a nation of immigrants. The liberty/freedom and vast opportunities available to us today are the result of the blood, sweat, toil, sacrifices, and other good works of our "nation of immigrants." Of **contributors** and **earners** — not the takers and assumed-entitled! Of principled people of many origins. Willing, for the greater good of all, to **assimilate** into a **common** U.S. culture . . . speaking a **common**-language — English. People dedicated to **building, protecting** and **preserving** this great nation. As opposed to those who strive to abuse, transform, and ultimately destroy it.

Some special aims of this section: **(1.)** *Share* constructive information that hopefully helps to dispel various misunderstandings about **migration, immigration,** and **emigration;** and **(2.)** Encourage and support an unrelenting and highly-visible movement of lawfully-constructive public outrage and feedback to our federal government. Until our political representatives and leaders pass, implement, and enforce policies, laws, and procedures, that:

(A.) Secure all U.S. borders; **(B.)** Stop "illegal" migration and immigration into our country; **(C.)** Execute a timely and humanitarian deportation of all illegal aliens from the U.S.; **(D.)** Establish, declare, encourage, and enforce "English" as our nationwide common-language; **(E.)** Vigorously embark upon a nationwide clean-up and correction of the social and cultural mess caused by the irresponsible and failed migration and immigration policies now in place. Starting with, immediately outlawing and putting a stop to: "sanctuary cities" and "sanctuary states;" issuance of drivers licenses to illegal aliens; and loop-holes that permit illegal aliens to receive U.S. benefits, vote in U.S. elections, etc.

Some Important Terms & Definitions

Migration generally means the temporary movement from place to place, such as the seasonal movement of Canada Geese and Monarch Butterflies, and movement of migrate workers and nomadic people, etc.

On the other hand, **immigration** and **emigration** commonly refer to a <u>permanent</u> move from one's native land to settle in another country. Therefore, while people, animals, and birds, can all **migrate**, we generally consider that only people **immigrate** and **emigrate**.

The difference between **immigration** and **emigration** is a matter of perspective, or point of view. That is, both **emigration** and **immigration** originate from Latin words: *emigratus* referring to "moving away," while *immigratus* referring to "moving into." So, their meaning is determined by the country of <u>origin</u> and the <u>destination</u> country.

In other words, to **emigrate** means to leave one country or region to settle in another. While, to **immigrate** means to come to a country which one is not a native of, and usually to permanently reside. For example: The Jones family *immigrated* **to** the U.S., while the Smith family *emigrated* **from** Europe.

Clearly then, almost all of us that now inhabit the United States are descendants of **immigrants** to the U.S., who **emigrated** from somewhere else. Think not? Then, possibly a friendly chat on the subject with our closest American Indian neighbor might be in order and meaningfully revealing.

Relationship to "Liberty & Survival"?

But, what do **migration, immigration,** and **emigration** have to do with "threats to our liberty and survival"? Quite a lot, of course. The doubters that this is so might benefit from a talk with Canada Geese, Monarch Butterflies, and other creatures that **migrate**. Starting with how and for how long would they likely survive without the freedom/liberty to routinely carryout their life-sustaining migrations.

And, a little closer to home — how important would **migration, emigration** and **immigration** suddenly become to us personally, in the unthinkable event that we should wakeup someday to a United States, or portions thereof, no longer inhabitable as the result of a nuclear disaster or other environmental catastrophe.

Think that we are immune to such threats? Then, a re-read of herein section titled *"Nuclear Energy — A Double-Edged Sword"* is strongly suggested. And/or, for much more eye-opening information on the subject — "Google" the "1979, U.S., Three-mile Island nuclear disaster," and "1986, Ukraine, Chernobyl disaster," and "2011, Japan, Fukushima disaster."

There are other examples, but the three suggested above should be a sufficient wake-up call. Enough to remind us that, in a heart-beat, any of us could be faced with the survival-driven need to **migrate** or **emigrate**. To immediately relocate to some other place in search of safety and the opportunity for life, liberty, and pursuit of happiness!

Consider also, if we were ever to be in the shoes of the untold millions of people elsewhere on this earth, who, in an effort to survive, have been forced throughout history to flee their homeland as a result of wars. Or, due to persecution by tyrannical government leaders, such as Germany's Hitler in the 1933-45 time frame. Or, more recently, from Syria's dictator, Assad. Or, from the present and widening atrocities carried out by terrorist threats such radical/militant Islamists under the black flag of ISIS.

So, whether **migration, emigration** and **immigration** are a benefit or threat, depends largely upon one's perspective — which side of the fence, border, or tragedy one is on.

On the *benefits* side, consider that the United States — the most powerful country on this planet in terms of military and economy, and the envy of the world in terms of liberty/freedom and opportunity — was built by immigrants. By people fleeing from tyranny, persecution, religious intolerance, economic depression, etc.

On the *threat* side, consider the fate of the estimated 30 to 75 million buffalo (bison) that once roamed North America before arrival of European explorers and settlers. Or, of the many American Indian tribes and clans — and their cultures, traditions, and languages — that had existed for thousands of years in North America, before driven from their homelands and replaced by our modern-day U.S.A., Canada, and Mexico.

Whether migration, emigration, and immigration are a benefit or threat to a host-nation depends upon that nation's related policies and laws and its enforcement thereof.

Unfortunately and most shamefully, due to bad and poorly-enforced policies and laws, our U.S. borders, common-language English, and culture, are being methodically destroyed before our eyes. For evidence, one need only to just "look," "watch," and "listen" around. In our neighborhoods, workplaces, schools, colleges, churches, shopping malls, streets, sidewalks, highways, parks, playgrounds, and in or local, state, and federal government.

Growing evidence of people entering the U.S. legally and illegally — NOT to accept and assimilate our country's culture, learn and use our common-language English, and contribute to this country's betterment. But, rather, to disregard and disrespect U.S. history, and abuse this great nation's generosity and hard fought for freedoms/liberties and opportunities.

Truly, nation-destroying behavior encouraged, aided, and tolerated by irresponsible U.S. government representatives; profit-driven business leaders; a liberal-biased news media; and too many legally eligible voters consumed with inattention, ignorance, apathy, complacency, denial, greed, and counter-productive fears.

Our U.S. Census data speaks for itself. Given the many hundreds of other legal-citizen ancestry groups in the U.S., one can only imagine the countless millions of people that justifiable feel betrayed and outraged. By, for instance, the special treatment being given to Spanish-speaking groups within our borders. And, by Muslim groups dedicated to promoting and applying Sharia-Law within our U.S. borders.

Overall, about 500 different self-identified ancestries were reported during the recent U.S. Census. Ranked by number, the top ten ancestry groups are as shown in the following chart.

Rank	Ancestry group	Number	Percent
1.	German	42,841,569	15.2%
2.	Irish	30,524,799	10.8
3.	African American	24,903,412	8.8
4.	English	24,509,692	8.7
5.	American	20,188,305	7.2
6.	Mexican	18,382,291	6.5
7.	Italian	15,638,348	5.6
8.	Polish	8,977,235	3.2
9.	French	8,309,666	3.0
10.	American Indian	7,876,568	2.8

"Immigration" involves many complexities. And whether it is helpful or harmful to any country, depends upon the kind of immigrants involved and the receiving country's (the host nation's) needs. For example, whether the immigrants under consideration are wealthy or poor, healthy or sick, young or old, educated or uneducated, skilled or unskilled, a single person or a family, from friendly countries or from hostile countries, or if they speak or do not speak the receiving country's language, etc. And, whether the receiving country has a need for the benefits offered by the type of immigrants available at a particular point in time.

So, depending upon their type, to the receiving country, immigrants can truly represent a possible benefit, burden, or risk. Certain immigrants may offer a positive contribution to the receiving country's social, economic, and technological progress, or to its world political standing, etc. While certain others may be a national/domestic security threat, health risk, crime risk, or possibly result in over-crowding hospitals, schools, and other infrastructure, or otherwise be a social, cultural, economic, and/or, security burden, etc. Again, and never to be forgotten, and cannot be repeated enough, a country is defined by—and cannot exist without—"its" **borders**, **language**, and **culture**. And, critical to protecting and preserving these three essential aspects is a proper, lawful, and strongly enforced immigration policy.

And here's a real (not-politically-correct) news-flash: All sane and in-touch-with-reality countries have and enforce immigration policies designed first and foremost to **benefit the receiving country**! Policies and enforcement practices founded in the reality that every country's resources are limited. And, upon the nation-survival fact that acceptance of immigrants must not be viewed as a service or obligation to the world at large. But, rather, <u>a lawful endeavor to satisfy the receiving country's self-interests</u>.

For, no country, the U.S. or otherwise, can feed, house, heal, and protect, all of the world's in-need and less fortunate. To ignore this reality is to defy logic and common sense, with ultimately a self-destructive outcome for the immigration-receiving country and its citizens. **Never to be overlooked also**, is a country's duty to not do an injustice to the countless **"legal"** immigrants who in the past have, and in the future will, lawfully play by the rules. The injustice of rewarding illegal immigrants with amnesty or other benefits from the receiving country's public treasury.

Crucial to remember also — the freedom/liberty and ultimate survival of the "receiving country," is truly dependent upon responsible, lawful, effective, and strongly enforced immigration policy! World history provides many examples of this reality. One such example is summarized below. Not one of fiction, hype, or exaggeration. But rather, a truly real-world example that "we the people" in the U.S., as well as other nations, should and must take serious note of. And, timely learn from, before suffering a similar fate.

Lebanon — Lost Liberty/Freedom & Struggle for Survival

(Please Note: The following account was taken in part from *"Because They Hate,"* by Brigitte Gabriel. In my view, a "must-read" for all U.S. Citizens; and what should-be "required reading" in all U.S. high schools, colleges, military installations, and branches of federal/state/local government. A truly eye-opening account of the threat of radical/militant Islam.)

= = =

At the end of World War I, the League of Nations gave France control over Lebanon and its neighbor Syria. In 1920 France divided Lebanon and Syria into separate colonies, with borders that separated the mostly Muslim Syria from the mix of religious communities in Lebanon, where Christians were at that time dominant.

Although Lebanon's independence from France was declared in 1941, its full independence came about in stages. By 1944 most of France's control over Lebanon had been transferred to Lebanon, and evacuation of French military was completed by 1946. Lebanon setup a representative form of government more similar to ours in the U.S. than any other country in Lebanon's region of the world.

At around that point in time Lebanon's population was estimated to be about 55 percent Christian and 45 percent Muslim. And, I was about four years old, living far away in the U.S. Midwest, and oblivious to anything but my child-perceived environment. An environment in stark contrast to the world a typical four year old child in Lebanon was then experiencing, or about to endure. For—by about 1970— around the time I had reached the age of 28, the Christians in Lebanon had become the **minority** and the Muslims the **majority**. All in the relatively brief span of less than 30 years since obtaining independence from France!

The reasons for this power shift (from Christian to Muslim) are many and complex. Such as, but not limited to: (1.)

Lebanon's acceptance of a wave of some 180,000 Palestinian refugees in connection with Israel's declaration of independence in 1948-49, followed by another wave of refugees from the 1967 Arab-Israeli War, and (2.) The imbalance between Lebanon's Muslim and Christian marriage practices and birth rates.

Typically, Lebanon Christians would marry one spouse until death did they part, and have two to four children. While, on the other hand, the Muslims' Islamic religion allowed up to four wives at the same time, and permitted husbands to end a marriage by simply declaring "you are divorced" three times in a row. The result being, many Muslim children from many Muslim wives. As one unsettling example: Osama bin Laden, the leader of al-Quada terrorists responsible for the devastating September 11, 2001 attack on the U.S., was reportedly one of fifty-three children, himself having twenty-seven children. With Osama bin Laden and his father siring at least eighty children—saying nothing about the countless off-springs from his fifty-two brothers and sisters.

Until the power shift from Christian to Muslim, the Christians in Lebanon never entertained the thought that their Muslim neighbors, doctors, teachers, soldiers, political leaders, etc., would ever murder them, torture them, bomb them, and blow-up their villages, towns, and cities. However, history shows that the very trusting and terribly naïve Christians and other non-Muslims of Lebanon and elsewhere in the region, tragically learned otherwise. For a tragic and shameful many, at the cost of their homes, businesses, schools, churches, freedom/liberty, and lives.

The above-described Lebanon tragedy offers a **critical lesson**. But most unfortunately, one that to this day is still being too-slowly learned. And, too-often ignored by the U.S. and other nations. Dangerously disregarded by the U.S. and other nations pursuing "political correctness," "multiculturalism," and "multinationalism" agendas. As radical/militant Islam continues its devastating spread and terror throughout the world. A world where some nation's borders are controlled and secured — and where other nations' are irresponsibly and self-destructively not!

To any country, immigration involves a mix of intentions. Not only the aims of the particular immigrants seeking entry and acceptance, but also those of politicians, government, businesses, religious groups, and employed and unemployed citizens; etc. Involving agendas often misunderstood, poorly communicated, concealed, distorted, and most always in conflict with one another.

In spite of the all the emotional and otherwise roadblocks, distractions, and barriers, the ultimate goals of our U.S. immigration policy must always be "**U.S. self-serving**." With primary considerations that, as a minimum, include the safety, security, and economic self-interests of our nation as a whole. And, given the reality of the times, an immigration policy especially focused on protecting our great nation and its citizens from the very real and spreading threat of radical/militant Islam. And, from Sharia-Law, regardless of the practitioner. For, at stake is nothing less than the sovereignty of our U.S. borders, English language, and culture. Truly, our very liberty/freedom and ultimate survival!

And, as these words were being finalized for this book, Europe's worst refugee crisis since the end of World War II continued to worsen. With millions fleeing the war and terrorist torn ravages of the Middle East, Africa, and Asia, etc. Fleeing on foot—by any available means—to any "elsewhere" opportunity for survival. Desperate human beings (men, women, children—of all ages and circumstance). Any of whom would unquestionably give anything to have a shot at the liberty, freedom, and opportunities that so many of us are blessed with. And, too often take for granted, waste, and abuse!

An on-going refugee crisis exemplified by Germany's plans to receive an estimated 800,000 in 2015; and with Britain, France, etc., struggling to accommodate countless others. A humanitarian crisis of unimaginable scope, that is overwhelming Europe and undoubtedly also heading for our shores. To an already much in-debt USA, struggling to handle a growing "illegal aliens" burden and threatened economy!

Senior officials within the United Nations (UN) have reportedly said that the UN's humanitarian agencies are close to bankruptcy. Leaving them unable to handle the basic needs of millions of people, resulting from the unthinkable size of the refugee crisis in the Middle East, Africa, and Europe. A crisis further worsened by new droves of refugees bound north-west towards Europe. Driven by rapidly degrading conditions in Jordan and Lebanon. Such as, lack of food and healthcare. Conditions becoming unbearable for countless of the some 4 million people who have so far fled Syria.

An ever-growing tragedy—in clear view of our "always media-connected" world. As countless millions "look the other way" in ignorance, apathy, complacency, denial, greed, and fear. And as President Obama, Hillary Clinton, Bernie Sanders, Pope Francis, and others, beat the socialist drum of *climate-change* and *income-inequality*, and call for the U.S. and the other "privileged" to do much more!

A rhetoric that—regardless of how compassionate or otherwise the intent—clearly neglects to acknowledge that the U.S. routinely takes-in more immigrants than all other nations combined. A rhetoric that ignores the fact that *socialism* eventually fails—because sooner or later it runs out of other peoples' money! A rhetoric that also fails to responsibly warn that, infiltrated within the countless thousands of desperate souls truthfully seeking refuge, can also be untold numbers of radical/militant Islamists and other terrorist-minded individuals. Those hell-bent to wreak horrific havoc on and ultimately destroy any nation in which they can establish a foot hold! A reality that, to our peril, we continue to ignore and fail to unrelentingly and successfully confront and defeat! Even as radical/militant Islamist terrorist atrocities continue to be suffered withing our U.S. borders!

"Illegal aliens have always been a problem in the United States. Ask any Indian." – Robert Orben

"The simple truth is that we have lost control of our own borders, and no nation can do that and survive. We ignore America's lost sovereignty at our own peril." – Ronald Reagan

"Our nation's immigration policy has been of top concern in recent years, and for good reason. With between eight and twelve million illegal aliens in the United States, it is obvious a problem out of control." – Chris Cannon

"Amnesty is a big billboard, a flashing billboard, to the rest of the world that we don't really mean our immigration law."

– Richard Lamm

"A simple way to take measure of a country is to look at how many want in. And how many want out." – Tony Blair

"In a world where various forms of modern tyranny seek to suppress religious freedom, or try to reduce it to a subculture without right to a voice in the public square, or to use religion as a pretext for hatred and brutality, it is imperative that the followers of various religions join their voices in calling for peace, tolerance and respect for the dignity and rights of others." – Pope Francis (Taken from his speech outside Independence Hall, Philadelphia, PA, September 26, 2015, on final leg of his six-day U.S. trip.)

"Change" We Can Believe In?

(Re: Candidate/President Barack Hussein Obama)

"We have a choice in this country. We can accept a politics that breeds division and conflict and cynicism . . . That is one option. Or, at this moment, in this election, we can come together and say, 'Not this time' . . . ."

"The first thing I will do as President will be to reverse the illegal and unconstitutional aspects of the Patriot Act, with the stroke of my pen."

". . . that means no more illegal wiretapping of American citizens."

"I don't want to pit Red America against Blue America. I want to be the president of the United States of America."

". . . I taught the Constitution for ten years, I believe in the Constitution, and I will obey the Constitution of the United States. We're not goanna use 'signing statements' as a way of doing an end-run around Congress."

"I pledge to cut the deficit we inherited in half by the end of my first term in office."

"I will sign a universal health-care bill into law by the end of my first term as president that will cover every American and cut the cost of a typical family's premium by up to $2,500 a year."

"I, Barack Hussein Obama, do solemnly swear that I will execute the office of president of the United States faithfully, and will to the best of my ability, preserve, protect, and defend the constitution of the United States."

"My administration is committed to creating an unprecedented level of openness in government."

. . . IRS targeting of political dissidents had "not even a smidgen of corruption".

"If you like your doctor, you will be able to keep your doctor. Period. If you like your health care plan, you will be able to keep your health care plan. Period. No one will take it away. No matter what."

". . . I believe in the Second Amendment, I believe in people's lawful right to bear arms, I will not take your shotgun away, I will not take your rifle away . . . ."

"If you've got a business – you didn't build that. Somebody else made that happen."

. . . U.S. will "do what we must" to stop Iran getting nuclear weapons.

= = =

"The future is not Big Government. Self-serving politicians. Powerful bureaucrats. This has been tried, tested throughout history. The result has always been disaster. President Obama, your agenda is not new. It's not change, and it's not hope." — Rush Limbaugh

Letters
"To" & "From"
The President

Beginning on the next page is a copy of a letter my wife Ann and I sent to President Obama, February 20, 2013. As shown at the end of this letter, copies were also mailed to our Kansas political leaders, the Speaker of The House, major news media, and selected radio talk show hosts. Like similar efforts of countless others—an attempt to "do what we can."

Immediately following our letter, is a scanned-copy of a May 28, 2013 response we received, showing it to be over President Obama's signature. A response that not only falls short on seriously acknowledging our expressed concerns, but also, from common-courtesy and professional-correspondence perspectives, fails to recognize that our letter to the President was submitted "jointly" by my wife Ann and me. While a certainly notable White House oversight—otherwise, in the big scheme of things, truly trivial. Also included is a scanned copy of Kansas Senator Jerry Moran's July 9, 2013 response. Which, in this author's view, is more appropriately addressed, more personal in tone, and its message more clearly related to the concerns expressed in our February 20, 2013 letter to the President.

(A Verbatim-Copy of Original Letter)

February 20, 2013

President Barack Obama
The White House
1600 Pennsylvania Avenue, NW
Washington, DC 20500

Mr. President:

At ages 70 and 68, this is the second letter we have written to a President of our United States. We should have written more. The first was to President Nixon, in 1972. You were about 11 years old at that time. There was war on this earth then, there is war now, and, sadly, history suggests that war will continue to be a terribly sad part of the human experience. An example of man's inhumanity to man.

As you well know, history also shows that devastating consequences can fall upon any nation failing to accept and prepare for this reality. You should receive due credit for appropriate measures you have taken, and take, to protect our

Country from national security threats, foreign and domestic. You must also be held accountable should you fail to do so.

Mr. President, you were elected as a result of many factors. Among them, a "special gift" you were blessed with, and the many freedoms and opportunities that only our Great Nation offers. Freedoms and opportunities that many before us have made great sacrifices for, and which are guaranteed by our United States Constitution.

The "special gift" we refer to above is of course your unique and obviously powerful oratory skills. Without which it is realistically inconceivable that you would have become President, regardless of your other attributes.

Supplementing your oratory skills was and is, in no small way, the "communications technology" born out of our Country's uniquely competitive and capitalistic economic system. The very system which you and many others seem to be hell-bent to destroy through radically liberal policies and agendas.

Mr. President, this Great Nation has provided you, your family, and countless others, a magnitude of opportunities enjoyed and taken advantage of. You, your family, and many others explored, compared, and considered other places on this good Earth, and chose to be here. Chose to take advantage of the benefits of this "one of its kind" Great Nation of fought for freedom and opportunity.

This Great Nation does not need "transformed". It does, however, need and deserve to be responsibly "protected", "maintained", and "preserved" for present and future generations. A responsibility shared by all U.S. Citizens. A responsibility which you and others have taken sworn oath to carry out. And, a task which you and other elected government officials are very well compensated for in many ways.

Mr. President, given your "special gift", you clearly share an "extra special" responsibility for the devastating course our country is now on. You could have used your gift to build upon many past efforts to "unite" our Nation on a "team effort" for the greater good of all.

But, shamefully, you have to date chosen to use your special gift of oratory skills to "divide" this Nation. To pit one against another. To create and perpetuate a growing population of "dependency" and "entitlement" constituents. And, to attack the very foundation of our Great Nation, that being the unique freedoms and opportunities afforded by our Constitution.

It is noteworthy that, when you delivered the keynote speech at the 2004 Democratic National Convention, *you emphasized the importance of "unity", and made veiled jabs at the Bush Administration regarding "diversionary use of wedge issues"*. What happened to the young man who spoke so eloquently and convincingly at that time? A gifted speaker, seemingly so sincere. Mr. President, as but one example of your leadership shortfalls, you could have made positive use of prime-time TV to routinely address and unite "all" U.S. Citizens with "team building" messages.

Instead, you have chosen to frequently spend valuable taxpayer money traveling to speak directly to your various special interest groups across the Country. With messages which all too often pit one of us against another.

As a result, while it is obvious that you are technically "the President", many, many citizens (including ourselves), who do not fall within one of your special interest categories, fail to see or acknowledge from a practical standpoint that you are also "our" President.

U.S. Presidents are of course elected, entrusted, and have the responsibility, to "lead" this Nation on behalf of "all" U.S. Citizens, and not to "rule" or otherwise act on behalf of any special interest element.

Mr. President, any one of our Nation's many successful sports coaches understands the importance of "leadership" and "teamwork". Teamwork focused on clear goals and objectives in support of a common good. Mr. President, no coach in his or her right mind would ever consider pitting his or her team members against each other.

No responsible coach, or other experienced and successful "leader", would ever create or tolerate controversy among their team based on race, religion, economic background, etc. Nor, would they ever promote or tolerate an atmosphere of counter-productive dependency, entitlement, or other attitude of "I'm owed a free ride at the expense of others".

Mr. President, just like our Great Nation, the typical sports "team" is of course made up of players from **"many"** walks of life. And, for a **"team"** to be successful, the coach must employ leadership that ensures **"unity"**. As you highlighted in your 2004 speech before the DNC, there can be no **"diversionary use of wedge issues"**. Our Nation requires and deserves nothing less from its President and other government leaders.

President Nixon resigned his second term as a result of conduct that, while clearly very improper, had per our view far less devastating ramifications to our Country than the **"division"** you, Mr. President, have perpetuated within our great Nation. Through the lack of proper "team" leadership, and the radically liberal policies and agenda you, your administration, your supporters, and many others, have imposed and continue to impose on this Great Country.

Radical policies and agendas which continue to be aggressively pursued, often in blatant disregard of the United States Constitution. Economic policies that represent unconscionable "generational theft", stealing from future generations. Setting our Nation on a self-destructing course.

Mr. President, you are certainly in no way alone in responsibility for the dangerous direction our Country is on. Too many elected government officials, in all parties, have for too many years placed "greed, power, and getting re-elected" ahead of what is best for our Country.

And, too many citizens (including ourselves) have for too long taken an inattentive and passive role in our Country's political processes.

While too many of us have been "asleep at the switch", our government has been progressively failing to: **"protect our borders", "protect our culture", "protect our language", "protect religious freedom", "protect taxpayer dollars through fiscally-sound and adhered-to budgets",** and **"protect and adhere to our U.S. Constitution".** At the same time, our government has grown to unsustainable size and cost.

And, has fostered a growing base of counter-productive and unsustainable "entitlement-minded" constituents. Which, will without any reasonable doubt, bankrupt and otherwise destroy our Great Nation, if not timely turned around through effective leadership and appropriately shared sacrifice and contribution by all. "Deserving and entitled to a free ride" must not be part of our nation's culture or government policies and agendas.

Mr. President, while the obvious "free pass" you have enjoyed and continue to receive from the so called major news media may work well for you, such is a very sad and damaging state of affairs for our Great Nation. As a result of shameful bias, political pandering, and professional corruption, <u>much</u> of our news media also shares <u>considerable responsibility</u> for the growing demise of our Great Nation, and the lack of "across the board" scrutiny of and accountability by "all" government officials, regardless of party affiliation.

Mr. President, your personal efforts, various life circumstances, and considerable taxpayer money, have now pretty much assured that you, your immediate family, and descendants will be very economically secure for years to come, and otherwise shielded in many ways from the consequences of failed Government policies and agendas.

Likewise, many other past, present, and future government officials will also benefit from the taxpayer's till, and escape the negative consequences of Government shortfalls. But, millions upon millions of the rest of us, and our descendants, will in no way enjoy the same such special favor.

In closing, we certainly recognize that it is very, very unlikely that you will ever see this correspondence, for a couple of reasons. One is awareness that any President receives much more mail than is humanly possible to personally deal with. Another reason being that, even if by some slim chance our letter should be selected through sampling and screening by the White House Staff, the length and challenging nature of this correspondence would most likely preclude you ever seeing it.

So, why even bother to write and send this letter? One explanation might be that doing so is an attempt to address a responsibility that we each have, that being to "do what we can". To do our best to communicate our serious concerns about the devastating direction that Government dysfunction and radically liberal policies and agendas are taking this country. And, to request and express hope that you, Mr. President, and our other elected government officials, will timely wake up and do the right things for this *"best hope for humankind"*, our United States of America.

Regards,

William J. Moore   *Cecilia A. Moore*

_____   _____

William J. Moore   Cecilia A. Moore

Copies furnished to: Governor Sam Brownback; Senator Pat Roberts; Senator Jerry Moran; Congresswoman Lynn Jenkins; Speaker John Boehner; CBS News, Attn: Scott Pelley & Charlie Rose; Fox News, Attn: Sheppard Smith & Bret Baier; NBC News, Attn: Brian Williams & David Gregory; Glenn Beck; Sean Hannity; Mark Levin; Rush Limbaugh; Gretta Van Susteren; Bill O'Reilly.

= = =

Re: "Response from The White House" on next page. According to www.whitehouse.gov, tens of thousands of letters, faxes, and emails from Americans across the country arrive each day at the Office of Presidential Correspondence. Reportedly, they do their best to reply to these in a timely fashion, and a handful—just ten a day—are chosen for President Obama to personally read and respond to.

(A Scanned-Copy of Response from The White House)

THE WHITE HOUSE
WASHINGTON

May 28, 2013

Mr. William J. Moore
Parsons, Kansas

Dear William:

Thank you for writing. I appreciate your perspective on the serious issues facing our Nation.

After years of grueling recession, we have cleared away the rubble of crisis. Our businesses have created over six million new jobs. Our housing market is healing and our stock market is rebounding. Consumers, patients, and homeowners enjoy stronger protections than ever before. We buy more American cars than we have in 5 years, and less foreign oil than we have in 20. And after a decade of grinding war, our brave men and women in uniform are coming home.

Today, we must match our achievements with a commitment to address the challenges that remain. It is our task as a Nation to reignite the true engine of America's economic growth: a rising, thriving middle class. It is our task to build ladders of opportunity into the middle class and to restore the basic bargain at the heart of the American dream—the idea that you can make it if you try, no matter where you are from, what you look like, or who you love.

In the days ahead, my Administration will work to make the United States a magnet for new jobs and manufacturing, to combat climate change while driving economic growth, and to reduce our deficit in a balanced way while keeping our promises to our seniors. We must pass comprehensive immigration reform, and we must take commonsense steps to reduce gun violence and get weapons of war off our streets. Government cannot solve every problem, but if we—as members of one American family—accept our obligations to one another and embrace the belief that our destiny is shared, I am confident that our country's best days lie ahead.

Thank you, again, for taking the time to share your views. I encourage you to explore www.WhiteHouse.gov to learn more about the ways we are moving America forward.

Sincerely,

= = =

Reference the above May 28, 2013 letter from President Obama, and his encouragement "to explore **www.WhiteHouse.gov** to learn more about the ways we [the President's administration] are moving America forward":

Respectfully, we U.S. Citizens of course do not need to visit The White House website to get a grasp of our country's status and direction. We need only to "look" and "listen" around us. To sadly witness our U.S. borders, English language, culture, economic system, and middle-class, etc., being methodically destroyed by the radical-left's "transformation of America." And by other self-serving agendas of "career-politicians" in **both** the democrat and republican parties!

= = =

"Those who stand for nothing fall for anything."
— Alexander Hamilton

"Bad politicians are sent to Washington by good people who don't vote." *— William E. Simon*

"All tyranny needs to gain a foothold is for people of good conscience to remain silent." *— Edmund Burke*

"The liberties of our country, the freedom of our civil constitution, are worth defending against all hazards: And it is our duty to defend them against all attacks." *— Samuel Adams*

(A Scanned-Copy of Response from Senator Moran)

JERRY MORAN
KANSAS

SEN. RUSSELL SENATE OFFICE BUILDING
WASHINGTON DC 20510-1606
P: 202 224-6521
F: 202 228-6966

COMMITTEES:
APPROPRIATIONS

BANKING, HOUSING, AND
URBAN AFFAIRS

VETERANS' AFFAIRS

United States Senate

July 9, 2013

Mr. and Mrs. William Moore

~~[redacted]~~

~~[redacted]~~

Dear Mr. and Mrs. Moore:

I appreciate the copy of your letter to President Obama, and your message of teamwork is one we in Washington should keep in mind. Congress must set aside the game of politics and work together to confront the enormous challenges before us. Whether we have the courage to tackle the pressing issues before us now – not later—will determine the course of our country for the next generation. There is much work to be done in the months ahead. I stand ready to work with my colleagues in the Senate to do what it takes to get our country back on track.

While serving Kansans in the United States Senate, I have continued to live in Kansas. Traveling home each week keeps me in touch with those I represent. When I am not back home, I rely on messages like yours to remind me of what is important to Kansans and give me direction as to where I need to focus my efforts. Thank you for sharing with me your thoughts and please let me know if I can be of service to you or your family in the future.

Very truly yours,

Jerry Moran

Jerry Moran

JM:NH

= = =

"We must not confuse dissent with disloyalty. When the loyal opposition dies, I think the soul of America dies with it."

— Edward R. Murrow

The Bottomless Pit
of
Our Federal Government

"In general, the art of government consists of taking as much money as possible from one party of the citizens to give to the other."
— Voltaire (1764)

"A government which robs Peter to pay Paul can always depend on the support of Paul." — George Bernard Shaw

"My reading of history convinces me that most bad government results from too much government." — John Sharp Williams

A **bottomless-pit** is "something that drains all one's energy or resources." **Broke** (bankrupt; insolvent; etc.) is "having completely run out of money." **Common-sense** is "good sense and sound judgment in practical matters."

Our Federal Government has become a bottomless-pit! As a nation—by any reasonable and sensible standards—we are broke! And, "we the people" and "our federal government" have lost touch with any resemblance of common sense!

Evidence that the above claims are true is all around us. Some of that "should-be-unsettling" evidence is summarized in this section. Factual information that should not only be very alarming, but also motivating! Prompting and otherwise supporting unrelenting demands for more responsible government! One not only focused on our "present-day needs," but also on our responsibility to future generations of Americans!

As reviewed in more detail in the earlier section titled *"Our National Debt & Unfunded Liabilities,"* . . . roughly speaking, "we the people" are already on the hook for a rapidly growing national debt of $18 trillion—that's about $57 thousand per citizen; or $154 thousand per taxpayer! And, for U.S. Unfunded Liabilities totaling some $97.5 trillion—that's over $820,000 for every man, woman, and child in the U.S. And these gut-wrenching numbers don't include our personal debt, which year 2015 Federal Reserve reporting shows to be over $52 thousand per U.S. citizen!

Now—again roughly-speaking--$57,000 plus $820,000 plus $52,000 seems to add up to a total outstanding debt of about **$929,000 per U.S. citizen**. And, if called upon to pay our shares today **(totaling $1,858,000)**, my wife and I would unquestionably have to default on this our "citizen-obligation." Likewise, considering our age and financial circumstances—in the absence of winning a major lottery—it is all but a life-certainty that paying such debt will never be a realistic option for us. And, of course, nationwide, we are far from being unique or alone in this this matter.

And, given the above summarized liberty and survival threatening realities, and as these words are being typed, the Obama administration and its supporters are out promoting and promising "free community college;" "amnesty for illegal aliens;" "free healthcare;" and "free accommodations for Europe's migration crisis;" etc. Never-ending "free stuff"!

Adding to the pile of already existing and unsustainable "free benefits" promised, and those already put in place, by our self-serving and otherwise irresponsible government. More and more "free" from an already broke and heavily in-debt public treasury — to buy the votes and support of likewise self-serving and irresponsible citizens! A truly unsustainable path that is dragging this nation deeper and deeper into a "bottomless-pit" of liberty and survival threatening debt!

And then there is Senator Bernie Sanders, a Vermont independent running for the democratic presidential nomination. Whose campaign rhetoric and income-inequality agenda reportedly amounts to another "$18 trillion in benefits!" "More promises" from — as earlier stressed — an already broke and in-debt public treasury! Pure and absolute, "liberty and survival-threatening" insanity! But, sadly, much appealing to the ears of his thus far growing numbers of greedy, out-of-touch, and otherwise irresponsible supporters. Similar to the nation-destroying "BS" being echoed by another democratic nomination seeker, Hillary Clinton, whose campaign rhetoric is likewise loaded with promises of more and more "free stuff." And, like that of Senator Sanders — straight out of the play-book of "socialism"!

At this point, with all this chatter about "free," for some reason the following quotation seems most fitting and appropriate: *"The trouble with Socialism is that eventually you run out of other people's money." – Margaret Thatcher*

According to September 2015 U.S. Census data, we are a nation of about **321.7 million**. Government records indicate that within this constantly changing number:

- Only 118.9 million (37%) are income taxpayers;

- Our workforce is about 149.1 million (46%); available private sector jobs are around 117.3 million (36.4%); manufacturing jobs only 12.4 million (3.8%); 8.07 million (2.5%) are "officially" unemployed; 16.1 million (5%) "actually" unemployed; 122.1 million (37.9%) full-time workers; 26.9 million (8.3%) part-time workers; 8.6 million (2.7%) self-employed; and 94.0 million (29.2%) are not in labor force;

- 23.6 million (7.3%) are government employees; 1.3 million (0.42%) U.S. armed forces; 14.9 million (4.6%) union workers; 48.8 million (15.1%) retirees; 21.2 million (6.5%) veterans;

- 57.0 million (17.7%) are Medicare enrollees; 76.4 million (23.7%) Medicaid recipients; 40.7 million (12.6%) without health insurance; 10.8 million (3.3%) disabled; 47.6 million (14.8%) living in poverty; 45.3 million (14.0%) Food Stamp recipients; 1.7 million (0.05%) homeless; 122 thousand unaccompanied-minors; 1 in 6 live on incomes at risk for hunger; 14 million American children rely on food banks; food insecurity exists in every county in the U.S.; about 2.3 million are in jail or prison; 6.6 million convicted felons; 21.6 million (6.7%) are living with a substance-abuse disorder; and about 157 million (49%) of us are presently receiving some type of "benefits" from the public treasury;

- Our U.S. median income stands at about $28.6 thousand; family savings $9.4 thousand; personal debt $52.6 thousand per citizen;

- Our U.S. national debt is over $18 trillion ($57.1 thousand per citizen); unfunded liabilities $97.6 trillion (over $820 thousand per taxpayer). $6.2 trillion of our U.S. national debt is held by foreign countries.

U.S. Gross National Product (GDP) is now about $17.8 trillion, and our largest federal budget items are: Medicare/Medicaid $96 billion; Social Security $881 billion; Defense/War $586 billion; Income Security $310 billion; Net Interest on Debt $250 billion; and Federal Pensions $256 billion. Given these numbers—you have a clue where the "big cuts" must someday come from? Voluntarily or involuntarily!

A glance at the "tax" numbers finds: Federal Tax Revenue to be $3.17 trillion ($9.8 thousand per citizen); State Revenue $1.67 trillion ($8.7 thousand per citizen); Income Tax Revenue $1.5 trillion; Payroll Tax Revenue $1.05 trillion; and Corporate Tax Revenue 327.7 billion.

Our military has been and continues to be critically-downsized; Social Security solvency is doubtful; our country's infrastructure is deteriorating; the middle-class is being destroyed; and a struggle is underway to find funds to cover healthcare obligations to our military veterans and others.

And yet we are surrounded by self-serving politicians and others still "promising" and "demanding" more and more "free stuff"! Tolerated and supported by citizens willing to load-up and pass-on to future generations a selfish and unsustainable U.S. debt!

In this age of high-tech global communications, rapidly expanding internet access, and always-connected social-media frenzy — little if any of this information should be "news."

And, faced with these and other social and economic burdens and challenges — **"common sense"** would say that no **responsible government** would ever create, tolerate, or let stand, laws or other circumstances that would allow our country to be flooded with millions of **illegal aliens**. But, being a **"bottomless pit of tax and spend"**, and void of **"common sense"** — our Federal Government has done just that!

And, **"both"** the democrat and republican parties, over several administrations, are to blame! As well as "we the people" for failing to responsibly carry out our obligations as voters and citizen-custodians of our country's affairs!

For years, our Federal Government has failed to establish and enforce responsible immigration policy and secure our borders. As a result, our country has been and continues to be flooded by countless illegals of known and unknown origins, backgrounds, and intents. Some that may wish to assimilate into U.S. culture, adopt our common-language English, and be positive contributors to our nation's wellbeing. While many others refuse to assimilate U.S. culture, disrespect and abuse our country's opportunities, and commit criminal acts, etc.

Our Federal Government's willful acceptance of millions of "illegals" over the years has irresponsibly further-burdened our already over-stretched resources. With burdens, such as, "billions of dollars" for food, clothing, housing, transportation, medical care, education, legal services, and even "spending allowances" for illegal alien minors, etc. And, among the many devastating consequences—a special insult to the countless "legal immigrants" who have gained, or now stand in line to gain, lawful entrance into the U.S. by respectfully playing by the rules.

And, as our Federal Government continues to accommodate and cater to "illegal aliens"—the long-standing hardships and concerns of U.S. citizens go unaddressed. And our military veterans wait in line for "earned" health care benefits; our country's infrastructure deteriorates; and gang violence and drug abuse spread throughout our cities. While the flood of "illegal aliens," and "irresponsibly-accommodated" legal immigrants, continue to be used to satisfy the nation-destroying agendas of "cheap labor," "secured votes," "demographics change," and otherwise "transformation of America"!

The Illusions of Unlimited Resources & Tolerance:

Given the truly liberty and survival threatening risks posed by irresponsible tax and spend agendas, and failed immigration policies, etc.—we must very timely pull our heads out of the sand and reject the self-destructive *"Illusion of Unlimited Resources"*! That being, the delusional-thinking that any nation of ever-growing numbers of **"takers"** and ever-diminishing numbers of **"contributors"** can forever last!

"We the people" and our government must also recognize and reject the *"Illusion of Unlimited Tolerance"*! That being, the likewise delusional-thinking that this country's hardworking "contributors" have "unlimited tolerance!" For a government that is unresponsive to the best interests of our country. Or, that there exists unlimited tolerance for a government that puts the welfare of "illegal aliens" above that of "legal immigrants" and law-abiding, tax-paying, U.S. citizens!

Regardless of our political affiliation, or lack thereof—we have ownership in our government's shortcomings and failings. We also have inescapable ownership in the consequences! At risk from "bad government"—nothing less than our great nation—as defined by its borders, English language, and culture! Among the major roadblocks (and purposely repeated throughout this book)—our voter-ignorance, apathy, complacency, denial, greed, and counter-productive fears!

= = =

"Our nation stands at the crossroads of liberty. Crushing national debt, rampant illegal immigration, insane business regulations and staggering national unemployment are pushing our nation into unchartered territory." — James Lankford

"The American people are not anti-immigrant. We are concerned about the lack of coherence in our immigration policy and enforcement." — Chris Cannon

"Dictatorship naturally arises out of democracy, and the most aggravated form of tyranny and slavery out of the most extreme liberty." — Plato

"While I support immigration regulated through a legal framework, I do not support rewarding those who broke the law to get here."
                                                              — Kit Bond

"Government is the great fiction, through which everybody endeavors to live at the expense of everybody else."
                        — Frederic Bastiat, French Economist (1801-1850)

"No man's life, liberty, or property is safe while the legislature is in session." — Mark Twain (1866)

"Real immigration reform must put security first because border security and homeland security are inseparable in the terrorists' war on us. The first responsibility of the federal government is to protect our citizens by controlling America's borders, while ending illegal immigration. We must restore integrity, accountability and the rule of law to our immigration system to regain the faith of the American people." — Rudy Giuliani

"Government's view of the economy could be summed up in a few short phrases: If it moves, tax it. If it keeps moving, regulate it. And if it stops moving, subsidize it." — Ronald Reagan

"I contend that for a nation to try to tax itself into prosperity is like a man standing in a bucket and trying to lift himself up by the handle." — Winston Churchill

"Just because you do not take an interest in politics doesn't mean politics won't take an interest in you." — Pericles (430 B.C.)

"Since the general civilization of mankind, I believe there are more instances of the abridgement of the freedom of the people by gradual and silent encroachments of those in power than by violent and sudden usurpations." — James Madison

The CFPB: Another "Agency" —
Another "Attack on Liberty"

"Politics is the art of looking for trouble, finding it whether it exists or not, diagnosing it incorrectly, and applying the wrong remedy."

— Ernest Benn

A few years ago a very competent, experienced, and trustworthy young banker — and most dedicated father — brought to his parents' attention one of the more recent and unrelenting attacks on our liberty. Seemingly another government "service" — once again imposed upon us under the political spin of "protecting" all Americans.

Thinking back to when our son Ryan shared the above concerns with us, our best recall is that his cautionary-predictions went something like the following very rough and generalized summation: ". . . given the very disturbing trends of federal government intervention into the U.S. financial services industry, it seems not far off until the "helping hand" of our government will in essence be calling-the-shots as to who will, or will not, be deemed eligible for loan services; from what bank; at what interest rate and other terms; and eventually, even what product or service a given loan can be used for and from what supplier it must be obtained, etc. Not to mention, the ultimate "federal government" say in what banks, other financial institutions, and other businesses, will be allowed to exist, and what products and services they will be authorized to make available to U.S. consumers—when, at what price, and per other government-determined terms."

The above-mentioned, very informal and non-business discussion within "family," was of course in reference to a maze of relatively new laws and regulations. Reportedly designed to "protect" us consumers from abuse and other shortcomings of our financial institutions, other businesses, products, services—and even from ourselves. **This time— coming to our recue**—the Dodd-Frank Act and Consumer Financial Protection Bureau (**CFPB**)!

Naturally, **"safety," "protection," "services," "free,"** etc., are attention-getters with often very comforting and enticing appeal. But, most unfortunately, when such come from our federal government, the often-associated "threats to our liberty" and "other costs" get lost in the maze of real or imagined danger, emotion, political spin, and propaganda. As each of us in our own way deal with our built-in "safety and security"' calls of human nature. A potentially self-destructive reality-of-life, so very wisely cautioned in the following wisdom from Alexander Hamilton many years ago:

"Safety from external danger is the most powerful director of national conduct. Even the ardent love of liberty will, after a time, give way to its dictates. The violent destruction of life and property incident to war, the continual effort and alarm attendant on a state of continual danger, will compel nations the most attached to liberty to resort for repose and security to institutions which have a

tendency to destroy their civil and political rights. To be more safe, they at length become willing to run the risk of being less free."
                              — Alexander Hamilton (1755-1804)

Without question, and as so eloquently expressed above — when our fears or deep concerns about something become great enough, we can and often do call upon or yield to "protection" by our government. Through its ever-growing number of agencies — "servants of the people." The same institutions, as stressed by Alexander Hamilton, that too often have a tendency and history of civil abuse and otherwise liberty-threatening intrusion in our lives.

At this point — in giving some serious thought to Alexander Hamilton's heads-up on this subject — what may come to mind are some of the liberty-threatening actions of such "servants-of-the-people" as: our FBI, CIA, NSA, DHS, EPA, etc. — as well as from Congress, Presidents, and the Supreme Court? Some unsettling matters that still come to mind in spite of life's many distractions, and being smothered by propaganda.

But, now — back to the Consumer Financial Protection Bureau (CFPB), and an overview of its origin, stated aim, and some consequences — so far.

The CFPB — an Overview of Origin & Aim

In brief, the Consumer Financial Protection Bureau (CFPB) is a federal government "agency" established by the Dodd-Frank Wall Street Reform and Consumer Protection Act of 2010.

Passed as a government response to the "Great Recession," among the consequences of the U.S. financial crisis of 2007-08 and subprime mortgage crisis of 2007-09. An agency with authorization to "enforce" new consumer financial laws — reportedly designed to protect consumers from unfair, deceptive, or abusive practices. Bringing with it the most significant changes to "financial regulation" in the U.S. since the Great Depression of the 1930's, and, "financial regulatory changes" affecting all federal regulatory agencies and about every part of our U.S. financial services industry.

At **http://www.consumerfinance.gov/the-bureau/**, the CFPB's official website, it is stated in part that: *"The Consumer Financial Protection Bureau (CFPB) is a 21st century agency that helps consumer finance markets work by making rules more effective, by consistently and fairly enforcing those rules, and by empowering consumers to take more control over their economic lives."*

A visit to the CFPB website is encouraged, where you will find access to an overwhelming amount of information regarding the CFPB's function and stated accomplishments, as well as an array of "services" available. A professionally designed website, prepared and maintained at no spared expense of we taxpayers. For those interested in such matters, the site even includes an easily accessible display of the CFPB's top-tier Organizational Structure (re: reduced-size copy inserted below).

CFPB: Top-tier Organization Chart
(Reduced-Size Copy of June 29, 2015 Update)

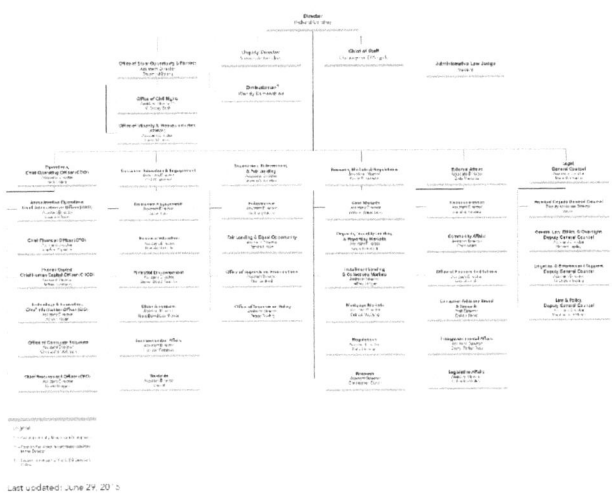

Last updated: June 29, 2015

But, contrary to the above (obviously to-small-to-read) reduced-size copy, the chart accessible at CFPB's website is of course very readable. For example, the June 29, 2015 update clearly showed a CFPB of 46 offices, led by: 1 Director; 1 Deputy Director; 1 Chief of Staff; 1 Administrative Law Judge; 1 Ombudsman; 33 Assistant Directors; 6 Associate Directors; 1 Deputy Associate Director; and 1 Staff Director.

All of course being "appointed" or otherwise "unelected" individuals, basically untouchable by and unaccountable to "we the people." In keeping with the hundreds of other federal government agencies—the CFPB's executives are most likely all overworked, underpaid, and unappreciated individuals—with ever-growing support staffs likewise burdened.   Each required to struggle with ever-growing budgets—as was required by the CFPB's FY 2015 budget estimate of $583.4 million, 2.4% above the FY 2014 budget level of $569.8 million.

Right now, you by chance may get the feeling that this writer is being "just a bit" cynical? If so, then please spend some time seriously reviewing the "Eight-Page Listing" of some 438 Federal Government Agencies included near the end of this book.   Take a quality moment to wrap your tax and regulation-burdened mind around our "tax dollars at work" listed there! And picture any business coping with such! No more than a basic awareness of the existence of such a bloated, parasitic, every-growing, and out-of-control bureaucracy **"should prompt"** a flood of public outrage and other appropriate citizen-feedback to our elected servants in Washington!

The "key words" in the above last sentence of course being— "should prompt." And the yet unanswered question being— "How much more lost-liberty must be suffered in order to prompt a meaningful response from we-the-people?"

The CFPB — Some Consequences — So Far

At **http://www.consumerfinance.gov/the-bureau/**, the CFPB's official website, access is provided to a detailed, professional display of its "achieved goals" and other stated "accomplishments." Therefore, space within this book will not be used to duplicate the CFPB's self-promoting spin.

Rather, this particular section of *Threats to Our Liberty & Survival* will strive to highlight some consequences very unlikely to receive much, if any, unfiltered attention on any federal government website. Consequences such as briefly summarized in the below random listing (which is <u>not</u> presented as, nor should be assumed to be, all-inclusive):

<u>Harmful rather than helpful</u>: Instead of helping to stabilize the U.S. economy, Dodd-Frank Act regulations and the CFPB's application of such, are creating greater costs and uncertainty for U.S. financial institutions, businesses, and consumers.

<u>Abusive and potentially unconstitutional powers</u>: Various powers granted by Dodd-Frank Act to the CFPB, FDIC, and the Treasury Department, may be unconstitutional. Such as, empowerment of the Treasury Secretary to liquidate a financial company "with little or no advance warning, under cover of mandatory secrecy" and without "meaningful legislative, executive, or judicial oversight." [Re: Related complaints filed in U.S. District Court for the District of Columbia by various state attorneys generals.]

<u>Barriers to establishment of needed new banks</u>: Dodd-Frank regulations and CFPB oversight are barriers to establishment of new banks needed to support growing consumer demands. For example, reports of no new bank charters in recent 5 year period, compared to 100 per year in the 30 years "prior" to Dodd-Frank Act. [Re: Related article, front page of 03/31/2015 publication of The Wall Street Journal.]

A benefit to—rather than ending of—"too big to fail' banks:
A government-stated primary-purpose of the Dodd-Frank Act
was to end the "too big to fail" banks. But, under Dodd-
Frank, such banks continue to thrive, and in 2010 Goldman
Sachs CEO Lloyd Blankfein reportedly expressed publicly that
his firm would be among the largest beneficiaries of subject
financial reform.

Consumers personal-data at risk: Provisions of the Dodd-
Frank Act and CFPB oversight call for federal government
collection, use, and storage of a growing amount of
"consumer data"—putting at risk U.S. citizens' personal data
and rights-to-privacy, etc. This unsettling reality is especially
alarming, when one considers the federal government's
atrocious track record of failures to responsibly use and secure
the personal-data of U.S. citizens. A prime example being,
July 2015 news reports of recent discovered data-hacking of
the U.S. Office of Personnel Management (OPM). A security
breach thus far believed to have resulted in some 22 million or
more people, inside and outside of government, likely to have
had their social security numbers and other personal
information stolen. And, there is absolutely no evidence or
right-minded thinking that CFPB's track record will be any
better, regarding personal information it collects or otherwise
has entrusted access to.

Community banks forced-out of consumer-lending services:
Community banks are being forced out of consumer-lending
(and in some cases out of business) by ever-growing
compliance costs driven by Dodd-Frank regulations and CFPB

enforcement. Including growing numbers of the "smaller" and "rural" banks that millions of U.S. citizens, nationwide, rely upon for physical access to mainstream banking services. Leaving the more flexible loan services, historically provided by community banks, no longer available to truly qualified and in-need borrowers. A devastating state of affairs for many truly trustworthy borrowers, who are often not able to get loans from larger, less-customer-aware banks that rely on more standardized and impersonal criteria.

As but one example of this consumer-devastating trend, a recent study by the Oklahoma Bankers Association notes that, 24% of the community banks in the state have decided to no longer offer home loans due to the ever-growing maze of Dodd-Frank Act regulations, administered through the CFPB. With those regarding "TRID" being "among the many" costly hassles pushing a growing number of our community banks over the edge. And just what does "TRID" stand for? Well, TRID is the TILA / RESPA Integrated Disclosure Rule. And, only our federal government—"servants of the people"— could make an acronym out of acronyms. So, here's a little further explanation . . . TILA is the Truth in Lending Act and RESPA is the Real Estate Settlement Procedures Act. And reportedly, the CFPB modified both of these rules in its "TRID final ruling." Almost enough to make one's head spin just reading this! One more despicable example of our tax dollars at work! And of our citizens' liberty slip, slip, slipping away!

= = =

Whether the above listed consequences are "unintended" or "otherwise," of course rests in the hearts, minds, and agendas of those who designed, sponsored, approved, and are enforcing the dictates of the Dodd-Frank Act and CFPB.

Furthermore, any doubts about the validity of the above listed threats to our liberty and livelihood may readily be put to rest by any of the sensible-minded among us, through little more than candid discussions with our banks and other businesses throughout our communities. And, during our next application for a home mortgage or other loan of significance.

"Government Intervention" — Too Often the Problem, Not the Cure!

It is most unfortunate for all Americans that, by way of the Dodd-Frank Act and CFPB, our federal government has once again imposed a "harmful" rather than "helpful" hand. Through a continuing flow of new regulations that are unnecessarily burdening most if not all businesses with costly overhead, and seriously road-blocking economic growth and job creation. All with the stated intent of preventing a repeat of financial disasters of years past.

Ironically, including disasters that were created in large measure by the same type of previous federal government meddling. Think not? Then get your U.S. citizen-rightful hands on (and actually read) a copy of: Staff Report, U.S. House of Representatives, 111th Congress, Committee on Oversight and Government Reform, July 7, 2009, titled "The Role of Government Affordable Housing Policy in Creating the Global Financial Crisis of 2008. The following excerpt taken from the Introduction of this very revealing Staff Report, is but a glimpse of the referenced committee's troublesome findings:

"The housing bubble that burst in 2007 and led to a financial crisis can be traced back to federal government intervention in the U.S. housing market intended to help provide homeownership opportunities for more Americans. This intervention began with two government-backed corporations, Fannie Mae and Freddie Mac, which privatized their profits but socialized their risks, creating powerful incentives for them to act recklessly and exposing taxpayers to tremendous losses. Government intervention also created "affordable" but dangerous lending policies which encouraged lower down payments, looser underwriting standards and higher leverage. Finally, government intervention created a nexus of vested interests – politicians, lenders and lobbyists – who profited from the "affordable" housing markets and acted to kill reforms. In the short run, this government intervention was successful in its stated goal – raising the national homeownership rate. However, the ultimate effect was to create a mortgage tsunami that wrought devastation on the American people and economy. While government intervention was not the sole cause of the financial crisis, its role was significant and has received too little attention."

And so, through the CFPB and growing hundreds of other regulations-armed, counter-productive agencies – our federal government continues to "pave our nation's road to hell" with its intentions and interventions. By government meddling in our businesses and lives – often assumed noble – with results that much too often involve nation-destructive, liberty-threatening, consequences!

Federal Agencies (in general) — Some Long-standing Pitfalls

In getting a serious grasp on downsides of the Consumer Financial Protection Bureau (CFPB) — and there are many — it is crucial that we clearly understand that our nation doesn't just have **"an agency"** threat to deal with. Instead, we truly face **"an agencies"** threat! And, in seeking a truly complete, clear and universally accepted "definition" or "list" of the extent of federal government agencies — good luck! For, any best efforts to find such will likely take you into an abyss of seemingly endless amounts of conflicting and confusing information.

A possible explanation for this dilemma may rest in the following background provided by Wikipedia, the free [Internet] encyclopedia: *"Legislative definitions of a federal agency are varied, and even contradictory, and the official United States Government Manual offers no definition. While the Administrative Procedure Act definition of "agency" applies to most executive branch agencies, Congress may define an agency however it chooses in enabling legislation, and subsequent litigation, often involving the Freedom of Information Act and the Government in the Sunshine Act, further clouding attempts to enumerate a list of agencies."*

Our federal government bureaucracy no doubt learned long ago that what is fuzzy and confusing, is also hard to track. Especially by citizens who may seek a responsible accounting of the use of their hard-earned tax-dollars. Although no one — especially our government — seems to agree on their definition or numbers — there are in fact "hundreds" of federal agencies.

In an effort to highlight this unsettling fact — about eight pages near the end of this book have been used to provide a glimpse at their number and type. A glimpse at what much of our ever-increasing tax dollars, and/or rapidly growing national debt, are financing. An **eight-page** or so alphabetical listing of some **438** federal agencies found during a July 2015 search at the official website for the Federal Register: **https://www.federalregister.gov/agencies**. Note that the Consumer Financial Protection Bureau (CFPB) is included within approximately 33 other agencies identified in the "C's" of this list. A sad and most alarming eight-page example of our ever-growing and "out of control" federal government bureaucracy. A conglomeration of agencies so structured that citizen (or government) tracking of responsibility and accountability has become all but impossible.

Among the best yet news coverages on this subject — of our growing maze of out-of-control federal government glut — was presented long ago. In a CBS broadcast, January 26, 1975, titled "MR. ROONEY GOES TO WASHINGTON." A printed version of that revealing work remains available in a book by the now deceased Mr. Rooney, titled, "The Most of Andy Rooney." Where, in vintage "Andy Rooney" style, the unmanageable bureaucratic maze of our federal government at that time was skillfully aired. The absurdities noted back then have of course worsened over time. Among the primary reasons CBS reportedly undertook that particular 1974-75 project, was to see what a nonpolitical reporter with no previous knowledge of Washington could find out about it.

For example, why our government has grown so big and why there are so many bureaus, agencies, departments, etc. in the bureaucracy. The following excerpt from Mr. Rooney's 1975 reporting offers at least a partial explanation—unfortunately one more true today than in years past: *"One of the reasons seems to be that almost every committee, every agency or every department is established by law, but there is never anything in that law about putting the agency out of business when its job is done. Once established, a government agency, like a government job, is practically immortal. If a committee or agency has a name that makes it sound out-of-date, it doesn't go out of business; it just changes its name."* — Andrew A. Rooney [Re: Book titled, "The Most of Andy Rooney" — Article titled, "Mr. Rooney Goes To Washington.]

Not to be forgotten, the CFPB and hundreds of other federal government agencies were each sold to, or imposed upon us as our "servants" and "rescuers." In fairness, many very likely were and are established with the intent of doing some good. Unfortunately, and more realistically, too often history showing the outcome much otherwise. Too often the legacy of a federal government agency is one of liberty-threatening harm.

Threats to our liberty as has at times been the outcome of trust placed in "services" such as: the Internal Revenue Service (IRS); National Security Agency (NSA); and Environmental Protection Agency (EPA) — to mention but a few. And bordering on gross ignorance and irresponsibility, would be any thoughts that the relatively new Consumer Financial Protection Bureau (CFPB), or any other federal agency, is immune from going down the paths of similar abuses of power and influence. Likewise, regardless of how noble-appearing their official charter, our government agencies can often be used as a destructive tool, by those hell-bent to make us ever more dependent upon our federal government for our every want and need. With the primary aim being, our continuing votes, tax dollars, and other support.

One way or another, all "agencies" are empowered to enforce policies, programs, and laws — and often able to modify or create such. All too many agencies likewise often duplicate or are in conflict with many of the functions of their agency-peers. And, all "agencies" are typically ran and staffed by "appointed" or otherwise "unelected" bureaucrats, making them essentially uncontrollable by and unaccountable to "we the people."

Unaccountable to the very same U.S. citizens called upon to fund this irresponsible glut of institutions, by way of ever-increasing taxes and a rapidly growing national debt. "Agencies" that, once established, become practically immortal — permanent government-fixtures and takers from the public treasury. Each driven to justify their existence and retain power and influence. Self-serving aims that receive ever-increasing priority attention. Making it all the more certain that none of our federal agencies—including the CFPB—will ever be truly disbanded or restricted from continuing growth. All the more certain that the resulting tax burdens and threats to our liberty will only continue to rise.

And, so it will continue to be! Until "we the people" develop and exercise responsible ways and means of "taking back our country." Until we overcome the roadblocks of voter-ignorance, apathy, complacency, denial, greed, and counter-productive fear—within ourselves and others. Until, in constructive ways we effectively demonstrate our unrelenting intolerance for any liberty-threatening Congress, President, or Supreme Court; and any failure to protect, defend, and preserve our U.S. Constitution, borders, common-language English, culture, and free-market economic system.

= = =

"A government big enough to give you everything you want, is big enough to take away everything you have." — Thomas Jefferson

"Somehow liberals have been unable to acquire from life what conservatives seem to be endowed with at birth: namely, a healthy skepticism of the powers of government agencies to do good."
— Daniel P. Moynihan

A Letter to Department of Health & Human Services (DHHS)

> *"As government expands, liberty contracts."* — *Ronald Reagan*

During the month of July 2014, my wife Ann and I were among the no doubt untold millions to receive (at considerable taxpayers' expense) a **twelve-page, ninety-question survey** from the Department of Health & Human Services (DHHS). Reportedly part of a four-year "CPC Initiative" seeking to improve primary [health] care practices.

It is noteworthy that, **"before"** Obama-Care was imposed on us and the rest of the nation, we didn't receive a "survey" from the President, Congress, DHSS, or other government agency, seeking our views about health care!

Beginning on the next page of this section is a verbatim copy of our July 26, 2014 **"response"** to the DHHS. A letter-response that is (with intent and by design) considerably harsh and abrasive. But, nonetheless, very serious citizen-feedback. To which, now surpassing a year later, the DHHS has not seen fit to even acknowledge receipt of, nor extend a courtesy response to, the concerns we aired.

Yet another example of arrogance and disrespect, from one of the hundreds of federal government "agencies" continuing to thrive from endless access to the seemingly bottomless-pit of our public treasury. One of the ever-growing federal government "servants of the people" shown in the approximate **eight-page list** near the end of this book.

"Before and after" reviewing the below-inserted copy of our feedback to the DHHS, the following question seems worthy of serious thought: "What might be the constructive outcome of a long-past-due wake-up call to our federal government . . . if correspondence similar in content and tone were to be communicated in serious citizen-feedback, from at least a mere 25 percent (29.5 million) of the yet remaining 118.9 million U.S. income-tax payers? Or, from at least an even more meager 10 percent (21.8 million) of our estimated 218.9 million eligible voters?" That is, feedback in the form of letters, phone calls, texts, tweets, and social media posts, etc. Not only in regard to government-imposed health care laws, but other issues of national importance. Protection of our U.S. borders, common-language English, culture, and free-market economic system, are a few that readily come to mind.

= = =

(A Verbatim-Copy of Original Letter Sent to DHHS)

July 26, 2014
<u>Subject</u>: CMS' "CPC Initiative" –
Patient Survey Questions & Answers."

DEPARTMENT OF HEALTH & HUMAN SERVICES (DHHS)

Centers for Medicare & Medicaid Services

7500 Security Boulevard, Mail Stop S2-24-25

Baltimore, Maryland 21244-1850

ATTN: Mr. Walter Stone, CMS Privacy Officer

Dear Mr. Stone:

Up front—this is a piece of serious U.S. Citizens-correspondence that we respectfully insist be handled and responded to as requested herein.

Firstly, the DHHS and other aspects of "our" government did not ask for input and preferences from us and other U.S. Citizens **"before"** imposing the devastating burdens of the "Affordable Care Act (ACA)" on us . . . so do not waste our time and tax dollars with the subject after-the-fact "CPC Initiative" and its twelve-page, 90-question Survey!

Secondly, the "CPC Initiative" is stated to be ". . . a four-year initiative that seeks to improve primary care practices . . . ." If such is the serious aim of the CMS / DHHS, here is our very serious feedback to the subject survey: Immediately scrap the ACA, get out of the government healthcare business, and let health insurance companies compete across state lines for our healthcare products and services. And, abolish the DHHS and all other redundant tax burdens connected to it.

Thirdly, "in addition to" recognizing that the subject CPC Initiative is just another costly way of perpetuating the existence of the ever-growing government-healthcare bureaucracy . . . we furthermore consider it **a blatant and inexcusable insult** that you would send correspondence addressed to us printed in Spanish! Your doing so is not only **disrespectful of us,** and **a waste of tax dollars**, it is further evidence of the **dangerous path** our once much greater country is now on. Our tax dollars, and that of our hard-working (English speaking) adult children, are being spent to print and otherwise handle correspondence in a **foreign language** — for people too damn inconsiderate and irresponsible to learn our country's common language — English! Why the pandering to one particular foreign language (Spanish)? . . . Votes, of course . . . in irresponsible disregard of our U.S. borders, language, and culture. On the present path, want to know what USA our descendants may well be living in but a relative few years in the future? . . . Just take a look at the chaos across our southern border!

Closing Request: (1.) Remove us from your mailing list for any/all future CMS / DHHS Surveys; (2.) Take positive measures to ensure that CMS / DHHS never again sends us any correspondence printed in anything other than English; (3.) Forward this letter to the Director, DHHS, with our request for written response to the concerns we have identified herein.

Sincerely, William J. & Cecilia A. Moore

Copy Fwd. To: Director, DHHS (*Through Mr. Walter Stone, CMS Privacy Officer*)

"Press 1" for English

"Language is a unifying instrument which binds people together. When people speak one language they become as one, they become a society." — S.I. Hayakawa

"Every immigrant who comes here should be required within five years to learn English or leave the country." — Theodore Roosevelt

Those with agendas aimed at doing so, clearly understand there are various ways of "transforming" or "otherwise destroying" any nation. And if an objective of any such agenda is to also do it without, so-to-speak, "firing a shot" — then the three primary targets are that nation's **borders**, **language**, and **culture**. The three "must-haves" that <u>define any nation</u>!

And any clear-headed and rational-minded "look and listen" around us reveals that our U.S. borders, common-language English, and culture, are undergoing unrelenting assaults! Attacks that, most unfortunately, are not resulting in public outrage and vigorous defensive measures. But, rather, self-destructive support of "political-correctness," "divide and conquer," and "transformation of America." Aided by voter-ignorance, apathy, complacency, denial, greed, and counter-productive fears of threatening numbers among us.

This great nation was built by, and yet survives as the result of, the many efforts of dedicated immigrants and descendants of immigrants. People respectful of and grateful for the unique liberty/freedom and opportunity offered by this "best hope for humankind." People who wisely and constructively blended (assimilated) into a "common U.S. culture" using a "common U.S. language—English," within a sovereign nation of defined and defended borders!

All of which are now being systematically dismantled by an irresponsible, power-hungry, self-serving, and self-perpetuating government. One that is fast-track pandering to various Spanish-speaking groups within and without our borders! Pandering **at the expense of U.S. taxpayers of "all" origins**! Pandering in blatant disrespect and disregard of past and present immigrants, and descendants of immigrants, who have done and continue to do the right thing—respect our U.S. borders, adhere to U.S. laws, assimilate U.S. culture, learn and use our common U.S. language—English, and otherwise "contribute" to our nation's wellbeing!

And "why" this pandering of "one" particular group? <u>The answer in brief</u>: To secure cheap labor, votes, and demographic changes in order to "transform" America! A liberty and survival threatening behavior that **"both"** the democrat and republican parties have had, and still have, their grossly-irresponsible hands in! Yes, driven by political and economic greed, our country has been put on a self-destructive path. Disregarding the earlier mentioned fact that our "nation"—any "nation"—is defined by, and cannot exist without . . . its borders, assimilated culture, and common language.

And, in but a relatively few more recent years, our "once" English-speaking America has been and continues to be progressively saturated with "Spanish." As our public areas are more and more filled with . . . "not" our common-language English, but, rather, a rapidly spreading foreign language . . . Spanish! Yes, "Spanish" in our schools, shopping malls, workplaces, fast-food outlets, youth-sports events, parks, playgrounds, etc., etc. **And "in America"** . . . **it's NOT "Press 1 for Spanish" . . . but, rather . . . "Press 1 for English"**! All, at U.S. taxpayers' expense — not only in dollars from the public treasury, but also in lost liberty.

As expressed at length elsewhere in this book, our *time* is precious and limited — and what we choose to do with it is of most importance. With such in mind I truly hope you choose to read this section and find within it, or elsewhere, the motivation to unrelentingly pursue your own vigorous ways and means of helping save and secure our U.S. common language — English! And, that by way of letters, phone calls, e-mail, newspaper articles, social media networks, informed-voting, or otherwise — you and millions of other concerned citizens send the President, Congress, and Supreme Court, a swift, clear, and unnegotiable message! **That we have had enough!** That we demand an immediate halt to any and all destructive "transformation" of America agendas. That we unrelenting demand the restoration, protection, and preservation of our U.S. Constitution, borders, culture . . . **and, our English language!** Shame on us should we fail to do so!

In likeness to no doubt countless others nationwide, over the years my wife Ann and I have tried to constructively support the above expressed aims. By way of word-of-mouth; public-mind articles to our local newspaper; and letters and e-mails to the president and our elected representatives; etc. Some examples are expressed throughout this book. Including, the copies of correspondence "to and from" executive management of our natural-gas utilities supplier (inserted at the end of this section).

Just as was encouraged in the previous section regarding correspondence to the DHHS . . . "before and after" reviewing the below-inserted copies of our feedback to the ONE Gas, Inc., the following question again seems worthy of serious thought: "What might be the constructive outcome of a long-past-due wake-up call to our federal government . . . if correspondence similar in content and tone were to be communicated in serious citizen-feedback, from at least a mere 25 percent (29.5 million) of the yet remaining 118.9 million U.S. income-tax payers? Or, from at least an even more meager 10 percent (21.8 million) of our estimated 218.9 million eligible voters?" That is, feedback in the form of letters, phone calls, texts, tweets, and social media posts, etc. Not only in regard to government-imposed health care laws, but other issues of national importance. Protection of our U.S. borders, common-language English, culture, and free-market economic system, are a few that readily come to mind.

The answer to the above question can be long-debated. However, obvious and unquestionable, are the ever-worsening results of the "irresponsible-silence" of countless U.S. citizens. As our liberty and ultimate survival continue to be threatened by the nation-destroying "transformation of America" taking place before our very eyes . . . and our ears!

= = =

(Partial-Copy of Original Letter Sent to ONE Gas, Inc.)

04/24/2014

Mr. Pierce H. Norton II,
President and Chief Executive Officer
ONE Gas, Inc., 100 West Fifth Street
Tulsa, OK 74103

Dear Mr. Norton,

First, I would like to offer you my congratulations on your promotion and new position with ONE Gas! I have read your bio and it of course clearly attests to your qualifications for the new and obviously considerable responsibilities you now have!

Next, I want to assure you that I very much understand and appreciate that you are a terribly busy executive, with an extremely tight schedule, and with countless people standing in line to catch your ear, etc. As such, I also understand that you may not ever personally see this letter or any response to same.

Nevertheless, it is my wish and respectful request that this correspondence be taken seriously, and that I be extended the professional courtesy of receiving a likewise serious response — if not from you, then from your designated staff representative. Someone authorized to officially speak on your behalf.

Before expressing subject concern, I feel obligated to share a little about myself — a retired management professional, college graduate, enlisted-ranks of USAF for 4 years, husband, father, proud grandfather of our ten year old grandson, employed since age 19, have been a natural gas customer for some 53 years, and am not in the business of wasting my precious time or that of others by writing "crank" correspondence.

Hence, this correspondence is very "sincere", as is the concern summarized below:

Enclosed is a copy of the back-page of the Monthly Billing Statement we routinely receive from the Kansas Gas Service. Its content deals with "Natural Gas Terms" and a safety caution for all customers. More than half of the page is printed in Spanish? My "very serious" question is, **"Why is <u>any</u> correspondence from my natural gas supplier printed in anything but our United States common-language — English?"**

Overall, about 500 different self-identified ancestries have been reported by the U.S. Census. Ranked by number, the top ten ancestry groups are shown below:

Rank	Ancestry group	Number	Percent
1.	German	42,841,569	15.2%
2.	Irish	30,524,799	10.8
3.	African American	24,903,412	8.8
4.	English	24,509,692	8.7
5.	American	20,188,305	7.2
6.	Mexican	18,382,291	6.5
7.	Italian	15,638,348	5.6
8.	Polish	8,977,235	3.2
9.	French	8,309,666	3.0
10.	American Indian	7,876,568	2.8

Our U.S. Census data speaks for itself. Given the many hundreds of other legal-citizen ancestry groups in the U.S., one can only imagine the countless millions of people that feel, as I do, betrayed and outraged by the special treatment being given to Spanish-speaking groups within our borders!

Mr. Norton, you and I know full well that this country was founded and built by people from "many different ancestries". By people who had great appreciation and respect for the special liberty and opportunity made possible by our one-of-its-kind constitutional republic. By people who put forth the effort to learn and use this country's language—English.

Through much personal effort, skill, and talent, you have achieved considerable success. However, you and I would have never enjoyed our respective successes without the special liberty and opportunity this great country has afforded us—and, without our being able to speak and our willingness to routinely use our English language.

It is not only just plain wrong, but also outrageous and irresponsible, for our political leaders and other persons of power and influence to turn their heads as our country's borders, language, and culture are being methodically destroyed before our eyes! My wife Ann and I and concerned others want to be justifiably confident that we, and good men like you, are doing their very best to pass-on a United States of America with its borders, English language, and culture securely intact!

Looking forward to your response . . . .

With Warm Regards,

William J. Moore

Enclosure: a/s

"Scanned Copy of Original"

(Back Page of Monthly Billing Statement from Kansas Gas Service)
Left-side of page (in English) - - - Right-side of page (in Spanish)

The above "reduced-size copy" is of course unreadable. However, recognizable and noteworthy . . . the "print space" on the *left* (for English) versus the *right* (for a "foreign language" — Spanish). A foreign-language printing expense of course passed on to "all" GAS One, Inc. customers.

May 30, 2014 Response from ONE Gas, Inc.
"Scanned Copy of Original"

= = =

100 West 5th Street
Tulsa, OK 74103
918-588-7000 • onegas.com

May 30, 2014

Mr. William J. Moore
~~████████████~~
~~████████████~~

Dear Mr. Moore:

Mr. Pierce Norton, CEO of ONE Gas, received your recent letter and asked me to reply on his behalf. We're always happy to hear our customers' ideas about how we can serve them better, so thank you for your letter.

Kansas Gas Service is proud to provide safe and reliable natural gas service to more than 630,000 customers in the state of Kansas. We are committed to ensuring that each customer is served well, and that includes clearly communicating with them. Our Hispanic customer base continues to grow; in recognition of this fact, we have chosen to include certain information about the bill, including important safety information, in Spanish. Since safety is our top priority, we want to do everything we can to ensure that our safety messages reach as many customers as possible.

Again, thank you for taking time to provide your input. We appreciate your business.

Sincerely,

Caron A. Lawhorn
Senior Vice President - Commercial

= = =

Please note, when one cuts through all the "politically-correct BS" in the above May 30, 2014 response from ONE Gas, Inc.,-- ***"because Our Hispanic customer base continues to grow"*** is the summed-up executive management answer to my question – *"Why is <u>any</u> correspondence from my natural gas supplier (ONE Gas, Inc.) printed in anything but our United States common-language – English?"*

<u>*June 07, 2014 Response to May 30, 2014 Response from ONE Gas, Inc.*</u>
<u>*(Verbatim Copy of Original Letter)*</u>

= = =

June 07, 2014
Ms. Caron A. Lawhorn
Senior Vice President – Commercial
ONE Gas, Inc.
100 West Fifth Street
Tulsa, OK 74103

Dear Ms. Lawhorn:

I have received your 05/30/2014 letter (copy enclosed) in response to my 04/24/2014 letter to Mr. Norton, CEO of ONE Gas. You being asked to reply on behalf of Mr. Norton is understandable and the task you were given appreciated. During my working years I often carried out similar responsibilities.

Being the professional you are, you did your best to represent Mr. Norton, ONE Gas, and yourself, in a very courteous, generic, and otherwise business-appropriate manner. From your business perspective you did well. The courteous tone and direct nature of your letter is also appreciated.

That being said, you will hopefully recognize that my feedback below is directed at your letter's business message and not at the messenger.

Up front please know that I recognize "business BS" and "insincerity" when I see it. Considering the nature of some customer feedback, ONE Gas nor any other business is of course <u>not</u> "always happy" to hear from their customers.

Secondly, my letter to Mr. Norton was <u>not</u> sent to share "ideas about how ONE Gas can serve their customers better." Rather, and with considerable background information — my letter to Mr. Norton simply asked the following very serious question: *"Why is <u>any</u> correspondence from my natural gas supplier (ONE Gas, Inc.) printed in anything but our United States common-language – English?"*

Via your letter and with emphasis on providing safe and reliable natural gas service to more than 630,000 customers in the state of Kansas, ONE Gas' answer to my question is: *because "Our Hispanic customer base continues to grow . . . ."* To which I submit the below very sincere comments and re-stressed concerns.

So now ONE Gas divides their 630,000 Kansas customers into "two bases" — your "Hispanic customer base" and "the rest of us"? "The Rest of Us" being <u>all the other ancestry groups</u> that learned and use our country's English language. "The Rest of Us" being all those other customers ONE Gas has in the past sent, and continues to send, billings and other correspondence printed in English — with the assumption that the recipients can read such — including any/all "safety related" information therein.

"The Rest of Us" being your English speaking customers who are also paying for the costs incurred in providing ONE Gas, Inc. correspondence printed in Spanish. "The Rest of Us" being your other ONE Gas customers that are justifiably outraged by the "special treatment" ONE Gas has chosen to extend those particular Hispanics that refuse to respect, learn, and use, our country's language—English.

So, more plainly put, ONE Gas has made a business decision to make sure that your safety information is understood by your growing "Hispanic base", while expecting the rest of your customers (regardless of ancestry, etc.) to just get off their butts and learn and use the English language!

A shameful "CYA" business policy that fits quite well with other agendas aimed at methodically destroying our nation's borders, language, and culture. Agendas that will eventually turn our once great nation into something all too similar to the environment that now exists south of our uncontrolled borders. A sad legacy being passed on to our children and grandchildren—and yours. By persons and businesses lacking the wisdom and courage to do otherwise.

As was the case with my 04/24/2014 letter to Mr. Norton, I full well recognize this piece of serious correspondence to also be an exercise in futility. So, rest assured your time and mine will not be further wasted by other letter correspondence from me.

Any further attention on my part will be directed elsewhere. Although I would prefer it to be otherwise, dinosaur correspondence such as this does little to draw meaningful attention to issues of serious concern—for this is the era of web-pages, social media tools, and use of political contacts, etc.

Sincerely,

William J. Moore

Enclosure: a/s

C/F: Mr. Pierce H. Norton II, President and Chief Executive Officer, ONE Gas, Inc.

= = =

"With all the divisive forces tearing at our country, we need the glue of language to help hold us together. If we want to ensure that all our children have the same opportunities in life, alternate language education should stop and English should be acknowledged once and for all as the official language of the United States."

— Senator Bob Dole

"Our common language is English. And our common task is to ensure that our non-English-speaking children learn this common language." — William Bennet

A Few "U.S. Language" Facts

An **"Official Language"** is generally defined as one given special legal status in a particular country, state, or other jurisdiction.

While **American English** is the "most common language" in the U.S., no "official language" exists at the federal level. Over the years various proposals to make English our national language have been pursued as amendments to immigration reform bills, etc., with no success so far. However, some 27 U.S. states and most U.S. territories have designated English the "official language," requiring that business regarding government services be handled in English — as public debate continues regarding whether to recognize Spanish or require that all business be carried out in English.

Then, in much contrast, "California" — permitting driving tests to be taken in more than 30 languages; issuing drivers licenses to Illegal Aliens; and even permitting Illegal Aliens to serve on some city council positions, etc.

Since passage of the 1965 Immigration Act, the Latin-American population in the U.S. has dramatically increased, and our nation now includes the world's fifth largest Spanish-speaking population (some 35 million or more). As of the 1990s, our U.S. population increase was more than 30 percent created by legal immigration and heavily added-to by illegal immigration (illegal aliens), from Latin America and other developing areas.

"We have a responsibility to make them [immigrants] welcome here, and they have a responsibility to enter the mainstream of American life. That means learning English and learning about our democratic system of government. There are now long waiting lines of immigrants that are trying to do just that. Therefore, our budget significantly expands our efforts to help them meet their responsibility. I hope you will support it. Whether our ancestors came here on the Mayflower, on slave ships; whether they came to Ellis Island or LAX in Los Angeles, whether they came yesterday or walked this land 1000 years ago, our great challenge for the 21st century is to find a way to be one America. We can meet all the other challenges if we can go forward as one America."

– President Clinton (from State of the Union Address, 01/19/1999)

Access to Health Care

"The Obamacare contraception mandate was never about freedom. It was always about pitting secularism against religion, and using the power of government to sponsor secularism." — Ben Shapiro

On June 30, 2014, the U.S. Supreme Court ruled against an Affordable Care Act requirement that employers cover certain contraception products at no extra charge, as part of preventive-benefits in employee health insurance plans. A ruling reportedly applying to certain closely-held for-profit businesses, whose owners object to being forced to pay for certain birth control methods considered in conflict with their religious beliefs. Soon after this ruling was announced, the White House Press Secretary reportedly expressed that the court's decision **"jeopardizes the health of women employed by such companies."** A related question would seem to be: "What about the millions of unemployed women? **And, on such note, here's a revealing newsflash to The White House . . . not every woman (or man, or child) is "employed by a company," or an otherwise "employee"!**

Some view this ruling as a long-past-due victory for personal liberty. Others see it as preventing access to contraception products. A debate and blame-game that no doubt will continue for a long time—and be a recurring agenda item in future elections. Regardless of where one stands on this issue, below are a few thoughts for consideration:

- Somewhere between birth and death most discover there are no "free-rides" in life. Someone pays.

- No "for-profit" company is in business to lose money.

- Like other "for-profit" businesses—providers of Home Owner's Insurance, Auto Insurance, Life Insurance, and Dental/Heath Insurance, do not exist to supply "free" products. One can therefore rest assured that, within the many pages of, and changes to, the Affordable Care Act and agreements with participating insurance companies— there is a "golden parachute" clause. That is, language that makes certain that any cost/loss suffered by an insurance company, as result of providing government-mandated "free" / "no extra charge" products, will be duly reimbursed from our tax dollars. Again, "somebody" pays. If not us—then someone else—such as our descendants to whom our national debt is passed.

- "So far", without government mandated access, we have available a wide range of products. We can, for example, purchase human food, pet food, bird food, clothing, soft drinks, tobacco, alcohol, appliances, entertainment, transportation, an array of heath care items, as well as life/home/auto insurance, etc. "Access" to these and countless other items is made possible by "money"— which we could have much more of if much less was taken from us by our ever-growing, ever intrusive, Federal Government.

Which brings to mind some no doubt "truly unique" ideas for government consideration! How about taxing us less, leaving more of our money with us to responsibly do with as we choose, and back-off on controlling our personal affairs.

Believe it or not, contraception products can be purchased in the same manner used to pay for the many other essential and nonessential products we have routine access to. This type of personal liberty has been around for countless years—and can be exercised without infringing upon the liberty of others. Again, just some "truly revolutionary" ideas to consider. But, if access to and money for our contraception products is too personally challenging—we can always rely upon our Federal Government to "manage" and "simplify" our lives. Provided, of course, we continue to provide "unlimited access" to our hard-earned money—and maintain our irresponsible tolerance for an ever-increasing National Debt. Which, by the way, is now over $18 Trillion (or, more clearly expressed, over $18,000,000,000,000 and climbing). Spend, spend, spend-away, America! Future generations will pick up the bill!

And, about that Obama-promised "**$2,500 per year savings**" a typical family will gain through the now imposed Affordable Care Act (ObamaCare) . . . well, it's now forecasted that, starting in **2016**, Medicare premiums and other health care insurance premiums and deductible, etc., are expected to **"increase" about 50 Percent!** Just some more of that "Change

We Can Believe In"! Nevertheless — **"spend-away," America!** And, every chance you get, vote for more "free stuff" from our already broke public treasury, and for more "transformation of America." Our nation's children, grandchildren, and great-grandchildren, etc., etc., will someday pick-up the tab!

= = =

"To compel a man to furnish funds for the propagation of ideas he disbelieves and abhors is sinful and tyrannical." — Thomas Jefferson

"Think for a moment about what Obamacare has done: The Federal Government has come up with its own (ever-evolving) definition of 'health insurance,' which now includes free access to sterilization, contraception, and certain abortifacients such as the morning-after pill." — John Cornyn

"For most women, including women who want to have children, contraception is not an option; it is a basic health care necessity."
— Louise Slaughter

"It pains me deeply to see members of my own party attempting to legislate women's health and contraception choices." — Linda Lingle

"One year they asked me to be a poster boy — for birth control."
— Rodney Dangerfield

"If men got pregnant, there would be safe, reliable methods of birth control. They'd be inexpensive, too." — Anna Quindlen

"Contraception doesn't define a woman." — Nikki Haley

Eat "FREE"

"In this country that grows more food than any other nation on this earth, it is unthinkable that any child should go hungry."
— Sela Ward

"There ain't no such thing as a free lunch." — Robert A. Heinlein

There is "good" in this world — lots of it — and, it can be seen if, with open minds, we just look around.

For example, an attractive sign posted near the entrance of our Parsons, Kansas Elementary School during the summer of 2015 that read: **"USDA "USDA SUMMER MEALS SERVED HERE! Children Ages 1 – 18 EAT FREE!"** An indicator of some of the too-often overlooked, unappreciated, and otherwise taken-for-granted "good" in our world — and of the many named and unnamed who make such possible.

It would truly be most shameful if such sharing were not available in this hard-earned and fought-for land of unequalled opportunity and plenty. Suffering, poor health, and death, caused by hunger are terrible things — especially when experienced by children and the other helpless among us.   World-wide, the statistics regarding hunger and malnutrition are staggering, disheartening, and shameful.

It would likewise be most unfortunate if the recipients and others benefiting from such taxpayer-funded programs did not, at some appropriate time in their lives, learn, acknowledge, and appreciate that there really is no such thing as **"FREE."** That, regardless of the offering—be it food, safe-to-drink water, clothing, shelter, medical care, security, transportation, mobile phones, entertainment, education, liberty, freedom, or otherwise—someone pays, someone sacrifices.   If not past and present generations, then future generations of Americans.

Of course, these are just some well-meant shared-opinions, with certainly no intent to be "politically-incorrect," or, worse yet, "offend" anyone.

For, it seems that more and more it is someone's "feelings" that are expected to be the focus of our priority concern.   As opposed to responsible attention to our uncontrolled borders; onslaught of illegal aliens; our nation's rapidly growing $18 Trillion National Debt; etc.   Or heeding the warnings provided by the current financial crisis in a relatively small and out of sight and mind bankrupt-country named Greece.

Regardless of how much we are threatened by our federal government's tax and spend insanity, and by our disregard of the realities of nature and the facts-of-life, we nevertheless continue to expend our limited energies on futile agendas such as trying to control the Planet Earth's climate. And liberty-threatening agendas, such as trying to rid our world of the right to offend and be offended. And irresponsible agendas, such as—regardless of how worthy the intentions— suggesting that somewhere on this earth food is **'FREE'**— when, for example:

(1.) The UN World Food Program reports over 900 million people world-wide do not have enough to eat—that's more than the entire population of the U.S., Canada, and European Union combined;

(2.) wfp.org reports about one in every eight people on earth go to bed hungry each night; and

 (3.) thp.org reports about every 10 seconds a child dies from hunger-related diseases.

But, again, choosing not to use the "FREE stuff" pitch might detract from the political agenda and sought-after votes.

Or worse yet, fail to measure-up to political-correctness aims and, as a result—"offend" someone!

= = =

"Thirty-five million people in the U.S. are hungry or don't know where their next meal is coming from, and 13 million of them are children. If another country were doing this to our children, we'd be at war." — Jeff Bridges

"Close to a billion people — one-eighth of the world's population — still live in hunger. Each year 2 million children die through malnutrition. This is happening at a time when doctors in Britain are warning of the spread of obesity. We are eating too much while others starve." — Jonathan Sacks

"When I was four years old, my brother and sister died of hunger, so I achieved my success through confidence, self-motivation and my hard work." — Chen Guangbiao

"We know that a peaceful world cannot long exist, one-third rich and two-thirds hungry." — Jimmy Carter

"My friends, some years ago the federal government declared war on poverty — and poverty won." — Ronald Reagan

Massacres at U.S. Military "Gun-Free Zones": Why?

> *"A free people ought not only to be armed and disciplined, but they should have sufficient arms and ammunition to maintain a status of independence from any who might attempt to abuse them, which would include their own government."* — *George Washington*

On June 1, 2009, Abdulhakim Mujahid Muhammad, an American born Carlos Leon Bledsoe, killed 1 soldier and injured another soldier, in a drive-by shooting at a U.S. military recruiting office in Little Rock Arkansas. On July 25, 2011, Muhammad was reportedly sentenced to life imprisonment without parole for capital murder, and received 11 additional life sentences plus 180 years in prison on other charges.

On November 5, 2009, Nidal Malik Hasan, a U.S. Army psychiatrist and Medical Corps Major, killed 13 people and wounded at least 30 others, in a "mass murder" he carried out at the Fort Hood Military Base, Texas. Reported at the time as being *"The worst shooting to have ever taken place on one of our American military bases!"*

Less than five years later, on April 2, 2014, Fort Hood suffered another similar tragedy. A U.S. Army Specialist and Iraq War Veteran, undergoing treatment for mental health issues, reportedly killed at least 3 people and wounded some 16 others – 3 critically — before killing himself.

Each of these tragedies being indescribable horrors! With no words doing justice to the pain and suffering experienced by the victims, victims' families, and the many others affected. And, as typically the case, many of our politicians and news media moved quickly to divert our attention to—"why" did these murderers do such horrific things?

Not that "why" someone would commit such atrocities does not matter—because it certainly does! But, there are some other very important questions that deserve equal press and our serious national attention.

For example: "Why" do so many of our politicians, news media, and out-of-touch others, continue to debate only whether the shooter's actions were the result of madness or ideology, and, how and where was the weapon obtained, etc.?

And, "why" does there seem to be no anger, outrage, or, even a question about "why" our military personnel and civilians are left defenseless as "sitting ducks on a pond"—especially on a military installation?

Just maybe a serious review of a related Department of Defense (DOD) Policy is long-past-due! A policy that was reportedly originally-approved by President Clinton upon taking office in 1993, and, left in place by President Bush and (so far) by the Obama administration. DOD Regulations creating "gun free zones" on various military bases and forbidding military personnel from carrying their personal firearms, etc.

Policies removing the right of personal protection and self-defense from our military men and women—the same people we put in harm's way to "protect us and others". We trust them to put their life and limbs at risk on our behalf, but not to routinely carry a weapon on a military base? What a way to say "thank you for your service"!

An Update

"Approaching six years after" the November 5, 2009 Fort Hood Massacre: As of 2015—Nidal Malik Hasan, the U.S. Army psychiatrist and Medical Corps Major, who has admitted and been convicted of fatally shooting 13 people and injuring more than 30 others in the Fort Hood massacre on November 5, 2009, **is still alive**.

Still alive, after a jury panel of 13 officers convicted him of 13 counts of premeditated murder, 32 counts of attempted murder, and unanimously recommended that he be formally dismissed from the Army and sentenced to death.

Still alive, after the Army irresponsibly failed to charge him with "terrorism." After the Department of Defense (DOD) irresponsibly classified his mass murders as "workplace violence." And, after a subsequently released Senate report described this atrocity as "the worst terrorist attack on U.S. soil since September 11, 2001."

Yes, this self-admitted and convicted killer—this despicable coward who massacred his "unarmed" victims; this obvious "terrorist," described by his military peers as "anti-American"—this prime example of radical/militant Islam—is still alive! Incarcerated at Fort Leavenworth, Kansas at U.S. taxpayers' expense. Representing an unconscionable insult to any resemblance of justice—awaiting execution while appellate courts "review" his case!

Yet, to date, there is no visible citizen-outrage, no marching in the streets in protest. And, no actions being taken to provide our military and civilian personnel with the option to carry a personal weapon on our military bases, in self-defense against such terrorist acts! **"Why?"** . . . should be a loud and unrelenting question ringing in the ears of the President and other political and military leaders, until true justice in this yet to be resolved and unspeakable tragedy is served! And, until our military personnel and other law-abiding U.S. citizens are afforded the undeniable right of self-defense!

= = =

"No freeman shall ever be debarred the use of arms."

— Thomas Jefferson

(Correspondence to Kansas Representative Jenkins & Senators Roberts and Moran)

"Verbatim Copy of Original"

= = =

August 6, 2015

Dear Representative Jenkins:
Dear Senator Roberts:
Dear Senator Moran:

In June, 2009, Abdulhakim Mujahid Muhammad killed 1 and injured another at a recruiting station in Little Rock, Arkansas...

In November, 2009, Nidal Malik Hasan killed 13 and injured 32 at the Soldier Readiness Center in Fort Hood, Texas...

In September, 2013, Aaron Alexis killed 12 and injured 3 at Navy Yard in Washington, DC...

In April, 2014, Ivan A. Lopez killed 3 and injured 16 marking the second mass-shooting in Fort Hood, Texas...

In July, 2015, Muhammad Youssef Abdulazeez killed 5 and injured 2 at a recruiting center in Chattanooga, Tennessee...

The above being stated, allow me to note that every one of these tragedies were facilitated by the federal policy that mandates "Gun-Free Zones" at bases and other military workplaces.

Seeing that "Gun-Free Zones" have consistently failed -- and at the expense of many American lives -- I urge you to work with your colleagues to eliminate the "Gun-Free Zones" currently existing at military establishments.

The fact is, "Gun-Free Zones" are nothing more than "Free-Fire Zones" for predators and terrorists.

Furthermore, rumors are circulating that our U.S. Navy may charge Lieutenant Commander (LCDR) Timothy White for "illegally" using his sidearm against Mohammed Abdulazeez – the terrorist who opened fire at a recruiting station and reserve training center in Chattanooga, Tennessee, July 2015. As demonstrated patriots of this great nation, you clearly recognize that any such action against LCDR White would be an outrageous injustice and a devastating and demoralizing insult to our past, present, and future military personnel. LCDR should be awarded an appropriate Letter and Medal of Commendation for his courageous act—not disrespectful hassle from the country he serves.

Please take immediate action on this.

Sincerely,
Mr. William Moore
 Street
, KS

$$= \quad = \quad =$$

A Scanned-Copy of August 10, 2015 Response From Congresswoman Lynn Jenkins

August 10, 2015

Dear Mr. Moore:

Thank you so much for taking the time to contact me with regard to H.R. 86. As your representative in Washington, I want you to know how much I value your thoughts and concerns.

Growing up a farm kid in rural Jackson County, I learned to respect and value our constitutional right to bear arms at an early age. I have memories of driving to school with guns in the gun rack in the back of the family pickup. I am opposed to any legislation that unnecessarily infringes on individual rights, including the right to keep and bear arms.

H.R. 86 seeks to repeal the Gun-Free School Zones Act of 1990 and amendments to that Act. This bill was referred to House Judiciary. Although I do not serve on this committee, please be assured I will keep your thoughts in mind should this bill come before the House of Representatives.

Thank you again for contacting me. Please never hesitate to call, email, or write if you have any issues or concerns on your mind. Also feel free to visit my website at www.lynnjenkins.house.gov where you can see what I have been up to and sign up for my weekly newsletter.

Sincerely,

Lynn Jenkins, CPA
Member of Congress

"And that the said Constitution be never construed to authorize Congress to infringe the just liberty of the Press, or the rights of Conscience; or to prevent the people of the United States, who are peaceable citizens, from keeping their own arms; . . ."

— Samuel Adams

"Today, we need a nation of Minutemen, citizens who are not only prepared to take arms, but citizens who regard the preservation of freedom as the basic purpose of their daily life." — John F. Kennedy

Experts See No Solution!

"Experts often possess more data than judgment." – Colin Powell

The Sat-Sun, April 5-6, 2014, publication of our local newspaper, the Parsons Sun, included an almost quarter-page Dallas (AP) article entitled *"Experts see no solution for violence on military bases."* It read in part: *"After three mass shootings at military bases in the U.S. over the last five years, security experts say the sad truth is that there is probably no practical way of preventing members of the armed forces or civilian employees from carrying guns onto big installations like Fort Hood . . . ."*

Although rightly never accused of being an expert on or about anything, a few thoughts and suggestions do come to mind. Ones that the "security experts" who continue to wrestle with this issue may wish to consider.

Such as:

(1.) After receiving required training and background checks a law-abiding Kansas resident can obtain a Concealed Carry License—presently honored in some 35 other states—including Texas. It borders on absurdity that, for example, a tourist from Kansas eating lunch in a Texas café would have a self-defense option not available to personnel on (or off of) a Texas (or other) military base.

So—"security experts"—how about strongly recommending that the President "use his pen" to void Department of Defense (DOD) policies that create "gun free zones" on some military bases . . . policies that also forbid military personnel from carrying their personal firearms. Policies that remove the right of personal protection and self-defense from our military men and women, as well as the civilian personnel employed at same locations.

(2.) How about giving some serious consideration to the fact that persons hell-bent on massacring a bunch of innocent souls, often seem to have the presence of mind to seek out the helpless and defenseless—"the known to be unprotected". For some reason they don't often challenge targets such as Local Police stations, State Trooper facilities, FBI/CIA Headquarters, the White House, etc.

(3.) When our "security experts" publically declare that they see no solution for violence on "military bases", it is time we strongly insist that they be timely dismissed and replaced by some new and much more competent individuals.

(4.) If we are powerless to prevent massacres on our "military bases" within our U.S. borders, what does that say about our prospects for protecting our defenseless school children, shopping centers, community activities, etc.? "To see no solution" is not an option—and must not be tolerated!

In most all other aspects of life we do not seem to have a deep-seated aversion to "defense". "Defense" is an essential part of all sports activities. We use "defense" against the weather, disease, automobile accidents, internet hackers, and threats from other countries. In protecting our political leaders no expense is spared. We also go to great measures to protect our property — our "stuff".

But, when it comes to affording law abiding civilians and military personnel the option — the constitutional right — to personal protection against massacres and other bodily harm, we continue to run into liberty-infringing obstacles that put the lives of countless vulnerable and unprotected souls at risk.

Some common sense is long past due — and, again, "no solution" is not an option!

= = =

"Don't be intimidated by people who seem to be experts. Hear their points of view and get their judgments. But at the end of the day, you've got to make a judgment because it's not their life that's going to be affected so much as your future."   *— Robert Dallek*

"The right of the citizens to bear arms is just one more guarantee against arbitrary government, one more safeguard against the tyranny which now appears remote in America, but which historically has proved to be always possible."

— Hubert H. Humphrey

"The greatest danger to American freedom is a government that ignores the Constitution." — Thomas Jefferson

"They that give up essential liberty to obtain a little temporary safety deserve neither liberty nor safety." — Ben Franklin

"I ask, Sir, what is the militia? It is the whole people. To disarm the people is the best and most effectual way to enslave them."

— George Mason, Co-author of the Second Amendment

"Boots on the Ground" — Overused & Distracting

"Older men declare war. But is the youth that must fight and die." — Herbert Hoover

"In war, there are no unwounded soldiers." — Jose Narosky

"Anyone who has ever looked into the glazed eyes of a soldier dying on the battlefield will think hard before starting a war."
— Otto von Bismark.

The expression *"boots on the ground"* has a lengthy history originally applying to the direct physical presence of military troops in a conflict area.

Over the years, many of our political leaders, military spokespersons, and media, have been using this particular expression more and more. As we struggle, stumble, and fumble with how to deal with the growing number of defense-related threats worldwide. Whether involving nuclear arms, conventional weapons, terrorists, or otherwise.

While some expressions or catchwords may at times be popular or fashionable, some can innocently or otherwise serve to distract our attention away from the real subject—an important issue—some very serious aspect of life.

For instance, years ago "air pollution" (from automobiles, factories, etc.) was noted over various major cities in the U.S. and elsewhere. Discovery of this health hazard was soon followed by a new word—*smog*. While *"smog"* sounds so much less threatening, and the word's origin often lost through time and continued use, the hazard hanging over various major cities and breathed by the residents and visitors therein is still, nonetheless, "air pollution"—a serious health hazard. The significance and severity thereof potentially masked by the use of unrelated and distracting catchwords.

In turn, when referring to our military men and women . . . clearly, we **should** use respectful and befitting words such as, our "military men and women," "military personnel," "troops," "soldiers," "fighting men and women," "etc." But, much too often we use insensitive and detached terms like *"boots."* Possibly the result of nothing more than innocent inattention, or copycatting the words of others. Or, possibly, a conscious or unconscious effort to seek, create, and use "kinder, gentler, and politically-correct" words and phrases. In order to **mask** the reality of war, military conflict, and other "use-of-force efforts" considered by some to be inappropriate, or too unsettling and distasteful—or, a bit too close to **reality**.

However, regardless of "why" words such as "boots," and catch-phrases like "boots on the ground," etc., are used . . . such can and do distract from, and otherwise misrepresent, the true nature of our U.S. military efforts. And of the contribution and sacrifice of the countless military personnel involved — past, present, and future.

For, at the end of the day, when it comes to war or military conflict — or whatever we choose to call *"fighting for our liberty, survival, and otherwise national interests"* — it is still **"human life"** — **"flesh and blood"** — **"someone's loved-one,"** that must be put in harm's way . . . **Not "boots."**

Yes, whether their military role is on the ground, in the air, or at sea — those wearing the "boots" will forever be someone's husband, wife, father, mother, daughter, son, grandchild, aunt, uncle, niece, nephew, friend, and otherwise loved-one. And, it is not "boots" that become wounded or disabled; risk capture, torture, and execution; lose their lives; and have to cope with an inexcusably flawed Veterans Administration and empty political promises. Nor, is it "boots" that have families, friends, or other loved ones, who are also touched by the sacrifices and tragedies of war or other military conflict.

It is our citizen-duty to never let the above-mentioned realities slip from our minds or be clouded by distracting words or behavior. Likewise, we must never tolerate our political and military leaders irresponsibly committing (or irresponsibly failing to commit) the as-required support of our military men and women. For, ultimately at stake — are not "boots" or "chosen words and catch-phrases" — but the **lives** and **welfare** of our military personnel. And, ultimately, our nation's cherished liberty, freedom, and prospects for survival!

"It is well that war is so terrible, otherwise we should grow too fond of it." – Robert E. Lee

"Until we're in the war front, we can never understand the sacrifices of soldiers." – Terry Ward

"The object of war is not to die for your country but to make the other bastard die for his." – General George S. Patton

"War is fear cloaked in courage."
                     – General William C. Westmoreland

"In the councils of government, we must guard against the acquisition of unwarranted influence, whether sought or unsought, by the military-industrial complex. The potential for the disastrous rise of misplaced power exits and will persist."
                     – Dwight D. Eisenhower

"Here in America we are descended in blood and in spirit from revolutionists and rebels – men and women who dare to dissent from accepted doctrine. As their heirs, may we never confuse honest dissent with disloyal subversion." – Dwight D. Eisenhower

"A politician is a fellow who will lay down your life for his country." – Texas Guinan

Signs Offer Limited Protection

> "Gun bans don't disarm criminals, gun bans attract them."
> — Walter Mondale
>
> "Those who hammer their guns into plowshares will plow for those who do not." — Thomas Jefferson

On March 06, 2014, the front page of our local newspaper, the Parsons Sun, included a nice photo and narrative about our Parsons Middle School students' rehearsal of *"10 Ways to Survive a Zombie Apocalypse."*

The picture depicted three "horrifying zombies" lurching across the stage in threatening manner towards two young people—a young lady defending herself with a (pretend) pistol and a young man equipped with a huge (plastic) ball bat.

So refreshing! An article suggesting that there just may be some hope after all! Indicating that "at least" some of our younger generation may seem to get it! That—alone— "zombie-free zone" signs and "laws that forbid zombie attacks," etc., offer little to no protection when actually confronted by such life-threatening beasts!

But, fortunately, for all concerned, our Middle School Play didn't include use of a make-believe "assault" pistol, an "assault" ball bat, an "assault" rifle, an "assault" knife, or, an "assault" anything.

Otherwise, our town may have been flooded with protests and other much unwanted interferences. Un-asked-for "help" from various individuals and special interest groups striving so terribly hard to rid our school systems and society of terrible threats. Such as those pointed out by the following headlines:

<u>01/31/2013, New York Daily News</u>: Six-year-old kindergartner at Alice Drive Elementary in Sumter County, SC, expelled for bringing her brother's toy gun to class for show and tell.

<u>03/18/2013, The Baltimore Sun</u>: Seven-year-old Anne Arundel County, Maryland, student suspended for nibbling a Pop-Tart breakfast pastry into the shape of a pistol.

<u>11/04/2013, The Washington Times</u>: Eight-year-old at Scottsdale, Arizona's County Day Scholl threatened with expulsion for drawing a picture of a soldier, ninja warrior, and Star Wars character, holding guns.

And, while our young Middle School Students responsibly demonstrated some common sense survival techniques against "make-believe" zombies, the play's audience enthusiastically watched-on. While no doubt well-assured that everyone present was safe, secure, and protected from any and all "real" potential threats.

Protection provided by declared "gun-free zones." And, by posted "signs" that further assured that no one in the audience had a "real" gun with them. Especially, law abiding citizens with a state of Kansas concealed carry permit, evidencing background checks and training prior to issue.

Probably a good thing some "real" zombies didn't show up during the play's rehearsal or formal showing. Because it's most unlikely that "real" zombies give a lot of thought about playing by "the rules," or honoring "Zombie-free Zone" signs, etc.

= = =

"Firearms stand next in importance to the constitution itself. They are the American people's liberty teeth and keystone under independence . . . from the hour the Pilgrims landed to the present day, events, occurrences and tendencies prove that to ensure peace, security, and happiness, the rifle and pistol are equally indispensable . . . the very atmosphere of firearms anywhere restrains evil interference — they deserve a place of honor with all that's good."
— George Washington (1732-1799)

"To preserve liberty, it is essential that the whole body of the people always possess arms, and be taught alike, especially when young, how to use them; . . . ." *— Richard Henry Lee (1732-1794)*

Gun Free Zone Sign (Black & White Depiction)

It is of course delusional, liberty-losing, and self-destructive thinking—that rules, laws, and signs, are alone true deterrents to those who are hell-bent to harm others. Whether the doers of harm are mentally-disturbed, murderous criminals, terrorists, or otherwise.

Self-defense—and our ability and willingness to carry it out—are ultimately the backbone of liberty and survival. This reality just may have been among the reasons our country's Founding Fathers had the insight, experience, and wisdom to constitutionally provide for—in addition to our right to "post signs"—our more important and more effective right to "bear arms." You think?

Had the Founding Fathers means-of-defense been "British-Free Signs,"—nonexistent would be this great Nation, as well as the *author* and *readers* of these hopefully meaningful words.

"Divide & Conquer"

> "It is not our differences that divide us. It is our inability to recognize, accept, and celebrate those differences." — Audre Lorde
>
> "When we train ourselves to attack our problems rather than people, we work our way toward healthy resolution without leaving casualties in our wake." — Elisa Morgan

On August 9, 2014, an 18 year old man was caught on security video camera stealing merchandise from a convenience store in Ferguson, Missouri, and shoving and otherwise intimidating (bullying) the shop owner in the process. A few minutes later, this young man died from gunshot wounds during a confrontation with a police officer. What should have been totally irrelevant—to anyone other than racists, race-baiters, and those with "divide and conquer" agendas—the officer was white, the 18 year old young man, black.

A tragedy not only resulting in the death of this particular young man, but also forever changing the lives of the police officer involved, as well as the lives of his and the deceased's family, friends, and affected others. A tragedy that offered the President, other political leaders, special interest groups, the Ferguson community, the news media, and the rest of us, an opportunity to improve our country's race relations—or , "to do otherwise."

Unfortunately, the choice of too many was "to do otherwise." Once again, in the thereafter hours, days, weeks, and months—the President, U.S. Attorney General, various other political leaders, many news media, activists, agitators, and opportunistic others, chose to exploit "this particular" tragedy.

By fanning the emotional flames of racism, race baiting, dissent, controversy, civil unrest, rioting, and further tragedy. In pursuit of "divide and conquer" agendas, greed, and other self-serving aims. While disregarding the liberty and security of others, and treating our country's many other tragedies with irresponsible neglect.

This "highly-publicized" death in Ferguson, Missouri represented a terrible loss and much pain and suffering for those affected. As is the case regarding most if not all tragedies. Including those "not-so-highly-publicized"—the countless others "not selected for exploitation." The countless other tragedies prompting headlines such as:

— 10/05/2014: "5 teens shot Sunday; Part of violent weekend in Chicago."

— 06/16/2014: "Teen wielding pellet gun shot by Anchorage policeman."

— 05/04/2014: "Alaska teen fired seven shots, killed two troopers from behind."

— 02/18/2014: "Ohio teen armed with AK-47 killed in shootout with officer."

— 10/23/2013: "13 year old boy carrying replica assault rifle shot and killed by Northern California Sheriff's deputies after repeatedly telling him to drop it.

Reportedly, there are about 57 million deaths per year worldwide. The result of everything from old age to the most horrific of circumstances. That's about 156,000 per day, 6,506 per hour, 108 per minute, or 1.8 per second. Mortality numbers of course often fluctuate, and are broken down into countless categories and endless details of data available through a growing number of sources.

However, regardless of statistical "category" or "circumstances" — to the affected families and others, "each" death represents a tragic loss, and indescribable heartbreak. From their personal perspectives, a loss and grief no less painful and otherwise no less significant than that suffered by others. While loved ones struggle to cope with this traumatic aspect of life, and many others offer and provide their heartfelt support and comfort — it is unlikely there will ever be a shortage of those who choose to "selectively exploit" such suffering.

The August 09, 2014 death of an 18 year old Ferguson, Missouri youth was without doubt a terrible misfortune, and the circumstances of his death certainly warranted special review and assurance of justice for all concerned being served.

But, with respect to the "greatest risks" to the lives of our nation's youth, this particular tragedy at Ferguson, Missouri is but one of many — and not the "elephant in the room."

For, on average, more than 16,000 youths, ages 12-19, reportedly die in the U.S. each year. That's about 45 per day! "Each" — regardless of the circumstances — a heartbreak to someone. The five leading causes of their deaths: accidents (unintentional injuries), homicide, suicide, cancer, and heart disease. Accidents are said to account for almost one-half of all teenage deaths — with **"texting while driving"** now reportedly being "the" leading cause of death among teenagers — surpassing those killed in drunk driving accidents.

Yet, when it comes to these and other very real and ongoing "elephants in the room," there will no doubt continue to be an absence of relative interest and passion on the part of much of our media, politicians, activists, and agitators. That is — until the next heartbreaking tragedy is "selected" for exploitation in support of "divide and conquer" agendas or other liberty threatening aims.

Tragedies of all types give rise to "mixed opportunities." The opportunity to extend sympathy, empathy, and a helping hand to the survivors. Or, through mob violence, rioting, looting, etc., an opportunity to take advantage of the vulnerabilities and other painful circumstances that come with such misfortunes. Devastating behaviors that are likely to remain a part of our society as long as such behaviors are encouraged and tolerated.

As long as we put up with biased and agenda-driven news media; incompetent and self-serving political leaders; and, foreign and domestic special-interest parties driven to abuse, take advantage of, and otherwise destroy our nation. Aided, through ignorance or intent by an ever-growing social media frenzy . . . clearly capable of conduct supportive of, or against, our country's best interests.

As an aid to our survival from every growing "divide and conquer" agendas, we must become ever more a united people—proud and unrelenting defenders of our envy-of-the-world constitutional republic. We must ensure always our right of public dissent and peaceful demonstration, but have zero tolerance for mob violence, rioting, and looting. Zero tolerance for those choosing to destroy our lives, property, businesses, and livelihood.

We must see, think of, treat, and respect one another as "Americans." And not as Black, White, Red, Yellow, Tan, African, Asian, Mexican, Latino, German, French, Chinese, Italian, Japanese, Russian, Polish, etc., etc. But, rather, each and all of us as—"Americans." In doing so, we must speak a common language—our U.S. English language—and, jointly strive to maintain a common U.S. culture. A culture built upon our county's history, and protected by responsible and strictly enforced immigration policies and secured borders.

Mutual respect and joint-efforts against the threat of "divide and conquer" agendas are truly not "options" for us. For the sake of our liberty and ultimate survival, they are now very real and critical "obligations" to ourselves, one another, and our descendants. We must "jointly" find our way in this ever more complex, challenging, and crowded social-fishbowl. A nation of liberty/freedom and opportunities that "we" must occupy, maintain, and preserve. For, "together" we shall succeed and survive—and "divided" we shall be conquered and enslaved. History's many examples show this to be true.

= = =

"Every right implies a responsibility; Every opportunity, an obligation; Every possession, a duty." – John D. Rockefeller

"Healing is a matter of time, but it is sometimes also a matter of opportunity." – Hippocrates

"We live in a world where unfortunately the distinction between true and false appears to become increasingly blurred by manipulation of facts, by exploitation of uncritical minds, and by the pollution of the language." – Arne Tiselius

"Divide and rule, the politician cries; Unite and lead, is watchword of the wise." – Johann Wolfgang

"Nature is based on harmony. So it says if we want to survive and become more like nature, then we actually have to understand that it's cooperation versus competition." – Bruce Lipton

"Nothing has done more to separate and divide human beings one from another than exclusivist organized religion."

– Neale Donald Walsch

Denial, Intimidation, &
Postponed Courage

> *"I learned that courage was not the absence of fear, but the triumph over it. The brave man is not he who does not feel afraid, but he who conquers that fear."* — Nelson Mandela

"Denial" is not admitting that something is true, real, or exists. **"Intimidation"** can render us fearful and lacking in courage and self-confidence. **"Courage"** is our ability and willingness to confront fear, danger, uncertainty, pain, and intimidation.

Paris, France, January 07, 2015 — as reported by various news media: "Masked gunmen armed with AK-47s and shouting "Allahu Akbar" stormed the offices of a French satirical news magazine Wednesday in a terror attack that left 12 people dead, including the editor and two police officers." ["Allahu Akbar" being a common Islamic Arabic expression, usually translated as "God is [the] greatest," or "God is great".]

October 31, 2015 — A Russian aircraft, Metrojet flight 9268, reportedly exploded in air over Egypt, killing all 224 people on board, including 25 children. As initial U.S. and U.K. reports had also indicated, finalized Russian investigations have reportedly revealed with certainty that a bomb planted by terrorists was the cause of this horrific tragedy.

Again . . . Paris, France, November 13, 2015—reportedly in the deadliest attack on France since World War II, at least 129 people are killed and 352 injured (including 99 seriously), during a series of coordinated terrorist attacks. Unspeakably savage acts that included mass-shootings, hostage-taking, and suicide-bombings, at some six targeted sites.

Then, on Wednesday, December 2, 2015, two terrorists, Chicago-born Syed Rizwan Farok, age 28, and his age 27 wife Tashfeen Malik (in the U.S. on a fiancé visa), jointly entered a social service facility in San Bernardino, California, Farok's place of employment, where they murdered 14 people and wounded another 21, before themselves later being killed in a shootout with police. According to police reporting, a search of the killers' home found other weapons, thousands of rounds of ammunition, tools and materials for making pipe bombs and IUDs, etc. The capability to have carried out additional horrific atrocities. That these murderers were "terrorists" is unquestionable. A reality confirmed by the FBI, and even (at least in this particular case) also acknowledged as being such by President Obama and others typically in a state of unrelenting public denial. Whether these terrorists were lone-wolf radical/militant Islamists, or had foreign influence and direction, etc., are subjects of ongoing U.S. investigations as of this writing.

But, we must not lose sight that this horrific, December 2, 2015, terrorist attack on U.S. soil in San Bernardino, California, has been preceded by many others. For instance:

- **February 26, 1993:** Bombing of North Tower of the New York City World Trade Center, during which six people lost their lives and over a thousand more were injured as a result of this (potentially even more so) gruesome act.

- **September 11, 2001:** al-Qaed Islamic-terrorists attacks on both towers at the New York World Trade Center and the U.S. Pentagon, using hijacked commercial aircraft; and a fourth attack originally intended for a Washington D.C. target, but prevented by the heroic passengers in an attempt to overtake the hijackers. Atrocities that overall took the lives of some 2,996 people, and caused over $10 billion in property and infrastructure damage.

- **April 15, 2013:** Horrific bombing during Boston marathon, carried out by two migrants who demonstrated appreciation for the generosity extended to them—by killing 3 people and crippling or otherwise seriously injuring some 264 other innocent Americans!

- **June 01, 2009:** Abdulhakim Mujahid Muhammad killed 1 and injured another at a recruiting station in Little Rock, Arkansas.

- **November 05, 2009:** Nidal Malik Hasan killed 13 and injured 32 at the Soldier Readiness Center, Fort Hood, TX.

- **July 16, 2015:** Muhammad Youssef Abdulazeez killed 5 and injured 2 at a recruiting center in Chattanooga, Tennessee.

The horrifying atrocities mentioned in this section are of course but a few of the growing number that continue to be carried out by rapidly spreading radical/militant Islamists. Unthinkable murderous acts, truly beyond the comprehension of those of us *not yet* personally touched by such evil. An evil now being openly recruited/influence by, and/or otherwise carried out in declared allegiance to, the black flag of ISIS.

And, self-defeating and suicidal is any thought that, in the absence of swift, unrelenting, victorious-opposition, such terror will cease on its own and that we are not in further jeopardy. The U.S. and other civilized countries must STOP **denying**, publically and otherwise, the existence of this very real and growing threat; STOP being **intimidated** by its barbarous acts; and STOP postponing the **courage** needed to rid our world of this darkest of evils.

We must not be distracted or misled—a "war" with long historical religious-roots "is" being waged. By an enemy whose primary targets include the U.S. and others it considers "infidels." The (our) enemy: "Radical/militant Islamists"— with goals that openly include world domination; with no creed, faith, or ethnic group beyond its sights. A barbaric enemy imposing on all opposition—conform to its ways—its radical/militant view and application of Islam! Or, be killed, be enslaved, or suffer other unthinkable savagery.

An enemy not swayed by "political correctness;" "multiculturalism agendas;" "cultural / ethnic / religious diversity;" and "apologies for our country's greatness or shortfalls." Or, by other exercises in futility seemingly aimed at bringing about "one big happy world-family" — providing for "diversity" and "inclusiveness." Insanely suggesting that we can co-exist with the most despicably evil among us. It is truly to the peril of our United States and other civilized societies, to not early-on grasp that **denial, intimidation,** and **postponed-courage**, can, does, and will continue to result in terrible "consequences."

The ongoing savage murders, destruction, and world-dominating aims of the recent resurgence of radical/militant Islam should be a sufficient wake-up call. If not, then a little reflection on some other not-that-long-ago world history should be helpful. Reference is of course being made to atrocities carried out only 80 some years. When another fanatic ideology, in Germany, had worldwide ambitions to establish a "master race." With horrific ambitions likewise born and carried out for years under the noses of the world's "civilized" societies. People, who, intentionally, or through ignorance, also turned their heads — for too long. As millions — under unspeakable and otherwise barbaric circumstances — lost their liberty, their dignity, their loved ones, their homes and other belongings, and their lives.

So, today, we and others can continue a self-destructive path of denial, intimidation, and postponed-courage. Or, we can act to save ourselves and others from devastation and ultimate destruction at the hand of radical/militant Islamists. Through dedicated worldwide effort led by political and religious leaders having the courage to rise to this critical need. Supported by the likewise critical courage of our news media;

social-media network; intelligence services; military; and the rest of us. One and all, mutually-focused on survival of our nation, our liberty, our way of life. We have the opportunity, and we can choose to be either the **victims** or **victors** of radical/militant Islam and other evil. That is, at least "so far," such freedom still exists. Facing us—a decision and commitment we must timely make. Truly, a war against an evil we and other civilized societies must jointly and unrelentingly fight—and win! For nothing less than the sake of our liberty and survival!

= = =

"Your fear is 100% dependent on you for its survival."

— Steve Maraboli

"Refusal to believe until proof is given is a rational position; denial of all outside of our own limited experience is absurd."

— Annie Besant

"The human mind isn't a terribly logical or consistent place. Most people, given the choice to face a hideous or terrifying truth or to conveniently avoid it, choose the convenience and peace of normality. That doesn't make them strong or weak people, or good or bad people. It just makes them people." — Jim Butcher

"Courage is what it takes to stand up and speak; courage is also what it takes to sit down and listen." — Winston Churchill

"Courage is being scared to death . . . and saddling up anyway."

— John Wayne

Surviving the Threat of Radical/Militant Islam

> *"Terrorism is not an expression of rage. Terrorism is a political weapon. Remove a government's façade of infallibility, and you remove its people's faith."* — Dan Brown, Angels & Demons

On February 26, 1993, in an attack planned and carried out by a group of terrorists, a truck loaded with some 1,336 pounds of explosive was detonated underneath the North Tower of the New York City World Trade Center. The explosion was meant to destroy both towers and kill thousands of people, by causing the North Tower to fall into the South Tower. Although the explosion failed to do so, six people lost their lives and over a thousand more were injured as a result of this (potentially even more so) gruesome act.

And, a little more than eighteen and a half years later—the unthinkable! On the **Tuesday morning of September 11, 2001**, both towers at the New York World Trade Center were destroyed in conjunction with "four" coordinated suicide attacks. Using four passenger airliners, hijacked by nineteen al-Qaeda Islamic-terrorists. Two of the aircraft being crashed into the North and South World Trade Center Towers; another crashed into our U.S. Department of Defense Headquarters—

the Pentagon; and the fourth originally intended for a Washington D.C. target, crashed into a Pennsylvania field after heroic passengers attempted to overtake the hijackers. Overall, these horrific atrocities took the lives of some 2,996 people, and caused over $10 billion in property and infrastructure damage. The lives lost included 2,507 civilians, 55 military personnel, 343 firefighters, 72 law enforcement personnel, and the 19 suicidal hijackers. And countless others who have and will yet die from disease and other health issues attributed to contaminated air, debris, etc., from these tragedies.

These 1993 and 2001 foreign-terrorist attacks on our U.S. homeland happened as over four-hundred taxpayer-funded Federal Government Agencies went about their various, and often self-serving, agendas. Many of which with aims of regulating and controlling almost every aspect of our lives. Many of which with responsibilities clearly including our personal safety and national security! And as terrible as these 1993 and 2001 attacks truly were and remain, it could have been much worse! Had either or both involved "nuclear material," the outcome would to this day, and for countless years to come, been one that could reasonably be described as in the realm of the "absolutely horrifyingly-unimaginable!"

Then (as also cited in the previous section), on Wednesday, December 2, 2015, two terrorists, Chicago-born Syed Rizwan Farok, age 28, and his age 27 wife Tashfeen Malik (in the U.S. on a fiancé visa), jointly entered a social service facility in San Bernardino, California, Farok's place of employment, where they murdered 14 people and wounded another 21, before themselves later being killed in a shootout with police. According to police reporting, a search of the killers' home found other weapons, thousands of rounds of ammunition, tools and materials for making pipe bombs and IUDs, etc. The capability to have carried out additional horrific atrocities. That these murderers were "terrorists" is unquestionable. Whether they were lone-wolf radical/militant Islamists, or had foreign influence and direction, etc., are subjects of ongoing U.S. investigations as of this writing.

And, how could these and other unthinkable atrocities have taken place on our U.S. soil? Again, the answer unquestionably has ties to the ignorance, apathy, complacency, denial, greed, and counter-productive fears – of "we the people" and "our federal government." Including President Obama, who, as of this writing, has yet to ever publically acknowledge the threat of, or utter the words of . . . radical/militant Islam. And, as stressed in the earlier section, titled *"Survival"* . . . to **survive**, we must not only be able to **recognize threats**, but also **have and apply effective defenses** against such. Life-sustaining basics that can get critically sidetracked when any government and its citizens become preoccupied with "self" as opposed to "country."

In speeches, March 03, 2015, before a special joint-meeting of our U.S. Congress, and six months prior, on September 29, 2014, to the United Nations General Assembly, Israeli Prime Minister Netanyahu delivered very strong, rational, and plain-spoken warnings about the growing threat of radical/militant

Islam, and why ISIS must be defeated and Iran must never be allowed to gain nuclear weapons capability.

In his September 29, 2014 speech he strongly cautioned: *"It's not militants. It's not Islam. It's militant Islam. Typically, its first victims are other Muslims, but it spares no one. Christians, Jews, Yazidis, Kurds – no creed, no faith, no ethnic group is beyond its sights. And it's rapidly spreading in every part of the world. You know the famous American saying: "All politics is local"? For the militant Islamists, "All politics is **global**." Because their ultimate goal is to dominate the world."*

In his March 03, 2015 speech he emphatically stressed his most deep concerns that, on their current path, U.S./Iran nuclear weapons negotiations could ultimately lead to Iran eventually having nuclear weapons capability. Posing an unthinkable threat to Israel, the Mid-East Region, and even our continental United States.

Each of these speeches by Israeli Prime Minister Netanyahu were of global importance. Each should have been echoed by President Obama and other world leaders. Each should have received positive media attention and strong public endorsement. But, none of these things happened. Largely because he spoke plainly, truthfully and bluntly about a very real and rapidly spreading worldwide threat— radical/militant Islam. A threat that is still too often being camouflaged by inattention, apathy, complacency, denial, greed, and a mix of conflicting political, religious, and other agendas.

Worse yet, the Prime Minister's speeches did not deal with the truly "top-priority concerns." Such as: political correctness, climate change (previously named global warming), some popular Hollywood actor's wedding, the grandchild of a U.S. political figure, or the need to mandate a name-change of a professional sports team, etc. Had he focused on any of these more important matters, his speeches most likely would have received overwhelming cheers and other accolades! But, he didn't. Instead, he rationally and responsibly warned us about dangers from the worldwide spread of militant Islam.

Views that the Prime Minister's warnings "exaggerate" the threat of radical/militant Islam, are often rooted in inattention or ignorance of past and present world events. Not exaggerated are the barbaric executions of countless men, women, and children, or the many raped, buried alive, and beheaded, or the other unspeakable atrocities carried out by this present-day and rapidly spreading fanatic ideology.

Some 80 years ago another fanatic ideology (in Germany) had ambitions to establish a worldwide **"master race."** Today, a radical/militant Islam menace openly declares the intent to establish a worldwide **"master faith."** This menace has a varied and long-standing history. Dating back to the 7th century (601 – 700, per Julian calendar), and the Muslim-conquests of: Persia (now called Iran), Syria, Palestine, Armenia, Egypt, and North Africa. But, what is now much different is "the truly unthinkable" — the growing potential of radical/militant Islamists access to biological, nuclear, and other weapons of mass destruction, via Iran. Or by other sources and supporters of radical/militant Islam ideology.

What is different also, is this fanatic ideology's use of likewise "truly unspeakable" weapons of mass murder. Such as, suicidal men and women, boys and girls, willing to strap explosive bombs on their bodies and blow themselves up in the presence of military personnel and innocent civilians, in order to carry out the heinous act of "mass murder." We now face an enemy that has no concern about losing its own life, wears not a recognizable uniform, and can be in a bodily form in likeness to our next door neighbor, or their children.

Effective defense against this spreading threat is unlikely until — as a nation and as individuals — we get in touch with some realities. Such as, no amount of political correctness will protect us from this truly evil ideology hell-bent to dominate the world at any cost; and we cannot be apologetic enough about our skin color, faith or lack thereof, sexual orientation, ethnic origin, economic status, strengths, weaknesses, achievements, or shortcomings, to ward off this barbaric enemy. Nor, can we ever demonstrate enough humility, sense of fairness, equality, or charity, to escape its wrath. Beyond "total submission" to radical/militant Islam, we can never be "accommodative enough" to this spreading evil.

The utter futility of any efforts to "co-exist" with radical/militant Islam ideology can be found in a real-world definition of "political correctness," — that being — "*the absolutely delusional proposition that it is actually possible to pick up a turd by the clean end."* A task that any right-minded person or attentive nation should have long ago determined as not doable — either through common sense or unforgettable experience!

World history has time and again shown that there are times when countering certain threats to the human race has called for "special leadership." This is one of those times. In addition to being a constitutional responsibility, our president and congress have a moral obligation to protect U.S. citizens from this rapidly-spreading foreign and domestic threat. Through a clear and effective strategy driven by uniquely strong, unifying, trustworthy, and plain-spoken "leadership."

But, as of this writing, President Obama and his administration have yet to reveal clear and successful national strategy and effective presidential leadership against the spreading threat of radical/militant Islam. For example, on February 5, 2015, and reportedly in reference to conflicting acts of compassion and cruelty often attributed to various religions over many centuries — President Obama's speech at the National Prayer Breakfast in Washington, D.C. included in part: *"Humanity has been grappling with these questions throughout human history." "And lest we get on our high horse and think this is unique to some other place, remember that during the Crusades and the Inquisition, people committed terrible deeds in the name of Christ. In our home country, slavery and Jim Crow all too often was justified in the name of Christ."*

It is noteworthy that the Crusades President Obama referenced above reportedly ended over "700 years ago," and were in large measure in response to Muslim conquests, etc. Hence, it can be logically viewed that the President's remarks were and remain an irresponsible attempt to distract from, and seemingly offer excuses for, radical/militant Islamist atrocities taking place on his watch — in this the 21st Century!

It is also noteworthy that President Obama's words were silent regarding "terrible deeds" committed by Muslim conquests prior to and after the Crusades he referred to. The intent of his no doubt specifically chosen words may long be debated. But, to many of us they are further unsettling evidence of an increasingly dangerous agenda of delusional denial of the existence and increasing curse of radical/militant Islam. And of failed presidential leadership.

But, as opposed to the many "hundreds of years ago" Crusades President Obama chooses to dwell upon, let us return to the here and now. Present-day human beings (adults and children) are being beheaded; burned alive; buried alive; enslaved, raped, crucified, and subjected to other horrific atrocities. And, the clear and indisputable facts are . . . these savage atrocities are **NOT** being carried out by radical/militant Protestants, Baptists, Catholics, Mormons, Christians, Hindus, Buddha's, Agnostics, Atheists, etc. Or by real/imagined U.S. racists; or otherwise in the name of Christ or Christianity. But, rather, by radicals/militants in the name of Islam . . . while shouting "Allahu Akbar." ["Allahu Akbar" being a common Islamic Arabic expression, usually translated as "God is [the] greatest," or "God is great".] Whether named al-Qaeda, ISIS, ISOL, or otherwise . . . it is nonetheless, "radical/militant Islam." Words (a fact-of-life, enemy, and evil) yet to be publically uttered and acknowledged by President Obama. Or, by Bernie Sanders, Hillary Clinton, and Martin O'Malley—all currently seeking nomination as the democrat party 2016 candidate for president.

And, given the hundreds-of-years track record of terror at the hands of radical/militant Islam . . . civilized people—including U.S. citizens—are not "getting on their high horse" when they wake-up to this very real and present threat, and demand their government have and execute a "successful strategy" to protect them from this foreign and domestic evil. Doing so is just the plain and simple exercising of good common sense and their natural instinct to survive!

The ability and willingness to recognize, acknowledge, and eliminate threats, are basic requirements for survival. Radical/militant Islam **"is"** a serious worldwide threat. Whether, in the form of ISIS, al-Qaeda, or Iran (the foremost militant-Islam state-sponsor of world-wide terrorism). Yes, the same Iran carrying out yet debated and highly controversial 2015 nuclear arms negotiations with the U.S. and other nations. The same Iran whose history of radical/militant Islam ideology strongly attest that negotiations, and best intentions of other nations, will not alone ever prevent Iran's strive for nuclear weapons capability.

As the U.S. and various other nations continue to pander Iran's negotiating demands, and apply confusing and un-united approaches to the threat of ISIS—radical/militant Islam continues its terror and territorial gains. And, as much of the not-yet-touched world continues to look away. Failing to aggressively confront and destroy an enemy of the darkest evil, made up of a rapidly-spreading number of well-organized, well-financed, internet and social-media savvy, and insanely-committed, despicable-beings. Recruiting followers and supporters from all corners of the earth—including the United States.

It is to our peril as a nation and as individuals, that we fail to understand and defend against the **"reality"** of radical/militant Islam. An unrelenting enemy that has openly declared war against western civilization! An enemy not seeking jobs, healthcare, improved race relations, U.S. apologies, political correctness, or anger management classes. But, instead, world domination, and death to the U.S., Israel, and all others considered "infidels."

Over the years "we the people" have not only tolerated, and continue to tolerate, disrespect and agenda-driven destruction of our U.S. Constitution, borders, common-language English, and culture. But, also, the continuing financial and social burden of millions of illegal aliens. Now compounded by the also financial and social burdens—**and national security risks**—of a continuing flood of untold thousands of immigrants from war-torn Muslim (Islam faith) countries.

With no means for us to ensure that terrorists are not embedded among them.

<u>Surviving the threat!</u> Truly, for the sake of our liberty and ultimate survival . . . of our free and open society . . . of our way of life, we must unrelentingly use our informed and responsible votes, phones, e-mails, social-media networks, town hall meetings, public protests, and other constructive means of communications, to flood the President and Congress with our uncompromising demand. That they immediately and jointly step up to the plate and do their constitutional and moral duty to protect our nation from foreign and domestic threats . . . first and foremost, those now posed by radical/militant Islam. And, likewise ensure that Iran never obtains nuclear weapons capability. Or, that our political representatives and president get out of the way and support those who will! "We" can and "we" must likewise exercise "our" constitutional duties and responsibilities as U.S. citizens! Our "obligation" to future generations of Americans.

Or . . . we can choose to seek "more comforting and entertaining" alternatives. Such as, further burying our heads in our smartphones, e-tablets, social media, reality-TV, virtual worlds, selfies, and other options of distraction and attempted-escape from reality. Until, that is, we are interrupted by the nuisance and inconvenience of the next unthinkable tragedy (somewhere else, of course)! Or, on U.S. soil, experience forever-lost liberty, savagery, and death—at the hand of radical/militant Islam. And, in the meantime, should we wish to pursue a more worthy cause, we can focus on what President Obama, Hillary Clinton, Bernie Sanders, the Pope, and others, have declared to be our most serious threat—**"climate change."** Focused on anything but the continuing spread of radical/militant Islam. And the public chants of "death to America!" . . . "death to the Infidels!" While of course sleeping peacefully, with trouble-free minds!

And, if the above message is taken as harsh, unsettling, and attention-getting . . . it was and is meant to be so.

= = =

"We are at war, and our security as a nation depends on winning that war." — Condoleezza Rice

"The purpose of terrorism lies not just in the violent act itself. It is in producing terror. It sets out to inflame, to divide, to produce consequences which they then use to justify further terror."

— Tony Blair

"Wanton killing of innocent civilians is terrorism, not a war against terrorism." — Noam Chomsky

"We have an American culture and we have an American constitution and anybody who's going to occupy our White House should be living in a pattern that is consistent with our constitution and our culture." — Ben Carson, Retired Neurosurgeon & Republican presidential candidate, September, 2015.

"In an interconnected world, the defeat of international terrorism – and most importantly, the prevention of these terrorist organizations from obtaining weapons of mass destruction – will require the cooperation of many nations. We must always reserve the right to strike unilaterally at terrorists wherever they may exist. But we should know that our success in doing so is enhanced by engaging our allies so that we receive the crucial diplomatic, military, intelligence, and financial support that can lighten our load and add legitimacy to our actions. This means talking to our friends and, at times, even our enemies." – Barack Obama, speech, Nov. 20, 2006

"Humanity has been grappling with these questions throughout human history." "And lest we get on our high horse and think this is unique to some other place, remember that during the Crusades and the Inquisition, people committed terrible deeds in the name of Christ. In our home country, slavery and Jim Crow all too often was justified in the name of Christ." – President Obama, February 5, 2015, taken in part from his speech at National Prayer Breakfast, Washington, D.C., reportedly in reference to conflicting acts of compassion and cruelty often attributed to various religions over many centuries.

*"It's not Islam. It's militant Islam. Typically, its first victims are other Muslims, but it spares no one. Christians, Jews, Yazidis, Kurds – no creed, no faith, no ethnic group is beyond its sights. And it's rapidly spreading in every part of the world. You know the famous American saying: 'All politics is local'? For the militant Islamists, 'All politics is **global**.' Because their ultimate goal is to dominate the world." – Israeli Prime Minister Netanyahu, in speeches Sept. 29, 2014, to the United Nations General Assembly, and March 03, 2015, before special joint-meeting of U.S. Congress.*

"The society that put equality before freedom will end up with neither. The society that puts freedom before equality will end up with a great measure of both." –Milton Friedman

*"When they took the **Fourth Amendment**, I was silent because I don't deal drugs.*

*When they took the **Sixth Amendment**, I kept quiet because I know I'm innocent.*

*When thy took the **Second Amendment**, I said nothing because I don't own a gun.*

*Now they've come for the **First Amendment**, and I can't say anything at all."*

–Tim Freeman

"Distorted Facts"

&

"False Assurances"

"How strangely will the Tools of a Tyrant pervert the plain Meaning of Words!" — Samuel Adams

Politically and otherwise, "we the people" face many challenges. Including, how to recognize and guard against the "distorted facts" and "false assurances" that continue to flow from our federal government. Regardless of political party.

For example, not so long ago the highest levels of our federal government assured us that the Ebola Virus disease responsible for taking thousands of lives in Africa would not find its way to the U.S.—but it did. And, following the October 8, 2014 death of a patient in a Dallas, Texas hospital—from an Ebola infection reportedly contracted during his visit to Africa—we were then assured that all was under control and there would be no outbreak of Ebola in the U.S. But, all was not under control. On October 12, the CDC reported that a "breach of protocol" at same hospital resulted in Ebola infection of a nurse, and that other caregivers could have also potentially been exposed. Reportedly "the first known case" of the deadly Ebola Virus contracted or transmitted within the U.S.

And, to date, our federal government has not yet been so forthcoming and assuring about another very dangerous health hazard — Entrovirus D68 (EV-D68). An especially rare virus, said to have been rapidly spreading across the U.S. at the same time of the U.S. Ebola exposures.

Exceptionally dangerous since Entrovirus D68 (EV-D68) can be contracted about as easily as the common cold and flu, and can include symptoms similar to both. A potentially life-threatening virus that, in 2014, had infected more than 600 people in well over 40 states by October, and was believed to have contributed to the death of 5 or more young U.S. children during the brief timeframe of late September to October of same year.

EV-D68 is said to be the most risk to young children, teenagers, and others with underdeveloped or compromised immune systems. And an even greater hazard to those with asthma and other respiratory issues. A threat that has been in the past, and may continue to be in the future, dangerously overshadowed by our government's and news media's focus on "Ebola" and other "more news worthy" and "politically convenient" subjects.

Unfortunately, we are certainly no strangers to distorted facts and false assurances from our federal government. Such as (to cite but a few): *"Not a smidgen of corruption in the IRS, NSA, VA, etc."* *"The Benghazi attack was a spontaneous demonstration prompted by a controversial video,"* *"You can keep your doctor and health care plan,"* *"Healthcare will cost less under the ACA,"* *"al-Qaeda has been destroyed,"* and, *"ISOL has been contained,"* *"etc."*

And, stepping back to 2003 timeframe, *"Evidence exists that Iraq has weapons of mass destruction."* And, a little further back in time to 1964, to the *"distorted facts by high U.S. Government officials"* about North Vietnamese and U.S. conflicts in the Gulf of Tonkin. Distorted facts, and deceptions of the American public, that led to full U.S. involvement in the Vietnam War! A war that caused some 4 million civilian casualties, and took the lives of over 58,000 of our U.S. Military Personnel and wounded more than 300,000!

But, as was so forcefully expressed by a departing U.S. Secretary of State during the early phase of Benghazi Terrorist-Attack Hearings – *"At this point, what difference does it make!"* Words uttered by the same now ex-Secretary of State who is, as of this October 2015 writing, under FBI investigation regarding her handling of classified correspondence intermingled on her personal e-mail server. The same ex-Secretary of State who, in addition to Bernie Sanders and Martin O'Malley, is now seeking nomination as the democrat party's 2016 candidate for president.

Well, as evidenced by the few examples mentioned above (from world history's countless many)—distorted facts and false assurances can and often do have serious consequences.

Unfortunately, the "source" is much too often our federal government. Elected officials and civil servants having the constitutional duty and moral obligation to do otherwise. A dangerous reality "we the people" must always be mindful of and on guard against. And, likewise remember and take into account, when we step into the voting booth. And, while on the subject of voting—shame on "we the people" if, out of a U.S. population of more than 322 million, we can't do better than another Bush or Clinton in The White House!

= = =

"Power tends to corrupt; absolute power corrupts absolutely."
— *Lord Acton*

"In order to become the master, the politician poses as the servant."
— *Charles de Gaulle*

"If we got one-tenth of what was promised to us in these acceptance speeches there wouldn't be any inducement to go to heaven."
— *Will Rogers*

"Some men change their party for the sake of their principles; others their principles for the sake of their party." — *Winston Churchill*

"Politics is supposed to be the second-oldest profession. I have come to realize that it bears a very close resemblance to the first."
— *Ronald Reagan*

"Bad officials are elected by good citizens who do not vote."
— *George Jean Nathan*

Information Overload

> *"In the age of technology there is constant access to vast amounts of information. The basket overflows; people get overwhelmed; the eye of the storm is not so much what goes on in the world, it is the confusion of how to think, feel, digest, and react to what goes on."*
>
> — Criss Jami

> *"Information overload is a symptom of our desire to not focus on what's important. It is a choice."* — Brian Solis

> *". . . a wealth of information creates a poverty of attention."*
>
> — Herbert A. Simon

To help connect this particular section to "liberty and survival," take note of the following very incomplete random list of some related news headings over recent years . . . and picture yourself in the voting booth making crucial decisions:

- "Students can't resist distraction for two minutes."
- "The effects of distractions on human performance."
- "Distractions at work."
- "Easily distracted: Why it's hard to focus."
- "How multi-tasking hurts your brain."
- "Modern technology is changing how our brains work."
- "Technology and the interrupted brain."
- "Social media networks are distracting students."
- "How background music affects our concentration."

In hearing or using the word "overload," we are generally thinking of *"more than something or someone can or should handle"* . . . an *"excessive load."*

We can and sometimes do overload our stomachs, backs, boats, home electrical circuits, national power grids, automobile and truck tires, machines, highways, bridges, communications systems, internet services, U.S. border security, schools, hospitals and emergency rooms, as well as our police, fire, and ambulance services, etc. It seems that nothing is truly immune to *overload*.

Of course *overloads* do not come without *consequences*. Such as, heartburn, obesity, back pain, ruptured discs, mental stress, capsized boats, drownings, electrical fires, disrupted electricity services, auto and truck tire blowouts, machine breakdowns, traffic jams and related accidents, collapsed bridges, disrupted phone calls, crashed internet services, compromised U.S. borders, uncontrolled immigration, overcrowded classrooms, and delayed or unavailable services regarding health care, police and fire protection, etc.

Reflecting upon such consequences, not a lot of deep thought should be needed to recognize how various *overloads* can also put at risk our **liberty and survival**. And in considering this reality, this section draws attention to one such potentially very serious overload-threat. One we may often be unaware of, deny, or otherwise just try our best to ignore. That being – *"Information Overload."*

More than 40 years ago Alvin Toffler fired a first warning-shot. In his bestselling 1970 book, *"Future Shock"*, Toffler theorized that there are limits to the amount of information our brains can deal with. That when overloaded, our decision-making becomes extremely difficult, defective, or not doable. Worse yet, Toffler posed that ***information overload*** can eventually result in physical and mental health issues. Considered science fiction at the time, today various scientists and research clearly support Toffler's views. The danger of continued exposure to excessive amounts of information is now widely recognized, viewed a serious concern, and an area of intense study.

An internationally recognized British author and psychologist, David Lewis, Ph.D., has even strongly suggested that some fatalities are actually the result of people encountering much more information than they know how to handle. Regarding this disturbing trend, Lewis has reportedly stressed that *"having too much information can be as dangerous as having too little . . . making it harder to find the right solutions or make decisions."*

Therein rests the issue, the threat! As touched upon in *"Survival"* and other sections of this book, and dictated by just plain old common-sense, our survival depends upon our being able to analyze issues, determine the right solutions, and make and act upon good decisions. In government and our personal lives. Anything that hinders our ability to do so represents a threat to our wellbeing. Including, but not limited to, both the <u>lack of</u> as well as <u>too much</u> — information!

Since the beginning of time, not having the right kind of factual information at the right time has posed a serious threat to countless millions. But now, more so than any prior generation, our problem is too often not the lack of information or limited access to it.

To the contrary, our present and future challenge is how to manage and properly use the ever-growing glut of now-available information. How to responsibly and constructively deal with the expanding mountain of information we are now *voluntarily* and *involuntarily* exposed to! A truly daunting challenge!

The Internet and digital-age continue to have a truly revolutionary impact on our complex society. To ever growing numbers of us worldwide, access to a rapidly expanding database of detail information on almost every conceivable subject is now available. Seemingly, a limitless source of knowledge — with the power and the problems knowledge can provide. By the end of 2014 the portion of our world population connected to the internet exceeded 42 percent. That represents 3 billion internet users — a number that has increased more than ten-times since 1999, and now forecasted to exceed 3.2 billion by the end of 2015. In 1995 less that one 1% had access.

During 2011, for the first time ever, shipments of desktop PCs and e-notebooks were less than shipments of smartphones and e-tablets. In 2013 Americans reported owning an average of about 4 digital devices; with some 80% of adults owning internet-connected PCs. By 2014, smartphones were owned by over 55% of American adults, and over 40% also owned e-tablets. 2015 research reports now show that children's access to e-tablet computers at home has more than doubled since 2012; use of e-tablets and smartphones is far exceeding that of desktop PCs and mobile phones; and interactive media usage is undergoing a rapid switch from the web to mobile apps.

Such devices and technology are increasingly considered to be "necessities" rather than conveniences. Expanding use of smartphones, e-tablets, wearable e-devices, etc., now make access to information truly mobile—ever present—always with us! Much in likeness to another *body-part* . . . a no doubt another also rapidly approaching reality.

We now have near-instant world-wide communication and increasing amounts of information transmitted at faster and faster speeds. Use of electronic mail, instant messaging, video conferencing, discussion forums, blogs, social networking, unlimited phone service, unlimited texting, e-commerce, e-books, online media 24/7, online shopping, online education, online research, online securities trading, online banking, and online entertainment, etc., are more and more commonplace in our daily lives. This being but a very incomplete snapshot of an extremely small portion of the rapidly changing digital-world of "information access."

Worldwide . . . governments, militaries, terrorist groups, etc., also continue to enjoy Internet-enhanced communications, surveillance, and "other" capabilities of our digital-age.

Capabilities, some we are aware of, some unknown to the average citizen, and many we should likely be much, much more concerned about. For example, there exists the ever-present potential for *information overload* to be used as a propaganda tool in liberty-destroying agendas. Therefore, how our government, and other parties, friend and foe, use information and information technology, are among a growing number of areas *we the people* must be especially attentive to.

It is to our peril that we ever *assume* that "any" government will always do the right thing; and will always use available information to the best interests of its citizens. History is loaded with liberty and survival threatening examples to the contrary.

Surprisingly (and I don't have a clue why) the previous couple of sentences prompted a bit of memory flash-back about some not-long-ago disclosures of yet unresolved abuses by our IRS, NSA, etc.? However, for now, back to our exposure to too much information—*information overload*. An also fact-of-life and rapidly-growing problem, evidenced by countless statistics, such as the following, but a few, YR 2014 examples:

- Over 2,000 new websites going online each day.
- Some statistics indicate that world-wide information is doubling about every two months.
- Estimates show that the mobile web is receiving more than 200 new users every minute.

- If internet website Wikipedia was a book it would reportedly include more than two billion pages.
- Over fifty percent of the phones in the U.S. are now smartphones — with mobile web *(information)* options.
- Our Library of Congress is said to be cataloguing more than 7000 new items daily.
- 14,000 or more books are being published each week.
- GOOGLE has reportedly estimated that so far more than 130 million different books have been published world-wide. This ever-growing number shows how truly challenging the search giant's ongoing project is "to organize all of the world's *information*."
- Researchers in the Department of Information Sciences at the University of California, Berkeley, have reportedly estimated that if the total amount of unique information generated in the world each year were to be divided up between every man woman and child on earth — each would receive a personal library of more than 250 books.
- On-line and brick and mortar book/music stores offer thousands upon thousands of book titles and music selections, as well as access to thousands of newspapers, periodicals, and magazines — domestic and foreign.
- Some estimates indicate that information/data storage is increasing at the rate of several hundred times yearly. Many businesses are collecting so much they are becoming overwhelmed, and a growing number of us are storing more photos and other information than we or our descendants will ever have time to deal with.

In the early 1900's, the average person wrote and/or received only a handful of letters in their lifetime. It is now commonplace for many of us to receive more junk snail-mail, e-mail, texts, tweets, photos, media news feeds, e-alerts, notices, offers, warnings, solicitations, advertisements, calendar reminders, reports, and other types of information, than we can effectively and responsibly deal with. Truly overwhelming! Truly **"information overload"**!

As a result, we often put-off making decisions, or make the wrong decisions. From the <u>overload of information</u> we are subjected to, we are often unable to distinguish factual information from falsehood. Or, unbiased government and media communications from agenda-driven propaganda. Or, information supportive of our liberty and survival from political spin that endangers such.

We humans have been using written information for several thousand years. A few hundred years ago the invention of the printing press made it possible to distribute larger amounts of written information to many more people and places. However, not until the creation of modern computers, the internet, and other supporting technologies, were we able to create, access, duplicate, and distribute vast amounts of information to countless millions worldwide. Not until these relatively recent innovations have we become able to create "information overload" — and spread it and its consequences worldwide.

Our human brain is the bottleneck—the limiting factor.
While we are able to create machines with increasing memory
and information-processing capability, we humans have some
very real limitations, too often being ignored.

There are limits to what and how much we can (and should)
eat, drink, lift, see, taste, hear, feel, etc. For the most part, we
recognize and accept these facts-of-life, these human
limitations. However, we too often fail to recognize or accept
that our brain also has limitations.

Remarkably, our brain can handle millions of signals from our
many senses each second! But, when it comes to reading,
writing, and talking, our brains can only process a relatively
small amount of information at a time. Our human brain has
not yet *evolved* the ability to fully focus on several subjects and
issues and the same time. It is not able to effectively and
responsibly process the "information overload" we are now
exposed to . . . voluntarily and involuntarily.

Failure to recognize these limitations is not only unwise and
unhealthy, but also threatening to one's survival.

Regardless of how organized, competent, and dedicated our
efforts—and how many "apps" are created to assist us—we
can still be overwhelmed by the ever-increasing glut of
information involved in our daily lives.

And, too often we are also burdened by expectations that we
should be able to "handle it all." Expectations imposed by

ourselves and others. And nothing in evolution or life today has prepared us to function in a world of overwhelming-exposure to a growing onslaught of information.

So far, there seems to be no simple or full-proof solution—no "magic pill"—for the ever-growing problem of **"information overload"** surrounding us. However, common sense and the reportings of many experts suggest there are some actions we can take to at least help minimize the problem. Some basic efforts that can help de-clutter our minds, improve our focus on the important issues, and thereby assist us in making better decisions, etc., in government and our personal lives. For instance:

- Making sure that we spend portions of each day fully focused on "one" thing for a significant period of time—while being "disconnected" from the interruptions of phones, internet, TV, radio, e-mail, texting, tweeting, social media, etc.

- Spending much more time on gaining only information truly needed "now"—and less on the nice-to-know stuff.

- Focusing on "quality" information by using brief, to the point, communications—in person, and via phone, e-mail, texting, etc. Likewise, applying the same guidelines to questions "we ask" and our responses to questions "asked of us".

- Striving to get out of the unrealistic and unhealthy rut of "multi-tasking" by keeping our minds focused on one problem at a time.

- Including appropriate exercise, relaxation, and sleep, in our daily routine.

- Treating ourselves and others with some uninterrupted "quite time" — some time for healthy meditation.

Clearly, the above are but a few very-summarized examples. With no suggestion or inference of being a full-proof solution or promise of flawless outcome. For, we are all "individuals" with varying needs and unique life-circumstances to deal with. Nevertheless, although the degree may be unique and personal for each of us, *information overload* is nonetheless a *common* problem and **growing threat**. One which we must not only *acknowledge* to exist, but also responsibly treat as a serious danger. And, wisely and unrelentingly develop and apply effective *defenses against*.

Informed and responsible voting, and ensuring a government properly focused on the best interests of our nation and its citizens, is a daunting challenge. Even with the benefit of uncluttered minds capable of required focus on crucial issues. Attempting to do so with minds threatened, damaged, or otherwise distracted by *information overload* . . . is a recipe for disaster. And in matters regarding the public trust . . . a present and growing threat to our liberty and survival.

= = =

"Unlimited choice is paralyzing. The Internet has made this form of paralysis due to option overload a standard feature of comfortable modern life." — Susan Orlean

"It is unquestionably true that man, left to his own devices, can gather a tremendous amount of <u>information</u>; so much, in fact, as to be smothered under the pile of facts he has heaped upon his own head." — FR Walter Farrell (1902-1951)

"There are many things of which a wise person might wish to be ignorant" — Ralph Waldo Emerson

"In the age of technology there is constant access to vast amounts of information. The basket overflows; people get overwhelmed; the eye of the storm is not so much what goes on in the world, it is the confusion of how to think, feel, digest, and react to what goes on."
— Criss Jami

"Information is the oxygen of the modern age. It seeps through the walls topped by barbed wire, it wafts across the electrified borders."
— Ronald Reagan

"Since Kodachrome made way for jpeg, pictures accumulate on hard drives like wet leaves in a gutter." — Jim Lewis

"I have a theory about the human mind. A brain is a lot like a computer. It will only take so many facts, and then it will go on overload and blow up." — Erma Bombeck

"We aren't in an information age, we are in an entertainment age."
— Anthony Robbins

Our State of the Union Addresses

Article II, Section 3, of our U.S. Constitution, requires in part that the President *"from time to time give to Congress information of the State of the Union and recommendations to their Consideration such Measures as he shall judge necessary and expedient."*

The Constitution is silent regarding "exactly how" this duty is to be carried out, and handling has varied considerably over the years. For example: 1790—President Washington used a "speech" to deliver the first "Annual Address" to Congress; 1801—President Jefferson, in what he considered a less imperialistic approach, used separate "written notes" to the House and Senate—a practice that continued for another 112 years or so; 1913—President Wilson put the tradition of "spoken delivery" back into play; 1923—President Coolidge broadcast his message by radio—until that time, public access to such information was limited to newspapers, word-of-mouth, etc.; 1935—President Roosevelt continued use of the radio, and started routine use of the term "State of The Union"; 1947—President Truman was first to broadcast his message by TV; 1966—Opposition parties began routine use of TV broadcasts in follow-up rebuttals to each State of the Union Address; 2002—President Bush delivered first address via live webcast on the Internet.

Nevertheless, over many years and different administrations, a simple requirement for common sense communication from our Presidents to our Congress has grown into a routine spectacle of rituals, propaganda, and wasted opportunities. That is, too often into little more than an extra dose of campaign propaganda—sandwiched between a beginning and ending comprised of self-absorbed pomp, ceremony, and an unsettling royalty-syndrome. Worse yet, into wasted opportunities to demonstrate crucially needed "nation-uniting" leadership.

"We the people" don't need a yearly dog-and-pony-show to grasp our nation's state-of-affairs—we need only open our eyes, ears, and minds to the world around us. Likewise, it is rather universally understood that our federal government is ever-growing, out-of-control, and dysfunctional—and our political leaders getting together in one big room once a year to further prove it, is not value-added.

Nor is, the routine practice of touting special guests, reportedly from the ranks of every-day-citizens, to demonstrate "being in touch" with our concerns—when the political record clearly shows otherwise.

Furthermore, a growing number of us are increasingly outraged by continued use of these yearly exhibitions (touted as State Of The Union Addresses) as platforms for more and more **"free stuff"** propaganda. While, irresponsibly ignoring our rapidly growing $18 Trillion National Debt (now exceeding $56,000 per citizen; over $150,000 per taxpayer).

However, **"Our National Debt"** never seems to make it as a serious agenda item in our "State of the Union Addresses." Although truly being a shameful and unconscionable issue of national importance. An importance that hopefully will one day outweigh current national concerns, such as: "need for more free stuff," "political correctness," "someone being offended," "drivers licenses for illegal aliens," "improperly-named sports teams," "climate change (earlier called global warming)," and, at some point, even outweigh the ongoing cries for more strict control of the "air pressure of NFL footballs!"

In the meantime, in critical need—a President, Congress, and Supreme Court, with the courage and support to stand before us and declare that there really is <u>no such thing</u> as **"FREE"**— someone pays. If not us—our children, grandchildren, and great-grandchildren!

= = =

"I predict future happiness for Americans, if they can prevent the government from wasting the labors of the people under the pretense of taking care of them." – Thomas Jefferson

"As government expands, liberty contracts." — Ronald Reagan

"I cannot undertake to lay my finger on that article of the Constitution which granted a right to Congress of expending, on objects of benevolence, the money of their constituents."
— James Madison

"Government exists to protect us from each other. Where government has gone beyond its limits is in deciding to protect us from ourselves." — Ronald Reagan

"A government big enough to give you everything you want is a government big enough to take from you everything you have."
— Gerald R. Ford

"Charity is no part of the legislative duty of the government."
— James Madison

"Dear Government . . . I'm going to have a serious talk with you if I ever find anyone to talk to." — Stieg Larsson

E-Mail "To" & "From" The President

"The greatest patriotism is to tell your country when it is behaving dishonorably, foolishly, viciously." — Julian Barnes

This section includes **"two"** messages. The first, concerns prepared for President Obama's attention, subsequently summarized in a March 2015 e-mail per message-size limitations specified by **WWW.WHITEHOUSE.GOV**. The second, a scanned-copy of President Obama's e-mail response, received May 20, 2015.

= = =

<u>Date</u>: 03/09/2015
<u>Topic</u>: "In short supply: Clear U.S. strategy & strong, unifying, plain-spoken leadership."
To: WWW.WHITEHOUSE.GOV, Attn: President Obama

The ability and willingness to recognize, acknowledge, and eliminate threats, are basic requirements for survival. "Radical/militant Islam" is a serious worldwide threat. Whether, in the form of ISIS, or Iran (the foremost militant-Islam state sponsor of worldwide terrorism), or otherwise. Treating this reality with apathy, complacency, and denial, is irresponsible — and will not make it go away.

As our government continues a confusing and un-united dealing (or not dealing) with this threat, and as much of the not-yet-touched world still looks away, radical/militant Islam continues its terror and territorial gains. Through unthinkably cruel acts of murder and other suffering, carried out by ISIS— a rapidly-spreading number of well-organized, well-financed, internet and social-media savvy, and insanely-committed, despicable-beings. And, by the radical/militant Islam state of Iran—as it continues distracting negotiations with the U.S. While Iran's history and radical/militant Islam ideology strongly attest that best intentions alone will never prevent Iran's strive for nuclear weapons capability.

Radical/militant Islam—an enemy not seeking jobs, healthcare, improved race relations, U.S. apologies, political correctness, or anger management classes. But, instead, world domination, and death to the U.S. and others considered "infidels."

World history includes times when countering certain threats to the human race has called for special leadership. This is one of those times. In addition to being a constitutional responsibility, our president and congress have a moral obligation to protect U.S. citizens from this rapidly-spreading foreign and domestic threat. Through a clear strategy driven by uniquely strong, unifying, trustworthy, and plain-spoken leadership.

In speeches, March 03, 2015, before a special joint-session of our U.S. Congress, and six months prior, on September 29,

2014, to the United Nations General Assembly, Israeli Prime Minister Netanyahu delivered very strong, rational, and plain-spoken warnings about the growing threat of radical/militant Islam, and why ISIS must be defeated and Iran must never be allowed to gain nuclear weapons capability.

These warnings of global importance should be taken as serious wakeup-calls by all world leaders; and receive broad media attention and strong public endorsement. Such outcome is not clearly evident. For example, on February 5, 2015, and reportedly in reference to conflicting acts of compassion and cruelty often attributed to various religions over many centuries — President Obama's speech at the National Prayer Breakfast in Washington, D.C. included in part: *"Humanity has been grappling with these questions throughout human history."* *"And lest we get on our high horse and think this is unique to some other place, remember that during the Crusades and the Inquisition, people committed terrible deeds in the name of Christ. In our home country, slavery and Jim Crow all too often was justified in the name of Christ."*

U.S. citizens are not "getting on their high horse" in demanding that their government execute a successful strategy to protect them from the foreign and domestic threat of radical/militant Islam. Doing so is merely exercising good common sense and the natural instinct to survive.

Respectfully, William James Moore, Parsons, KS.

= = =

"Scanned-copy of President Obama's e-mail response, Received May 20, 2015"

From : The White House <noreply@whitehouse.gov>   Wed, May 20, 2015 11:04 AM
Subject : Response to Your Message
To : wj██moore@████████.███

THE WHITE HOUSE
WASHINGTON

Dear William:

Thank you for writing. I appreciate the thoughtful messages I receive from Americans with deeply-held views that may not always align with mine. Dialogue on a broad range of issues is critical to moving forward in areas that matter to all of us. When we disagree, even fiercely, it doesn't mean we don't each love this country and want to make it better.

As it has for more than two centuries, progress comes in fits and starts. It's not always a straight line or a smooth path, and recognizing we have shared hopes and dreams won't end all gridlock, solve all problems, or substitute for the painstaking work of building consensus. But we must find common ground and make difficult compromises to reach a better tomorrow.

Again, even if we don't see every issue the same way, I want you to know I am listening and I appreciate your perspective.

Sincerely,

Barack Obama

= = =

In due respect of the office, and given the ever-flowing and truly massive amount of correspondence The White House deals with, the significance of President Obama's response is certainly recognized and appreciated. Nevertheless, in terms of substance, the President's message leaves little to no promise that his administration and its supporters will ever be detracted or waver from their radical-left "transformation-of-America" agenda. An agenda that—as stated in his May 20, 2015 response—President Obama considers to be "progress" involving "fits and starts." While, in reality, one that has brought and continues to bring great harm to our nation. Including, but not limited to, destruction of our U.S. borders, common-language English, culture, and middle-class. Whether the result of intent or ignorance—a devastating agenda that is taking our nation down a most dangerous path! One that truly threatens our liberty and ultimate survival.

"But, it's never too late to learn!" President Obama's May 20 e-mail response also provides a prime example of it never being too late to learn. For instance, until respectfully contemplating the President's response, I (like no doubt countless others) have obviously failed to understand. I have just plain and simply failed to grasp that our country's stumbling and fumbling on the world political stage; the expanding scourge of radical/militant Islam; growing racial/civil unrest in our country; demise of our borders, English language, and culture; political correctness gone mad; etc., are each and all actually nothing more than examples of the "fits and starts" of "progress." Not to mention the failure of myself and others to grasp that climate-change (i.e., earlier called global-warming) is our most serious security threat!

How in the world could well-meaning folks such as I have ever been so inattentive and irresponsible to have not recognized and duly appreciated the many examples of "the fits and starts of progress" all around us?

Possibly, John Adams, our 2nd U.S. President, was on target when he reportedly said, *"Old minds are like old horses; you must exercise them if you wish to keep them in working order."* Possibly, I and countless others are among an ignorant many who have short-changed our minds of essential exercise? Possibly, that is?

In wrapping-up this section it seems fitting and proper to especially note, that the less-than-complementary remarks in this section, and elsewhere within this book, are not shared in ignorance of the awesome burdens and many limitations that our U.S. Presidents have to deal with. Nor in ignorance of the roles that self-serving "power and influence-hungry" leaders in **"both"** the democrat and republican parties have played, and continue to play, in our country's demise. Nor, of the ownership of **"we the people"** . . . and the voter-ignorance, apathy, complacency, denial, greed, and lack of political wisdom and courage, etc., we sadly continue to demonstrate year after year. For, **"we"** are ultimately responsible for who **we** designate (and tolerate) to represent us. And "we" shall also certainly reap what "we" sow . . . as will our descendants!

= = =

"I do the very best I know how — the very best I can; and I mean to keep on doing it until the end. Nearly all men can stand adversity, but if you want to test a man's character, give him power."

--Abraham Lincoln

"Trojan Horses" — A Growing Threat!

> *"In order to become the master, the politician poses as the servant."* — *Charles de Gaulle*

As we know, the term **"Trojan Horse"** typically means someone or something with the deceptive aim of defeating, weakening, or destroying, a target from within.

As legend has it, a "Trojan Horse" once helped conquer the ancient city of Troy. According to classical mythology, the Greeks abandoned a huge hollow wooden-horse during their attempted siege of Troy. After the Trojans took the left-behind wooden horse into Troy, Greek soldiers hidden inside this deceptive (Trojan) horse slipped out at night and opened Troy's gates to the awaiting Greek army, who then conquered the city.

Today, we must be on constant guard against other types of "Trojan Horses." Such as:

"Computer" Trojan Horses — The countless "appearing to be useful" computer programs masquerading as legitimate games, utilities, antivirus programs, etc. But, are actually programs containing concealed code (instructions) that, when activated, carryout malicious actions, such as destroying the victims' data files, etc.

"Government" Trojan Horses — Those, at all branches and levels of government, that masquerade as "servants of the people," while using their positions of power and influence to carryout self-serving and malicious actions that contribute to the destruction of our nation (e.g., destruction of our borders, English language, culture, liberty, freedom, employment opportunities, security, etc.). As well as those **"Trojan Horse"** laws, policies, regulations, programs, agendas, agencies, etc., that masquerade as being in our best interests, while in reality being otherwise. And especially **"Trojan Horse"** political leaders who, underneath it all, are actually tyrants, dictators, autocrats, authoritarians, bullies, etc., in disguise.

"Terrorists" Trojan Horses — Such as, the truly threatening and common-sense-certain potential of **Radical-Militant Islamist Terrorists** disguised as **Trojan Horses**. Imbedded within the growing thousands of immigrants attracted by our uncontrolled U.S. borders and failed immigration policies! Posing a threat of growing magnitude, with unthinkable consequences that are today and historically-predictable! A world-crisis especially worsened by the mass-fleeing of peoples from Syria and other areas of the war-torn and ravaged middle-east.

"Deceit-disguised-as-truth" Trojan Horses — For example, to mention but a few: "...... (President Johnson) --*North Vietnam attacked our ship in international waters* ...... (1st President

Bush) — *Read my lips — no new taxes ......* (President Clinton) — *I never had sexual relations with that woman ......* (2nd President Bush) — *Iraq has weapons of mass-destruction ......* (President Obama) — *My administration will be one of transparency; I will be the President of all the people; You can keep your doctor and health care plan; your medical insurance and other health care costs will be less; I will not put ground troops back in Iraq or in Syria; Iran will never be allowed to possess a nuclear bomb; ISOL (ISIS — radical/militant Islamists) has been contained ....*

We spare no concern, expense, and effort at trying to protect ourselves from the ever-growing threat of **"computer" Trojans.** It is truly to our peril that we fail to also unrelentingly guard against **"government"** Trojans, **"terrorist"** Trojans, and **"deceit-disguised-as-truth"** Trojans. **"Any and all"** Trojan Horses that pose a threat to our liberty and survival. That this citizens'-duty is crucial and endless in scope, is clearly supported by world history — and is further stressed by the wisdom, experience, and warnings, contained in various of the quotations inserted at the end of this section and elsewhere throughout this book.

= = =

"This and no other is the root from which a tyrant springs; when he first appears he is a protector." — *Plato*

"The tree of liberty must be refreshed from time to time with the blood of patriots and tyrants." — *Thomas Jefferson*

"Ignorance has always been the weapon of tyrants; enlightenment the salvation of the free." — *Bill Richardson*

"The welfare of the people in particular has always been the alibi of tyrants." – Albert Camus

"War kills men, and men deplore the loss; but war also crushes bad principles and tyrants, and so saves societies."

– Charles Caleb Colton

"When the shepherd is a wolf, the flock becomes only so much meat."
– Brian Herbert & Keven J. Anderson

"Of all tyrannies, a tyranny sincerely exercised for the good of its victims may be the most oppressive." – C.S. Lewis

"Tyrants have always some slight shade of virtue; they support the laws before destroying them." – Voltaire

"Experience hath shewn, that even under the best forms of government those entrusted with power have, in time, and by slow operations, perverted it into tyranny." – Thomas Jefferson

"The accumulation of all powers, legislative, executive, and judiciary, in the same hands, whether of one, a few, or many, and whether hereditary, self-appointed, or elective, may justly be pronounced the very definition of tyranny."

– James Madison, Federalist 47, 1778

"Communism is the death of the soul. It is the organization of total conformity – in short, of tyranny – and it is committed to making tyranny universal." – Adlai E. Stevenson

The "Selective Exploitation" of Tragedy

On 08/26/2015, a Virginia reporter and cameraman were shot to death, and their interviewee seriously wounded, during a live TV broadcast. Another tragedy that was swiftly "selected" from the worldwide many, for exploitation through agendas driven by profit, politics, and otherwise. Including, but not limited to, renewed focus on "gun-violence."

Well, at the risk of being forever-barred from the growing ranks of "Political-correctness Gone Mad" — here's another noteworthy news-flash that just never gets much if any attention by our liberal-media and closed-minded others: **"Guns" are not the problem! "Wrong-minded People" are the problem!** "People" <u>use</u> guns, knives, axes, ball bats, automobiles, airplanes, fire, poisons, rocks, clubs, pressure-cookers, fertilizers, social-media posts, and countless other things "as weapons" to harm or kill others. We have a worldwide problem of **"wrong-minded people"** — not one of "guns," "shortages of gun-free zones," and other "things."

And, if we seriously crave to put a meaningful dent in the worldwide "tragedies of death," the ongoing atrocities carried out by the ever-growing ranks of **radical/militant Islamists**, both foreign and domestic, would seem to be a more fitting and priority target.

One might also find a most worthy cause to pursue within the many readily-available mortality statistics. For instance, according to the World Health Organization, **the top 10 "yearly" causes of death "globally" are:**

(1.) Ischemic heart disease (coronary artery disease), over 7 million deaths — the leading causes: smoking, genetics, high blood pressure, lack of exercise and **stress; (2.) Stroke**, 6.7 million deaths; **(3.) Chronic obstructive pulmonary diseases (COPD)**, over 3 million deaths; **(4.) Lower respiratory diseases** such as pneumonia, bronchitis and influenza, over 3 million deaths; **(5.) Lung cancer**, 1.6 million deaths — the leading cause: cigarette smoking in 80 to 90% of all cases; **(6.) HIV/AIDS**, over 29 million deaths since discovered about 30 years ago, with 1.5 million dying in 2013 alone; **(7.) Diarrhea-related disease**, 1.7 billion cases, 760 thousand deaths of children under 5; **(8.) Diabetes mellitus**, 1.5 million deaths; **(9.) Road injury (non-health related)**, 1.3 million; **(10.) Hypertensive heart disease**, such as angina and coronary heart disease, 1.1 million (the top killer associated with high blood pressure)—the risk factors including overweight, getting little exercise, eating fatty foods regularly, and smoking.

But, unfortunately, headlines, talk shows, and speeches about death, suffering, and other tragedies related to the above statistics, <u>or caused by the following</u>, just don't yet have the attention-getting and radical-liberal-agenda supporting appeal of **"gun-violence," "gun-control," or "gun-anything"**:

"Radical/militant-Islam violence," "beheading-violence," "mob-violence," "tobacco-violence," "alcohol/other drugs-violence," "sex-violence," "texting-while-driving violence," "sugar-abuse violence," "fatty/salty-foods violence," "over-eating/obesity-violence," "fire-violence," "airplane-violence," "stress-violence," "hunger-violence," "knife-violence," "bullying-violence," "car/truck-violence," "stone-violence," "poor-sanitation violence," "lack-of-exercise violence," "social-media violence," "illegal-alien violence," etc.

Nor, would "selecting the above for exploitation" be all that helpful to agendas aimed at **"disarming law-abiding Americans"**!

= = =

"The Constitution shall never be construed to prevent the people of the United States who are peaceable citizens from keeping their own arms." — Samuel Adams, Massachusetts Ratifying Convention, 1788

"In a perfect world you wouldn't need guns. This is not a perfect world." — Sheriff Ben Johnson, Volusia County, Florida

"The gun control extremist has at least two things in common with the Islamic extremist. He has a willingness to die for his fundamental beliefs. And he has the sanctimony to demand that others go with him." — Dr. Mike Adams

A Dangerous
Refusal to Accept Reality

> *"How many legs does a dog have if you call the tail a leg? Four. Calling a tail a leg doesn't make it a leg." — Abraham Lincoln*

"Reality" is *"the world or the state of things as they **actually exist**, as opposed to an idealistic or notional idea of them."*

Life, nature, and other aspects of our world involve countless unavoidable "realities." Such as, our limited life-span, and what it takes to survive.

As was expanded upon in a prior section, titled "Survival" — the ability of any life-form to survive depends upon, not only being able to **recognize** and **acknowledge** threats, but also **having** and being **willing to use** effective defenses against them. As is the case throughout nature . . . when we refuse to accept, or otherwise fail to effectively deal with, these and other basic realities of life . . . there are consequences. Potentially very serious consequences, such as, injury and death. And, at times, even the loss of liberty/freedom and destruction of a culture, nation, civilization, or species, etc.

Any refusal to accept the "realities of life" is truly a most unwise and dangerous behavior—at any time! Including, each time we have the opportunity (the responsibility) to exercise our right to vote! In any election concerning any aspect of our local, state, and federal government!

A complete "list of realities" that truly warrant our unrelenting attention leading up to, throughout, and after our country's many elections, would be long, varied, and growing. And would include issues and challenges dangerously unattended as a result of our ongoing **"refusal to accept reality."** Such as (to mention but a few):

- Since any nation is defined by its **borders**, **language**, and **culture**—agendas aimed at destroying a nation, **DO** overtly and/or covertly target these three critical aspects.

- Unsecured U.S. borders and irresponsible immigration policies **DO** expose U.S. Citizens to security threats, economic burdens, crime, diseases, and overcrowding of our schools, hospitals, and other institutions, infrastructure.

- The pandering of Spanish or other foreign language **DOES** serve to destroy our common U.S. English language—and ultimately, our U.S. culture and nation.

- Political-correctness gone mad, **IS** serving to destroy our freedom of speech and expression, our right to offend and be offended—and ultimately, our other liberties, U.S. culture, and nation.

- Refusing to fittingly use words like murderer, terrorist, militant-Islam, radicalized-Islam, radical/militant Islam, war, etc., will **NOT** prevent or change or prevent the realities of murder, terrorism, and war.

- Changing the name of environmental agenda "global warming" to "climate change" will **NOT** reduce related government bureaucracies and tax burdens. And will **NOT** truly change human control over the Planet Earth's earthquakes, volcanic activity, movement of continental plates, or other natural "climate changes" that have been underway — without our help — for well over 4 billion years.

- Policies instructing school teachers at Lincoln Nebraska Public Schools and elsewhere, to **NOT** use phrases such as "boys and girls," "ladies and gentlemen," and similarly gendered terms, and to instead call kids "purple penguins," etc., **DO** involve dangerous, idealistic, nation-destroying agendas. That ignore the reality that children and adults must strive, thrive, and survive in a world that in fact includes gender, race, ethnicity, etc. — a world that is **NOT** always fair, equal, considerate, inclusive, safe, and politically correct.

- Guns, military/kitchen knives, hatchets, fertilizer, pressure cookers, and even automobiles, **ARE** among various "weapons" used to commit murderous acts within our U.S. borders and elsewhere. Laws and agendas aimed at eliminating any single one or all of such items, and/or the declaration of weapons-free zones, will **NOT** rid our world of murderous acts.

- Creating a nation "free" of "offensive" names, symbols, remarks, behavior, and thoughts, is **NOT** realistic—or a proper role of our federal government.

- Willfully, or through policy and agenda, calling *"illegal"* immigrants/aliens *"undocumented"* immigrants/aliens, etc., **IS** a dangerous denial and cover-up of laws broken, and an affront to "all" law-abiding people.

- A nation of ever-growing "dependents" and ever-declining "contributors" is **NOT** sustainable.

- An ever-growing, ever-intrusive, ever-regulating federal government—feeding off of a disappearing middle-class and declining taxpayer-base, is **NOT** sustainable.

- Most (if not all) politics **IS** truly "local," and while politicians with honorable intentions and upstanding records **DO** exist, others **WILL** do, say, and promise most anything to get elected and retain positions of power, influence, and privilege.

And, before closing this particular section, inserted below is another "reality" that—to our peril—we continue to treat with ignorance, apathy, complacency, denial, greed, and counter-productive fear:

- If present and future generations of Americans continue to tolerate within our government, leaders, representatives, and officials, that are ignorant of, and unsupportive of, "realities" such as summarized above . . . the ultimate outcome **WILL** most certainly be some additional and "most unforgiving realities." Including, the "loss of" our precious liberty/freedom, nation, and prospects of survival.

= = =

"I have a very firm grasp on reality! I can reach out and strangle it any time!" — *Author Unknown*

"There is no point in using the word 'impossible' to describe something that has clearly happened." — *Douglas Adams*

"I believe in a real, physical world. I figure if the world existed only in my mind, it would pay more attention to me." — *Robert Brault*

"There is a fine line between dreams and reality, it's up to you to draw it." — *B. Quilliam*

"Reality is the leading cause of stress amongst those in touch with it." — *Jane Wagner*

"We all die. The goal isn't to live forever, the goal is to create something that will." — *Chuck Palahniuk*

"We all see only that which we are trained to see."
— *Robert Anton Wilson*

"The eye sees only what the mind is prepared to comprehend."
— Robertson Davies

"Reality is that which, when you stop believing in it, doesn't go away." — Philip K. Dick

"Thinking something does not make it true. Wanting something does not make it real." — Michelle Hodkin

"Insanity is doing the same thing, over and over again, but expecting different results." — Narcotics Anonymous

"The first responsibility of a leader is to define reality. The last is to say thank you. In between the leader is a servant." — Max de Pree

"The strong mother doesn't tell her cub, stay weak so the wolves can get you. She says, toughen up, this is reality we are living in."
— Lauryn Hill

"When the people fear the government, there is tyranny. When the government fears the people, there is liberty." — Thomas Jefferson

A popular definition of "**Political Correctness**": *"A doctrine, fostered by a delusional, illogical minority, and rabidly promoted by an unscrupulous mainstream media, which holds forth the proposition that it is entirely possible to pick up a turd by the clean end."* — Author Unknown

"Those who expect to reap the blessings of freedom, must, like men, undergo the fatigue of supporting it." —Thomas Paine

"Cyber-Attacks"

Regarding Warfare and Cyber Attacks: *"Cyber war skips battlefields. Systems that people rely upon, from banks to air defense radars, are accessible from cyberspace and can be quickly taken over or knocked out without first defeating a country's traditional defense."* – R. Clarke & R. Knake

Regarding Identity Theft: *"There are only three groups of people in the U.S.: those whose identities have been stolen, those who do not know their identities have been compromised, and the identity thieves. My advice: put a freeze on your credit now."* – Joy Gumz

Definitions: A much over-simplified definition of "cyber-attack" is *"an attempt by hackers to damage or destroy a computer or network system."* A more meaningful explanation is the following, taken from Techopedia.com: *"A cyber-attack, also known as a Computer Network Attack (CNA), is a deliberate exploitation of computer systems, technology-dependent enterprises and networks. Using malicious code to alter computer code, logic or data, resulting in disruptive consequences that can compromise data and lead to cyber-crimes, such as information and identity theft."*

Cyber-attacks can, for instance, range from a hacker installing spyware or other malicious code on a Personal Computer (PC), to attempts to destroy the infrastructure of an entire country.

A "cyber Apocalypse" would be *"a cyber-attack that could, for example, bring about havoc to the U.S. by bringing down our critical information infrastructures," "electrical power grids,"* etc.

The Hackers (Cyber-attackers): Today's hackers (cyber-attackers) can potentially be the adult or child next door, business-competitors, foreign and domestic terrorists, our government, foreign governments (both friendly and foe), social media and internet search engine enterprises, etc. Almost anyone—anywhere on the earth—with the technical knowledge, means, motive, and willingness to do so.

The Targets (Victims): Hackers' targets—victims—can now include almost every aspect of our world. Such as the random few identified in the following very incomplete listing: individuals, families, businesses, organizations, financial and other institutions, fire protection/police/medical facilities and systems, transportation systems and vehicles, infrastructures, communication and entertainment networks and user-devices; military weapons facilities and control systems, our federal/state/local government, foreign governments, etc.

The Threat (potential consequences): Growing numbers of us are becoming more and more aware of the loss and other compromise of personal/business information. And of the serious damage to the identities, reputations, finances, and otherwise welfare of individuals and businesses that can and do result from hacking (from cyber-attacks).

But, what a larger number of us may not be in touch with, or just don't want to think about, are the **"much more potentially devastating"** consequences of cyber-attacks. For example, major disruption or destruction of our information systems, telecommunications trunk lines, electrical power grids, gas and oil pipelines, water treatment facilities, nuclear power facilities, financial institutions network, and other critical infrastructures.

And, the loss of life and property from the resulting widespread and long-lasting electrical power blackouts; mob violence and other civil disobedience; compromised nuclear materials facilities; and disrupted water, food, medical, and fuel supplies; as well as disabled fire and police protection, transportation services, essential businesses, medical facilities, and financial institutions; etc.

Of extra-special concern is the fact that some cyber-attacks can be carried out without initial evidence that attacks have taken place. Such as, attacks on computer software applications and databases, whereby critical information is stolen, or malicious instructions are embedded to wreak havoc at some "later" point in time.

Cyber-Attacks — A Few "Actual" Examples

- **2001: Nuclear Plant in Ohio.** A cyberattack "worm" named the Slammer, compromised a private computer network at non-active Davis-Besse nuclear plant in Ohio, causing an about five-hour failure of facility's safety monitoring system.

- **U.S. Infrastructure Facility:** Although reportedly unsuccessful to date, computer network of Constellation Energy Group, Inc.,--a critical U.S. infrastructure facility – has been target of large number of cyberattacks.

- **January 2014: Target (retail).** Target announced additional 70 million individuals' contact information taken during December 2013 breach, during which 40 million customers' credit and debit card information were stolen.

- **April 2014: AT&T (communications).** For period of two weeks AT&T was hacked from inside by personnel who accessed user information, including social security information.

- **August 2014: Community Health Services (health care).** At community Health Service (CHS), personal data for 4.5 million patients were compromised between April and June. CHS warned that any patient visiting any of its 206 hospital locations over the past five years may have had their data compromised. Attack reportedly originated in China, and FBI warned other health care firms may also have been attacked.

- **October 2014: J.P. Morgan Chase (financial).** A cyberattack in June not noticed until August. Contact information for 76 million households and 7 million small business was compromised. Hackers may have originated in Russia and may also have ties to Russian Government.

- **September 2014: Home Depot (retail).** Credit card information of roughly 56 million shoppers compromised in Home Depot's 2000 U.S. and Canadian outlets.

- **September 2014: Google (communications).** Five million G-mail usernames and passwords reportedly compromised; about 100,000 released on a Russian forum site.

- **September 2014: Apple iCloud (technology).** Hackers reportedly used hacked-passwords and third-party applications to access Apple user's online data storage, resulting in posting of celebrities' private photos online.

- **July 2015: Economic Espionage.** FBI reportedly said economic espionage cases it handled in the preceding 12 months were up 53 percent from a year earlier, with China the biggest offender.

- **August 2015: IRS (U.S. Government).** In May, IRS reported hackers accessed 114,000 tax accounts through IRS "Get Transcript" application, a program for acquiring information about your tax returns. Today IRS acknowledged that recent review shows hackers may have had access to about 220,000 more tax accounts, bringing total number of victims up to 334,000, or three times originally reported amount.

- **September 2015: Apple's App Store (technology).** Apple said it is taking steps to remove malicious code added to several apps commonly used on iPhones and iPads in China. Thought to be first large-scale cyber-attack on Apple's App Store. Hackers created counterfeit version of Apple's software for building iOS apps, which developers were persuaded to download. Thereafter, apps compiled using the counterfeit tool allow hackers to steal users' data and transmit it to servers they control.

- **Personal Information "NOW ON SALE"!** There have been so many "successful" breaches in the U.S. from cyber-attacks (over 800 in 2014, and more than 600 by October 2015) that cyber-attack-stolen personal information is now "on sale"! Reportedly, one can now buy a stolen credit card on the black market for about $30. Along with social security numbers, passwords, etc.

Of course, the examples given above are but a brief snapshot of the countless millions being attempted worldwide each day. While the numbers are ever-changing and rapidly growing, here are a few related reportings: 50,000 cyber-intrusion attempts a day experienced by energy company BP; U.S. Pentagon the target of 10 million attempts daily; and National Nuclear Security Administration recording 10 million attempted hacks a day. With, in 2014, cyber-attacks costing the global economy and estimated $445 billion!

In October 2014 The Heritage Foundation stressed in part that, as cyber-attacks on retail, technology, and industrial companies increase, so does the importance of cybersecurity. Companies and their customers need to secure their data; and to improve the private sector's ability to defend itself, Congress should: (1.) Create a safe legal environment for sharing information; (2.) Work with international partners; and (3.) Encourage Cyber Insurance.

As a rapidly increasing rate and severity of cyber-attacks are targeted at all aspects of our nation, we must institute the right policies, and implement advanced technologies, to establish sound and effective cybersecurity for both the private and public sectors.

However, the overwhelming need and challenge will be for "we the people" and "our government" to do so, without creating regulations and other conditions that hinder our businesses more than help; or put at risk our national security, right to privacy, and individual liberty/freedom. A most daunting challenge for all, but one that must be met—and unrelentingly monitored by we U.S. citizens—the ultimate custodians of our nation's affairs, and of our cherished liberty!

And as we now and in the future struggle with "cyber-security," it seems that the following long ago "heads-up" from Alexander Hamilton should never be forgotten:

"Safety from external danger is the most powerful director of national conduct. Even the ardent love of liberty will, after a time,

give way to its dictates. The violent destruction of life and property incident to war, the continual effort and alarm attendant on a state of continual danger, will compel nations the most attached to liberty to resort for repose and security to institutions which have a tendency to destroy their civil and political rights. To be more safe, they at length become willing to run the risk of being less free."
                                    — Alexander Hamilton (1755-1804)

Furthermore, before leaving this section, it would be a grossly irresponsible oversight not to highlight that even the **medical devices** we depend upon, and the **automobiles** we drive and ride in, are also vulnerable to hacking—to cyber-attacks. Hence, the following two examples for consideration:

August 5, 2015: FDA Issues Warning About Hackable Medical Devices. As reported by Popular Science and other media, the Food and Drug Administration (FDA) has issued a safety notice, that an infusion pump, used in hospitals all over the country, is vulnerable to cyber-attack. As a result, the FDA has strongly encouraged hospitals to discontinue their use.

Referenced pump is one of several devices crucial to patients' lives. Reportedly, some 10 million Americans use devices like pacemakers, insulin pumps, cochlear implants, etc.—many of which a hacker could, for example, increase or decrease the device's function, resulting in catastrophe for the patient.

February 8, 2015: Cars Are Vulnerable to Wireless Hacking. As reported by The Detroit News and other media, millions of cars and trucks are vulnerable to hacking through "wireless technologies" that could jeopardize driver safety and privacy. As vehicles are increasingly connected through wireless networks and more dependent on sophisticated electronic systems, the U.S. Congress and federal regulators are worried about potential for hackers to interfere with vehicle functions. Studies show hackers can get into controls of some popular vehicles, causing them to suddenly accelerate, turn, kill the brakes, activate the horn, control the headlights, and modify speedometer and gas gauge readings. As well as record and send location or driving history information, etc.

An unnerving hypothetical: Picture, if you will, as the result of prank-hacking, or cyber-attack by an enemy nation — thousands of cars traveling down our nations streets, bridges, and highways, suddenly receiving remote (not over-rideable) instructions to immediately "go full-throttle" and "turn-hard left"! Unthinkable? Yes! Beyond the realm of present or future possibility? Certainly not! But, for now, I think I'll take a break from this unsettling subject, and let the reader envision some other similar hypotheticals. Such as — in addition to our vehicles — prank, terrorist, or enemy-nation hacking of our "medical devices," "home security systems," "commercial aircraft," "electrical power grids," "storm/emergency warning systems," etc.

And just in case you have been assured by your anti-virus software supplier, or someone else, that you are "un-hackable" — the following headline may be of interest.

October 20, 2015: CIA Director's e-mail Hacked! As reported by CBS Evening News, October 20, 2015: The "personal e-mails" of two of the highest-ranking National Security Officials in the U.S. have been hacked—CIA Director John Brennan and Homeland Security Secretary Jeh Johnson. The hacker claimed to be a high school student.

= = =

"One hundred twenty countries currently have or are developing offensive cyber-attack capabilities, which is now viewed as the fifth dimension of warfare after space, sea, land and air... ."
— *Jamie Shea, NATO Director of Policy Planning*

"Governments tend to move slowly but with cyber-security we need to move fast." — *T. Scully*

"If you want to hit a country severely, you hit its power and water supplies. Cyber technology can do this without shooting a single bullet." — *Isaac Ben-Israel [Major General, Israeli Air Force]*

"The amount of control you have over somebody if you can monitor Internet activity is amazing. You get to know every detail; you get to know, in a way, more intimate details about their life than any person that they talk to because often people will confide in the Internet." — *Tim Berners-Lee*

"Just as drivers who share the road must also share responsibility for safety, we all now share the same global network, and thus must regard computer security as a necessary social responsibility. To me, anyone unwilling to take simple security precautions is a major, active part of the problem." — *Fred Langa*

"Privacy" — Gone Forever?

> *"We are rapidly entering the age of no privacy, where everyone is open to surveillance at all times; where there are no secrets from government."* — William O. Douglas
>
> *"Instead of a government that seizes your emails and your cell phones, imagine a federal government that protected the privacy rights of every American."* — Ted Cruz

June 5, 2013: British daily newspaper, The Guardian, reports the leak of National Security Agency (NSA) documents, starting with an order from Foreign Intelligence Surveillance Court (FISC) requiring Verizon to turn over metadata from millions of Americans' phone calls to the Federal Bureau of Investigation (FBI) and NSA.

June 13, 2015: CNN reports that hackers may have stolen from U.S. government computers, security clearance applications from government employees, including those in military and intelligence communities. Including "top secret" clearances, among the highest levels of clearance. This disclosure of a second breach of U.S. government computers comes just one week after reports of some four million federal employees' personal information being hacked during a cyber-attack blamed on the Chinese.

The disclosures cited above are only two examples of the ever-increasing breach of data-security systems! Of the unrelenting, wide-spread "intrusion on our privacy" and theft of our "personal information!" Think not? Then take a look at the news headlines below, which are but a random snapshot of the ever-growing numbers being experienced worldwide!

(Small Sample of Actual News Headlines)

"Hospital network hacked, 4.5 million records stolen;" "Sony Hack Exposed Personal Data of Hollywood Stars;" "LivingSocial Hacked, 50 Million Customers' Accounts Personal Data Breached; "European Central Bank hacked, personal data stolen;" "Hacker Breached HealthCare.gov Insurance Site;" "Cheating website Ashley Madison hacked, personal info posted;" "123,000 Thrift Savings Plan accounts hacked;" "Postal Service breach;" "For Target, the Breach Numbers Grow;" "U.S. government hack could actually affect 18 million;" "Adobe Is Hacked: Customer's Personal Data, Product Source Code Compromised;" "School hacked by 15 year-old pupil broke data protection act—exposing personal details of 20,000 people, including medical info of over 7,000 pupils; "Officials warn 500 million financial records hacked; "How Hackers Can Take Control Over Your Car;" "State Department Computers Hacked;" "Largest single personal data hack ever? 360 million stolen account credential found online;" "Toymaker VTech says data on 6.4 million kids taken in unprecedented hack;" "Pentagon Source Says China Hacked Defense Department;" "Etc.;" "Etc.:" "Etc."

And, if the above headlines fail to get your attention, possibly the following one will (repeated from earlier section, titled, "Cyber-Attacks"):

October 20, 2015:   CIA Director's e-mail Hacked!   As reported by CBS Evening News, October 20, 2015:   The "personal e-mails" of two of the highest-ranking National Security Officials in the U.S. have been hacked — CIA Director John Brennan and Homeland Security Secretary Jeh Johnson. The hacker claimed to be a high school student.

And "a little closer to home" and "much more personal": Below is a partial copy of an October 08, 2015 e-mail message my wife Ann and I received from Scottrade regarding a breach of our account and personal data.

= = =

(Re: E-Mail received from Scottrade — Page 1 of 5)

Scottrade
Important Security Alert

October 8, 2015 9:01 AM
Dear Client:

We are writing to share with you important information about a security compromise involving a database containing some of your personal information, as well as steps we are taking in response, and the resources we are making available to you.

What Happened

Federal law enforcement officials recently informed us that they've been investigating cybersecurity crimes involving the theft of information from Scottrade and other financial services companies. We immediately initiated a comprehensive response.

Based upon our subsequent internal investigation coupled with information provided by the authorities, we believe a list of client names and street addresses was taken from our system. Importantly, we have no reason to believe that Scottrade's trading platforms or any client funds were compromised. All client passwords remained encrypted at all times and we have not seen any indication of fraudulent activity as a result of this incident.

Although Social Security numbers, email addresses and other sensitive data were contained in the system accessed, it appears that contact information was the focus of the incident. The unauthorized access appears to have occurred over a period of several months between late 2013 and early 2014. We have secured the known intrusion point and conducted an internal data forensics investigation on this incident with assistance from a leading computer security firm. We have taken appropriate steps to further strengthen our network defenses.

(Re: E-Mail received from Scottrade — Page 3 of 5)

What Happens Now

Federal authorities had requested that they be allowed to complete much of their investigation before we notified clients. In coordination with them, we are now able to alert you of this incident. We are fully cooperating with law enforcement in their investigation and prosecution of the criminals involved. Notices like this one are being sent to all individuals and entities whose information was contained in the affected database, and we have included here information about steps you can take to protect yourself.

Information about this incident is available online at **https://About.Scottrade.com/CyberSecurityUpdate**, and we will update that web page if new data becomes available.

What You Can Do

As always, we encourage you to regularly review your Scottrade and other financial accounts and report any suspicious or unrecognized activity immediately. As recommended by federal regulatory agencies, you should remember to be vigilant for the next 12 to 24 months and report any suspected incidents of fraud to us or the relevant financial institution. Please also read the important information included on ways to protect yourself from identity theft.

(Re: E-Mail received from Scottrade — Page 4 of 5)

We encourage clients to be particularly vigilant against email or direct mail schemes seeking to trick you into revealing personal information. Never confirm or provide personal information such as passwords or account information to anyone contacting you. Please know that Scottrade will never send you any unsolicited correspondence asking you for your account number, password or other private information. If you receive any letter or email requesting this information, it is fraudulent and we ask that you report it to us at **phishing@scottrade.com**. Be cautious about opening attachments or links from emails, regardless of who appears to have sent them.

Identity Theft Protection

As a precaution, Scottrade has arranged with AllClear ID to help you protect your identity at no cost to you for a period of one year. You are pre-qualified for identity repair and protection services and have additional credit monitoring options available, also at no cost to you.

You can call AllClear ID with any concerns about your identity at 855.229.0083. This hotline is available from 8:00 am to 8:00 pm (central) Monday through Saturday. We have also included additional steps you could consider at any time if you ever suspect you've been the victim of identity theft. We offer this out of an abundance of caution so that you have the information you need to protect yourself.

(Re: E-Mail received from Scottrade — Page 5 of 5)

We are very sorry that this happened and for any uncertainty or inconvenience this has caused you. We know that incidents like these are frustrating. We take the security of your information very seriously and are committed to continually strengthening and evolving our defenses based on new and emerging threats.

Sincerely,
Scottrade

= = =

In the interest of space-saving herein, omitted from the above "copy" of Scottrade's notification, are other pages that deal with a long list of steps we are encouraged to take to protect ourselves from this breach of our personal information. Including our purchase of Identity Theft Protection from "AllClear," — which Scottrade graciously offers to pay the <u>first</u> year of premiums thereof. What a deal! Scottrade fails to protect our personal information, so, after a year of Scottrade's generosity, we should then suffer thereafter the cost for Identity-Theft Protection — or worse!

Remarkably, on November 27, 2012 we received an almost mirror-image "Security Alert" from Nationwide Mutual Insurance Company. A company we had never had an account with. Nevertheless, we received the same "we are so very sorry this happened . . ." pitch. Along with their generous offer to pay for <u>one-year</u> of Identify-Theft Protection — from one of their financial affiliates, of course.

In the case of above-mentioned Nationwide Mutual Insurance company's security breach, we spent considerable time and effort airing our concerns through correspondence with the Kansas Attorney General and Kansas Insurance Commissioner. Very formal and fact-supporting correspondence that included, but was certainly not limited to, the following still yet unsatisfactorily answered question:

"The [11/27/2012] security breach reported by Nationwide Mutual Insurance Company, demonstrates that they are not trustworthy custodians of Personal Information (including ours, which their correspondence acknowledges to be in their system). As such, Why should a failure on the part of Nationwide Mutual Insurance Company [or other company, or our government, etc.], to effectively secure Personal Information in their systems, become a financial liability and/or otherwise burden on us or any other consumer? "They" [the information-thieves and irresponsible information-custodians], not us, should shoulder the burden and consequences! As applicable, for failure to protect, and for theft of, our Personal Information — and that of countless aware and unaware others!"

The above question of course applies to any and all custodians of our "personal and private" information. And, is a question and "privacy concern" all U.S. citizens should unrelentingly demand appropriate response to. By way of our votes, correspondence with our government representatives and leaders, and the products we spend our money on.

For, the loss of our "privacy" truly is a threat to our liberty and survival! Stolen personal/sensitive-information from U.S. citizens or our government can (and does) lead to identity-theft, blackmail, fraud, ruined credit-ratings, stolen bank accounts and retirement funds, destroyed reputations, comprised decisions by government representatives and leaders, and risks to our domestic and national security, etc. To list but a few of the devastating consequences of our rightfully-cherished "privacy" — being gone forever?

= = =

Some Things We Can Do In Trying To Protect Our Identity

Review Our Accounts and Credit Reports:

Regularly review statements from our accounts and periodically obtain our credit report from one or more of the national credit reporting companies.

We may obtain a free copy of our credit report online at www.annualcreditreport.com, or by calling toll-free 1.877.322.8228, or by mailing an Annual Credit Report Request Form (available at www.annualcreditreport.com) to: Annual Credit Report Request Service. P.O. Box 105281, Atlanta, GA, 30348-5281. We may also purchase a copy of our credit report by contacting one or more of the three national credit reporting agencies listed below.

• Equifax, P.O. Box 740241, Atlanta, Georgia 30374-0241. 1.800.685.1111. www.equifax.com

- Experian, P.O. Box 9532, Allen, TX 75013, 1.888.397.3742. www.experian.com

- TransUnion, 2 Baldwin Place, P.O. Box 1000, Chester, PA 19016. 1.800.916.8800. www.transunion.com

Further information can reportedly be obtained from the FTC about steps to take to avoid identity theft through the following paths: http://www.ftc.gov/idtheft; calling 1-877-IDTHEFT (438-4338); or write to Consumer Response Center, Federal Trade Commission, 600 Pennsylvania Ave., N.W., Washington, D.C. 20580.

= = =

But The Story Doesn't End With "Hackers"!

"Hackers" and "government surveillance (spying) on its citizens" are not all that threatens our "privacy."

In this digital-media age of rapidly-advancing technology, "always-connected" mindset, and social-media frenzy, we are also surrounded by a number of other existing and potential invaders. For example:

- **Cameras and sound-recording devices — everywhere!** In smartphones, e-tablets, PC screens, TV's, businesses, automobiles, parking lots, wearable-devices, drones, etc. In the hands of adults and children; military and civilian, friend and foe. Devices of a broad range of sizes, appearances, and capabilities. Some easily recognized, some small enough to be concealed most anywhere. Devices that can be "hacked." Turning our TV's, automobiles, smartphones, PC Monitors, etc., into potential video and audio spies—infringing upon the "privacy" of us unaware citizens.

- **GPS technology.** Technology routinely a part of our smartphones, e-tablets, automobiles, etc., capable of tracking, recording and sharing our location. Where we are, where we going, and where we have been.

- **Through-the-Wall Surveillance (TWS).** Technology able to detect—through walls (even concrete)—motions as slight as breathing, and of transmitting information about the particular location in a room the motion is from.

- **Satellite Imagery and Street View Mapping.** Making satellite and street view photos of our residences "accessible to the world." Another "mixed blessing" of benefits and risks from ever-evolving technology.

- **Apps ("free" and otherwise).** Unknown or ignored by too many of us, the many "Apps" that drive the endless functions and features we use by way of our smartphones, e-tablets, etc., are sophisticated intruders upon our privacy. Depending upon respective "download settings," these seemingly harmless "Apps" can and do provide untold others access to our contacts lists, photos, messaging, Internet-search history, GPS location and associated records, purchase history, etc., etc., etc. And, in some cases, also provide a doorway for malicious software take up residence in our smartphones and other e-devices, potentially compromising our passwords, bank accounts, retirement accounts, medical history, and carrying out other privacy-destroying actions.

- **"Drones" – Spies & Stalkers in the Sky.** Rapidly growing untold-thousands – soon to be millions – of remotely operated aircraft (drones), owned and operated by our government, private citizens, and foreign parties. Drones of every conceivable size, appearance, and function. Some deceptively small, such as the size and appearance of a humming bird.

  Spies and stalkers in the sky--capable of being equipped with cameras, weapons, or whatever technology their legal or illegal-use calls for. Capable of silently hovering overhead, and if necessary, high enough to be out of sight. As a weaponized military drone, capable of remotely destroying a terrorist-facility and enemy combatants.

  From hundreds of feet in the air, able to read our lips, and video-record facial expressions, people mowing their yard, or swimming clothed or unclothed in their private pool. Using infrared cameras, able to track movement in the dark, and sensitive enough to detect a lit cigarette.

  We can now be under constant surveillance – virtually everywhere. Video-recorded every time we enter or exit a building, take a walk or jog, drive a car, or use a train, bus, boat, or plane. And when equipped with technology able to peer through walls, gone also is privacy in our own homes. This is not about science fiction—but today's reality. And, that which looks like a cute little humming bird fluttering around our patio, or perched on a nearby tree limb, may actually be a remotely-operated, camera-equipped, miniature-drone aircraft. Operated by the CIA, FBI, Local Police, or the kid next door.

For sure, the "privacy-cat" is now out-of-the-bag (so to speak), and our ability to ever once-again catch it, not to mention get it back in the bag, is beyond any sensibly-envisioned likelihood! Yes, the nature of "privacy" we once enjoyed, assumed, abused, and too-often took for granted, is likely gone forever. This not being exaggeration or just an opinion— but, rather, now among our many liberty and survival threating "realities." A crucial part of our ever-changing world. One that we now must find ways and means of responsibly dealing with. A loss of privacy that, where and when necessary, we must confront and defend ourselves against. As we continue to weigh the ever-growing benefits against the ever-increasing risks—of ever-evolving technology. Forever mindful of the ever-present and rapidly-growing invaders and abusers of our cherished and unalienable right to . . . our "privacy."

= = =

"The American people must be willing to give up a degree of personal privacy in exchange for safety and security." – Louis Freeh (Fifth Director of FBI from September 1993 to June 2001)

"Those who desire to give up freedom in order to gain security will not have, nor do they deserve, either one." – Benjamin Franklin

"Privacy is not something that I'm merely entitled to, it's an absolute prerequisite." – Marlon Brando

"The fantastic advances in the field of communication constitute a grave danger to the privacy of the individual." – Earl Warren

"A decade after intelligence leaders secretly created a program to violate the privacy of millions of law-abiding Americans, we are on the verge of finally shutting it down."

– Democratic Senator Ron Wyden

"Drivers have come to rely on these new technologies, but unfortunately the automakers haven't done their part to protect us from cyberattacks or privacy invasions." – Edward Markey

"I don't believe there is a trade-off between privacy and security; I think they go together, if you have a society which evades and abuses privacy, then ultimately there will be a reaction against the damage to your security." – Edward Snowden

"It is the first responsibility of every citizen to question authority."

– Ben Franklin

"Make-believe Guns"

vs

"Clocks Mistaken for Bombs"

> *"Common sense is not so common." – Voltaire*
>
> *"Responsibility is the price of freedom." – Elbert Hubbard*
>
> *"Judgement comes from experience. Sometimes experience comes from bad judgement." – Christian Slater*

On September 16, 2015, an Associated Press reporting included the following headline: **"Muslim teen detained over homemade clock is invited to White House."** A story about a 14-year old Irving, Texas student, Ahmed Mohamed, who became a sensation on world-wide social media; received outpouring support from Silicon Valley executives; and reaped Washington's attention, including a personal "Tweet" message from the President and an invitation to the White House.

Accolades received and forthcoming after word spread that he had been placed in handcuffs and suspended for coming to school with a homemade electronic clock apparatus that teachers thought resembled an actual or hoax bomb.

Reactions—public, private, and political—that are in stark and conspicuous contrast to those associated with the following school-related headlines, not so long ago:

<u>01/31/2013</u>, New York Daily News: **Six-year-old kindergartner at Alice Drive Elementary in Sumter County, SC, expelled for bringing her brother's toy gun to class for show and tell.**

<u>03/18/2013</u>, The Baltimore Sun: **Seven-year-old Anne Arundel County, Maryland, student suspended for nibbling a Pop-Tart breakfast pastry into the shape of a pistol.**

<u>11/04/2013</u>, The Washington Times: **Eight-year-old at Scottsdale, Arizona's County Day Scholl threatened with expulsion for drawing a picture of a soldier, ninja warrior, and Star Wars character, holding guns.**

I don't recall these six, seven, and eight-year olds spending anytime at the White House . . . or getting any congrats from Silicon Valley for their show-and-tell support, artwork, and otherwise "expressions of creativity." But, let us now return to the "object of special attention by the President," the "social-media hero of the moment," in Irving, Texas. That our nation's schools have been, and will likely continue to be, the target of various horrifying atrocities, <u>should not be news to anyone</u>. Especially our mobile/social-media connected children of all ages. Especially, those in their teens. Especially the parents of teens. Especially the parents of a teen who has put together something that can reasonably be mistaken for a real or hoax bomb. And, at a time when our teachers, law enforcement personnel, and others, are struggling to prevent mass-murders and other horrific abominations in our schools — it defies all resemblance of reason and responsibility that any teen would show up at school with anything that could even remotely be mistaken to be a weapon — especially, a bomb. Anything "weapon-looking-thing" that could create dangerous false-alarms and panic situations, etc. It could be that the answer to "Why?" . . . relates in some way to the following November 23, 2015, Washington Post headline: "Clock Kid Seeking $15 Million in Damages." You think?

But, even more puzzling, why should any 14-year old student (or anyone of common-sense age) doing such a careless act be recipient of any attention beyond some appropriate-discipline and much-earned and past-due "common-sense" counseling!

Likewise, with all the truly major issues facing our country, it would seem that the President, The White House, Silicon Valley, the main-stream media, the courts, and others, could find something more constructive to do. Than to "selectively reward," what certainly appears to be, a classic example of teenage "irresponsibility" and "lack-of-common-sense." And of, as a minimum, some "very inattentive parenting."

= = =

"Common sense is the knack of seeing things as they are, and doing things as they ought to be done." — Josh Billings

"Affirmation without discipline is the beginning of delusion."
           –Jim Rohn

"Two things are infinite: the universe and human stupidity; and I'm not sure about the universe." – Albert Einstein

"Adolescence is society's permission slip for combining physical maturity with psychological irresponsibility." – Terri Apter

"Common sense is genius dressed in its working clothes."
– Ralph Waldo Emerson

"People demand freedom of speech as a compensation for the freedom of thought which they seldom use." – Soren Kierkegaard

"Whenever a man does a thoroughly stupid thing, it is always from the noblest motives." – Oscar Wilde

"The eye sees only what the mind is prepared to comprehend."
– Robertson Davies

"There are things known and there are things unknown, and in-between are the doors of perception." – Aldous Huxley

"Our blunders mostly come from letting our wishes interpret out duties." – Author Unknown

"Good judgment comes from experience, and a lot of it comes from bad judgment."
–James Merrow

"Beneficial" vs "Harmful" Discrimination

> *"First there is a time when we believe everything, then for a little while we believe with discrimination, then we believe nothing whatever, and then we believe everything again — and, moreover, give reasons why we believe." — Georg Christoph Lichtenberg*
>
> *"Prejudice, not being founded on reason, cannot be removed by argument." — Samuel Johnson*

"Harmful discrimination" is the practice of unfairly treating a person or group of people differently from other people or groups of people.

In contrast, **"beneficial discrimination"** is an essential "survival tool." That is, our ability to <u>recognize the difference</u> between things safe, healthy, trustworthy, and otherwise good — from those that are not.

Unfortunately, history shows that individuals, groups, and governments, worldwide have never been short of methods and a willingness to carry out **"harmful discrimination."**

Often to an unconscionable extent. Hitler's barbaristic murder of millions of Jewish people, in the not so distant past; and the likewise barbarism experienced in more recent times from the worldwide spread of radical/militant Islam — are but a couple of the more extreme examples.

Fortunately, at times there are signs of progress in some parts of our world at becoming more civil, compassionate, understanding, and tolerant of one another. Unfortunately, there is also no evidence we will ever be absent of those with the desire, ability, and willingness to be otherwise. Those driven to carryout, sponsor, and encourage **"harmful discrimination."** Including some within government, to support political, self-serving, or other (intentionally or otherwise) nation-destructive agendas.

Being able to distinguish between **"harmful"** and **"beneficial" discrimination** often seems to be an on-going struggle — and for some, a real "road block." As evidenced by the wide-spread inability (or unwillingness) for some to see, accept, and respect, the difference between **"harmful"** and **"beneficial"** people, places, things, behavior, and circumstances. Below are a few close-to-home examples of this reality. Of our too often failure to recognize and responsibly react to the **"difference between"**:

— Law abiding citizens and right-minded law enforcement officers — **and those who are not;**

— People respecting the rights, property, and wellbeing of others, — **and those who do not;**

— Constructive methods of dissent and demonstration — **and those that threaten and destroy the lives, property, and wellbeing, of others;**

— Political representatives and leaders who are capable, trustworthy, and nation-uniting — **and those who are not;**

— Policies and agendas supportive of our liberty, U.S. Constitution, borders, common-language English, and culture, — **and those that threaten such;**

— Beneficial education methods, foods, medications, environments, and entertainment, — **and those that are harmful;**

— Worthwhile and affordable healthcare agendas — **and the "unaffordable" Affordable Care Act (Obama Care) born out of political lies and deception, and more about wealth-redistribution, dependency on federal government, and voter demographics, than about "healthcare."**

— Meaningful, nation-improving, employment agendas — **and policies promoting attitudes and behaviors of entitlement and dependency, through tax-payer funded**

food stamps, housing, healthcare, transportation, mobile phones, etc.

— <u>Serious foreign/domestic security efforts</u> — **and political correctness agendas (that are more concerned about apologizing for America's greatness and preventing us from "offending" someone, than from losing our liberty, our heads and our country at the hands of radical-militant Islamists and other terrorists).**

As rioting, looting, and other unlawful and outrageous behavior continue to be fanned through ignorance and intent, by parties within and without our government, and by irresponsible agenda-driven news and reckless social media . . . we continue down the self-destructive path of **"harmful discrimination."** Of unfairly treating and doing harm to one another.

And, if we are to retain our cherished liberty/freedom, and ultimately survive in this ever-shrinking world — this social fishbowl of growing complexity — we truly have no choice. But to, with clear heads and open minds, very soon start recognizing and responsibly reacting to the **<u>difference between</u>** . . . **"harmful"** and **"beneficial"** discrimination.

= = =

"I have a dream that my four little children will one day live in a nation where they will not be judged by the color of their skin but by the content of their character." – Martin Luther King, Jr.

"The five essential entrepreneurial skills for success: Concentration, Discrimination, Organization, Innovation and Communication."
— *Harold S. Geneen*

"The way to stop discrimination on the basis of race is to stop discriminating on the basis of race." — John Roberts

"The moment a little boy is concerned with which is a jay and which is a sparrow, he can no longer see the birds or hear them sing."
— *Eric Berne*

"Collective fear stimulates herd instinct, and tends to produce ferocity toward those who are not regarded as members of the herd." — Bertrand Russell

"The one thing that the racist can never manage is anything like discrimination: he is indiscriminate by definition."
— *Christopher Hitchens*

"The test of courage comes when we are in the minority. The test of tolerance comes when we are in the majority." — Ralph W. Sockman

"It is not discrimination to treat different things differently."
— *Maggie Gallagher*

"Peoples of the world are subject to nuclear discrimination, as many countries possessing nuclear technology are seeking to monopolize this knowledge and deprive the rest of the world from this scientific capacity." – Mahmud Ahmadinejad

"We want the [IAEA] to end discrimination against us and allow all member states equal access to nuclear technology."

– Gholamreza Aghazadeh

"Whenever you find yourself on the side of the majority, it is time to pause and reflect." – Mark Twain

"When a political opponent resorts to the racist card, it's a sure sign of moral bankruptcy: there's no decent argument left in the armory." – Alex Morritt

"Illegal aliens have always been a problem in the United States. Ask any Indian." – Robert Orben

"We have an American culture and we have an American constitution and anybody who's going to occupy our White House should be living in a pattern that is consistent with our constitution and our culture." – Ben Carson, Retired Neurosurgeon & Republican presidential candidate.

"Teachers' Tenure,"
"Student Misbehavior,"
& "Drugging Our Kids"

"Success is a lousy teacher. It seduces smart people into thinking they can't lose." – Bill Gates

"The productivity now at universities is terrible. Tenure is a terrible idea. It keeps them around forever and they don't have to work hard." – Jack Welch

"I'm a tenured professor. But I'd get rid of tenure."
                                                    – Francis Fukuyama

The April 30, 2014 publication of our local newspaper, the *Parsons Sun*, included an article from the Clay Center *Dispatch* entitled "Teacher tenure." As with most subjects, there can be various points of view—pros and cons. The *Dispatch* article highlighted some justified concerns about serious student-misbehavior in our schools, as well as related obstacles posed by irrational parents, etc. The *Dispatch* article also expressed an affirmative perspective about teacher tenure. What follows are some other thoughts for consideration.

Referenced *Dispatch* article stated in part that *"School administrators are all too often teachers who couldn't make it in the classroom."* If such a claim were to have validity it certainly would not speak well for the education system that certifies our school administrators, or for the folks that subsequently hire them to run our schools.

Referenced *Dispatch* article also stated in part that *"The Kansas Legislature's right-wing made it easier to fire teachers,"* and *"The legislation signed by Gov. Brownback invites and encourages abuse by administrators."* Again, if such tenure-related claims are correct and represent serious job-security concerns for qualified and competent teachers, then there should be an even deeper concern for our graduating children! Why? Because by far the vast majority of them will at some point step out into a "real world" that is essentially without tenure! Into a world of opportunities, choices, and consequences — justly experienced by some, and unjustly by others. Into a world that — in addition to fairness — also includes abuse, unfairness, lawsuits, etc. All without the protection of tenure.

To ever be independent and self-supporting, at some point our children must also enter and compete in an "At-will"/"Free-Will" employment world. Meaning that, as an employee, they and their employer can at any time for any reason (except an illegal one) terminate their working relationship without incurring legal liability. This is the "real world" that most of us — and eventually our children — must deal with, must work in, pay bills in, raise a family in, and continue our education and other aspects of life in.

As have and do countless others, a world absent the protection of tenure was the reality I personally worked in, from about age 18, for at least 48 years. During which time I had the opportunity to work for and with some fair, courteous, and professionally competent people respected by me and others. As well as for and with some considered to be otherwise. Each experience was enjoyed or otherwise survived — all without tenure. Such will be the real-world circumstances that the vast majority of our children will encounter and hopefully prosper in. Such also represents a crucial life-lesson our children should be taught early-on by parents and educators through personal example. That is, how to live and prosper in a world without tenure.

Tenure is often defined as *"a senior academic's <u>contractual right</u> not to have his or her position terminated without just cause."* Something not afforded to most other occupations and the working majority. Regardless of occupation — any "<u>contractual right</u>" lawfully worked out between an employee and employer could reasonably be viewed as being the sole business of the respective parties, and not the concern of our federal or state government. It could also be reasonably viewed that, when it comes to job security, our senior academics and other educators should have to seek and maintain employment under the same job protection measures afforded to their graduating students. That being, where job security is a competition matter — and not a given occupation-privilege, government-mandate, or otherwise assumed right.

Contracts of various types obviously play an important part in our society of growing complexities. However, history and experience has yet to show that *"tenure"* and other *"contracts"* are the answer to misbehaved, disruptive and otherwise undisciplined students; or to parents that are missing, irresponsible, or irrational; or to frivolous lawsuits, incompetent teachers, incompetent school administrators, incompetent school boards; or to unconcerned citizens; or to an over-reaching federal government's increasing control of our education system.

"Tenure" and other *"contracts"* also have not yet resolved or explained why intelligent adults can have a deep-seated aversion to reasonable and common-sense discipline at home, in public, and at school. While, on the other hand, having little to no concern about the growing use of mood/mind-altering drugs on our children. Drugs that can inhibit little boys and little girls from behaving like little boys and little girls. Psychotropic and other drugs potentially much more harmful to the physical and mental well-being of our children than some old-fashioned and otherwise appropriate consequences for misbehavior. "Appropriate consequences" like I and countless others received at school and at home — which we not only deserved and survived, but also benefited from.

But instead, our "naturally" rowdy and misbehaving children continue to be "legally drugged" with dangerous medications that can often mask major problems. Such as the lack of appropriate diet, exercise, rest, discipline, entertainment, adult role models, etc. — as well as irresponsible adults at home, at school, and elsewhere. Drugs that financially benefit the "adults" involved in the production, marketing, sales, and administration of such potentially harmful substances. Medications with known and yet-to-be-discovered side effects — often disregarded by professionals and others pursuing the almighty dollar. As well as by those seeking a "prescribed-for-children" pill to replace their parenting role and other adult responsibilities.

Yes, our federal and state governments, school systems, and we parents, grandparents, and others certainly have much bigger and more important fish to fry than **"tenure."** For example, how about an unrelenting agenda for protecting our children from the on-the-street pusher of "illegal" drugs. And, likewise from the drug industry, various medical and education professionals, parents, and others who are subjecting our kids to "legal" psychotropic and other harmful drugs. Furthermore, how about some "serious" attention to appropriate diet, exercise, rest, common-sense discipline, entertainment; and positive adult role-models, etc. All pursued with the same level of drive, enthusiasm, and political clout heretofore dedicated to "teachers' tenure."

= = =

"Who dares to teach must never cease to learn." – John Cotton Dana

"The government cannot overcome bad parenting. What our leaders can do is publicly condemn irresponsible parental behavior in vivid terms." – Bill O'Reilly

"If you think your teacher is tough, wait until you get a boss. He doesn't have tenure." – Bill Gates

"To the extent that tenure supports academic freedom, I support tenure. I want no person or system to have any power, real or apparent, to chill academic freedom." – James E. Rogers

"Anytime you encourage critical thinking you risk offending somebody, ... I think the basic idea of tenure is to shelter people from political ups and downs." – Andrew Kirk

"The mediocre teacher tells. The good teacher explains. The superior teacher demonstrates. The great teacher inspires."
– William Arthur Ward

"Those who educate children well are more to be honored that parents, for these only gave life, those the art of living well."
--Aristotle

"Education is the most powerful weapon which you can use to change the world." – Nelson Mandela

"Never try to teach a pig to sing. . . .it wastes your time and annoys the pig." – Anonymous

"Good teachers are costly, but bad teachers cost more." – Bob Talbert
"The difference between school and life? In school, you're taught a lesson and then given a test. In life, you're given a test that teaches you a lesson." – Tom Bodett

More than Anything—
"Protect the Institution"?

> *"Experience hath shown, that even under the best forms of government those entrusted with power have, in time, and by slow operations, perverted it into tyranny."* — Thomas Jefferson
>
> *"All men having power ought to be distrusted to a certain degree."*
> — James Madison

On September 25, 2015, House Speaker John Boehner announced he would be resigning from Congress and giving up his House Seat at the end of October. In doing so, he expressed various reasons for his decision, including that: ". . . **more than anything**, my first job as Speaker is to protect the Institution." It is purely assumption on my part that the referred-to "Institution" is the U.S. House of Representatives.

While there is no intent herein to disregard any positive aspects of Speaker Boehner's long tenure in public office—the view that "Protecting the Institution" was his most important role is not only very troubling, but also a prime example of what has become a critical problem in Washington. Too many "career politicians"—of all political parties—permitted to stay on the taxpayers' teat for too long. So long that many have lost touch with much of the "real world" and have forgotten what their most important jobs really are as "servants of the people."

How refreshing and nation-saving it would be to have a Congress, Supreme Court, and President, that truly recognize and demonstrate that their **"more than anything"** public-servant roles have something to do with protecting our U.S. Constitution, liberty, freedom, and we-the-people. Something to do with protecting, defending, and preserving our U.S. borders, common-language English, and culture. Something to do with protecting us from an out of control and rapidly climbing $18 trillion national debt, and from the growing foreign and domestic threat of radical/militant Islam, etc.

But, **"Protecting the Institutions"** seems a little less complicated. And possibly more deserving of nation of politically uniformed, misinformed, and disengaged voters. Preoccupied with voter-ignorance, apathy, complacency, denial, greed, and counter-productive fears. Burnt-out by an unrelenting barrage dangerous and distracting "divide and conquer" agendas. As too many of our "servants of the people" continue to focus their energies and our public treasury on their positions of power, influence, and personal gain. On **"Protecting the Institutions."**

= = =

"Liberty may be endangered by the abuse of liberty, but also by the abuse of power." – *James Madison*

Fifth- & Sixth-Graders
Should be Joined by Washington!

> *"Knowing what's right doesn't mean much unless you do what's right."* — Theodore Roosevelt
>
> *"Never doubt that a small group of thoughtful, concerned citizens can change the world. Indeed it is the only thing that ever has."*
> — Margaret Mead

On October 07, 2015, the front page of our local newspaper, the Parsons Sun, included a most interesting and encouraging article entitled, *"Fifth-graders learn leadership skills."* About a new leadership development program started by the Wildcat Extension District. A special team-building and leadership-learning initiative designed for fifth- or sixth-grade students. One that emphasizes playing safe, fair, and hard; and in doing so, have fun and respect the environment. A unique "knowledge for life" program that stresses "six pillars of character"—trustworthiness, respect, responsibility, fairness, caring, and citizenship. Where the fortunate participants have a unique opportunity to learn about "talking versus communications," "importance of listening," "verbal and non-verbal communications," "importance of communications to problem-solving," "group consensus," and "leadership."

Oh, if only we had it within our citizens' power to mandate that all existing and future members of our federal government join our fifth- and sixth-graders in this so-much-needed learning experience. But, in our government officials' case, on a stringent "pass-fail" basis. With the consequences of failure requiring, as a minimum, an immediate and permanent departure from Washington. In order to "go home" and "live with" the deteriorating, liberty-threatening mess they have helped create over their years of "serving the people." And, upon their retuning home, have a "down-sized" life-style that at least somewhat resembles that of their average constituent.

And, while this pie-in-the-sky thought is most unlikely to ever become reality, all is not lost. For, hopefully, required numbers of our now fifth- and sixth-graders, and other youth nation-wide, will learn and take seriously the leadership training mentioned above. And will someday be carrying out responsible roles in government. Government duly-focused on protecting and preserving our national security, U.S. Constitution, borders, common-language English, culture, and a viable economic system.

A government that one day may even include a President who uses his or her leadership and communications skills for "nation-building" aims. Rather than, for taking "selected tragedies" as opportunities to pursue divide-and-conquer agendas. And for arrogantly lecturing, talking-down-to, and otherwise scolding law-abiding citizens for their efforts to retain their constitution-guaranteed liberties. The rights of free speech, religion, privacy, and personal protection, being a few of those liberties that readily come to mind.

How to Succeed in Politics!

Having never personally sought or held a job in politics, in no way discouraged development of the following Five-Step Plan on "*How to Succeed in Politics!*" A historically-proven plan made possible by qualifications gained from the "university of life" . . . while observing, helping to pay for, and living with the results of, those who have done and continue to do so. Including those who (in conflict with the intent of our country's founders) have turned "serving the people" into a "life-time career" and "an array of self-serving benefits."

A plan herein offered to the general public, "free-of-charge," with only the following basic conditions:

That I be recipient of untraceable life-time political favors commensurate with each respective user's level of success achieved as a result thereof. While, in accordance with political custom, such favors and their source will be categorically denied to exist—that is, until it being of benefit for me to do otherwise. *[While this obviously includes a bit of satire . . . much, much more than a bit, is a resemblance to a nation-destructive amount of our political reality.]*

STEP 1: Be born in, move to, or otherwise establish citizenship in, a most unique constitutional republic—a country providing unequaled liberty/freedom—a worldwide envy of countless people deprived of liberty. In the first and yet only nation governed by a unique constitution that establishes a separation of powers through three separate *but equal* branches of government: An Executive Branch (*headed by the president*), a Legislative Branch (*headed by Congress, which includes a House of Representatives and a Senate*), and a Judicial Branch (*headed by a Supreme Court*). A government of checks and balances—with each branch having its own responsibilities to uphold the constitution, work with the other branches of government, and to protect the liberty/freedom of each citizen. In a nation where sovereignty (supreme power and authority) rests with its citizens.

In—the best hope for humankind—a nation established by wise, insightful, and courageous, framers who worked hard to avoid the risk of dictatorship or tyranny. A most precious republic resulting from human needs and sacrifices—all too often disregarded due to innocent ignorance or intentional agenda. One's search will of course readily reveal that our

"United States of America" is the only place that satisfies these long-standing and much sought after expectations.

<u>**STEP 2:**</u> Never hesitate to do "whatever it takes" to get elected to the political office you seek. You will get a lot of help. Largely from voters absorbed with ignorance, apathy, complacency, denial, greed, and counter-productive fear— especially concerning their country's national and international best-interests. And from those who, "in consideration for" their votes and otherwise support, expect in kind special favors from your position of power and influence. Always remember that constant diversion and distraction from the real issues can also be a valuable aid to your success.

STEP 3: Once elected, your first and foremost aim must always be keeping your job and maintaining and expanding any power it provides you. Important even above the oath you have taken to uphold your constitutional role. And, while "serving the people," always make sure that your salary, healthcare, retirement, and overall benefit package far exceed that of your average constituent and private sector counterparts.

STEP 4: Should you ever be forced to actually deal with any of your respective constitutional duties, make sure that you readily delegate those tasks to one or more of the existing hundreds of government-funded agencies, departments, bureaus, or commissions. Such as, those in the eight-page listing near the end of this book. More preferably—create a "new" one that duplicates one or more of the untold hundreds of tax-payer burdens already in place.   In doing so, the VA, IRS, EPA, CFPB, USDHS, NSA, DNI, NRLB, BLA, NRC, and OSHA, are but a few of the countless existing models to consider.   But, in any case, make sure that the functions you delegate your responsibilities to have union representation, and without fail also provide their government employees with salaries, bonuses, healthcare, retirement, and other benefits that exceed that of their private sector counterparts.

It is also important that you entrust your passed-on responsibilities to folks who — similar to your circumstances — also have job security, bonuses, and an overall benefit package, duly protected from any efforts by "the voters" to control the cost of government. As well as protection from any attempt to hold anyone accountable for waste, fraud, abuse of power or for basic unsatisfactory job performance. Recent scandals involving the VA, IRS, NSA, and BLA, can serve as good role models. If supporting funds run short for these or other agencies, bureaus, departments, and commissions — make certain to readily increase taxes as required to at least maintain the status-quo. As well as cover any cost-of-living increases, etc.

Once you get your political agenda implanted in one or more of these functions you are pretty much home free. Because these bureaucracies are headed up by and staffed with people not elected by or realistically accountable to "the people." But, ever so important also, is to never forget to remind the government bureaucracies which you create and/or perpetuate, just how important it is that they remember to whom they owe their existence and longevity. That, being to you, of course.

STEP 5: Last but not least and regardless of political affiliation—NEVER accept responsibility for anything. Make sure you blame any and all shortfalls on the other party, the previous administration, or someone else. Or, if need be, to an act of God, or a "computer glitch". Keep in mind that in selected cases a politically biased and agenda driven news media can also be very, very supportive of such efforts. As can an electorate consumed with ignorance, apathy, complacency, greed, fear, class warfare, social-media frenzy, or other distractions and diversions. And relax—after your time of "serving the people" has passed, you will probably be able to get by and make ends meet through the various opportunities that await you—as a lobbyist, political advisor, author, guest speaker, corporate board member, talk show guest/host, government appointee, or maybe your own Reality TV Show—to list but a few struggling opportunities.

Nonetheless . . . a few words of caution! The above "Five Step Plan" will not appeal to everyone. Fortunately, there still exists . . . truly good, honest, hardworking, competent, informed, responsible, and self-sacrificing citizens. Within the young and old; rich and poor; and in between. Patriotic politicians, media personnel, and folks from all other walks of life—that are positive contributors to society and truly have our country's best interests in mind. Such persons will be too busy trying to do the right thing, to have anything other than justified contempt for the above Five Step Plan. And, it is to our U.S. citizens' shame and misfortune that such scarce, deserving, and often publically scorned folks, are not more often recipient of our unrelenting support and appreciation.

= = =

"One of the penalties for refusing to participate in politics is that you end up being governed by your inferiors." — *Plato*

"What is success? I think it is a mixture of having a flair for the thing that you are doing; knowing that it is not enough, that you have got to have hard work and a certain sense of purpose."
— *Margaret Thatcher*

"If you put the federal government in charge of the Sahara Desert, in 5 years there'd be a shortage of sand." — *Milton Friedman*

"A man who has never gone to school may steal from a freight car; but if he has a university education, he may steal the whole railroad." — *Theodore Roosevelt*

"In politics, stupidity is not a handicap." — *Napoleon Bonaparte*

"If there is ever a fascist takeover in America, it will come not in the form of storm troopers kicking down doors but with lawyers and social workers saying, "I'm from the government and I'm here to help."
— *Jonah Goldberg*

"All Politics is Local"

> *"One of the great mistakes is to judge policies and programs by their intentions rather than their results."* –Milton Friedman

Our SE Kansas hometown has one of the (if not "the") highest real estate/property tax rates in the state. And it is unlikely one would have to look very long or hard around town to find a large measure of strong, justified, and otherwise passionate, opposition to another tax-payers' bail-out of "General Motors," "the Big Banks," "Wall Street," etc.

But . . . in keeping with **"all politics is local"** . . . a reported $12,000 yearly subsidy of a particular local golf-course business has seemed of little concern to various of our city's already over-burdened tax-payers. Nevertheless, not long ago a concerned citizen did raise the subject during a regularly scheduled open-meeting of our elected City Commissioners. And, shortly thereafter, a related November 18, 2015 article entitled *"Golf club owner responds to comments,"* appeared in our local newspaper. Within which, it was explained that the city pays the subject subsidy *". . . to the only golf course in city limits to help keep the course open to add to the quality of life in Parsons."*

After reading this explanation, for some reason a couple of questions came to mind. For instance: (1.) When and how are we taxpayers going to "make it right" with all the other businesses in the city limits—by also giving them (retroactively) an equivalent yearly bailout of $12,000 . . . to likewise, "help keep them open"? And, (2.) When, how, and by whom was it determined that this particular business "adds to the quality of life in our city"? Or, more appropriately put, "adds to the quality of life for specifically whom"? These question will likely be pondered for some time yet. Questions one would think many of the other "unsubsidized" businesses in town would have long ago "passionately" asked and demanded responsible answers to?

In the meantime, in lieu of arbitrarily dipping into taxpayers' funds, maybe those who truly experience, or otherwise personally benefit from, the "quality of life" offered by this particular business venture, will at some point find it more appropriate to personally "bear the costs-of-doing-business"—for their chosen activity. Unless, that is, our town's taxpayers ultimately choose to subsidize "everyone's respective choices" of recreation, exercise, hobby, relaxation, sport, social intercourse, or aside business-venture, etc.

This type of activity is likely being played out nationwide at many government levels, involving tax dollars of lessor and much greater extent. Driven and enabled in some way by the ignorance, apathy, complacency, denial, greed, and counter-productive fears of "we the people." An ongoing reminder that truly, all politics is not only "local"—but, also warranting ever-mindful voter scrutiny and responsible oversight.

Consequences
of
"Knee-jerk Blames & Fixes"

"Without reflection, we go blindly on our way, creating more unintended consequences, and failing to achieve anything useful."
–Margaret J. Wheatley

"Remember one thing about democracy. We can have anything we want and at the same time, we always end up with exactly what we deserve." –Edward Albee

"Wisdom consists of the anticipation of consequences."
–Norman Cousins

On the night of May 23, 2014 a mass-murder took place in Isla Vista, California—a coastal community adjacent to the University of California, Santa Barbara.

Before killing himself, the murderer claimed the lives of seven innocent people and injured some 13 others. Three of his victims were <u>shot to death</u>, three were <u>stabbed to death</u>, and thirteen more were <u>injured either by gunshots or the automobile</u> he used as a battering ram against bicyclists and skateboarders.

According to news reports, the murderer was identified as 22-year-old Elliot Rodger, the son of an assistant director of "The Hunger Games." Reportedly, the murderer had been treated for mental illness since early childhood and suffered from extreme feelings of rejection. His killing spree seemed to closely follow intentions he had communicated in various public postings.

Postings in which he in part stated plans to silently kill as many people as he could around Isla Vista—by luring them into his apartment, knocking them out with a hammer, and slitting their throats. Although this murderer's horrifying acts involved planned and actual use of **knives, hammers, guns, and his automobile**—once again, our focus was diverted primarily to **"guns"**—by various news media, political leaders, and others. Through ignorance, apathy, or intent.

On another Friday night, February 23, 2001—in the same (as above) coastal California community, another mass killing was carried out under similar circumstances. According to news reports, David Attias, the son of a Hollywood director, and reportedly suffering from mental illness and intense feelings of rejection, **used his car to kill four people and injure another**. He was arrested, sentenced to a mental institution, and ruled to be released in 2012. He carried out this atrocity with an **"automobile"**—**not a knife, hammer, or gun.**

On Saturday, October 24, 2015, Oklahoma State's Homecoming parade in Stillwater, Oklahoma ended in tragedy. As a driver reportedly "on purpose" ran a red light, went around a barricade and drove over a police motorcycle before crashing into the helpless spectators. Killing 4, including a 2-year old, and injuring more than 40. According to related news reporting, the driver has admitted having a history of suicidal attempts and has been treated for mental health issues in the past.

In above-referenced tragedy, the "weapon" was an "automobile." The deterrents and safeguards for public safety: traffic lights, temporary motor barricades, and drivers' licenses, etc. All of which of course mean absolutely nothing to anyone (mentally-ill or otherwise) choosing to ignore such. Nor, is it likely that conspicuously-posted "Automobile-Free Zone" signs would have been helpful in preventing this truly horrific tragedy. And, in contrast to tragedies that involve a "gun" as the "weapon," The White House, major news media, and anti-gun agenda-driven others, have failed to ask some important questions. Such as, Where, when, how, and specifically from whom, etc., did the driver obtain the automobile? Furthermore, given the driver's reported mental-health history, was a valid or invalid Drivers' License involved? If so, where, when, how, and specifically from whom, etc., was such obtained? Would a smaller vehicle have resulted in less tragedy? Furthermore, could it be there are actually "too many" automobiles, and that possibly "everyone" should not have the right to have one? And if so, what make, model, etc.? But, of course, these types of questions will likely not be asked until the next tragedy involving a "gun" as the "weapon."

As will other "important questions" likely not be asked for a while. For instance: When are we as a nation going to "seriously" acknowledge and "responsibly" address the subjects of "mental health" and irresponsible use and abuse of "psychotropic drugs," etc.? And, "who" is ultimately going to pay for our existing and rapidly growing $18 trillion National Debt (possibly $20 trillion in 2016)? Just a couple of questions concerning issues we seem to think will just "somehow, someday, go away" — if we can just keep focused on "more free-stuff-for-all." And, on "getting rid of guns," and on other "self-destructive agendas" aided by voter-ignorance, apathy, complacency, denial, greed, and counter-productive fear.

But, returning to our country's "mental health crisis." According to national numbers, about 1 in 4 of adults struggle with some form of mental health every year. Various sources indicate that people with mental illness are "generally" no more violent than the rest of the population. Experts on the subject seem to "generally" agree that most (certainly not all) mass murderers tend to be young loners with a history of pent-up frustration. Socially isolated and vengeful individuals who blame others for their failures and unhappiness. Often with a history of mental illness, but no prior criminal record. Deluded thinking persons who "snap" and go on killing sprees, leaving devastated families and countless others with unimaginable pain and suffering.

But, as we know, "most" lonely and angry people do not commit violent acts, let alone mass-murder. And, the above examples barely begin to scratch the surface of this terribly tragic and unsettling subject. Of mass-murders, which have become much too common-place in our society. As our nation continues to suffer mass-murders in our schools, on our military installations, and during public events—such as the horrific bombing during our April 15, 2013, Boston marathon! Carried out by two migrants who demonstrated appreciation for the generosity extended to them—by killing and crippling innocent Americans!

Try as we may it is most doubtful we will ever be able to reliably predict specifically who will turn violent and commit such atrocities. Nonetheless, the radical/militant Islam "Trojan Horses" within our borders. Or, in any resemblance of full-proof manner, be able to prevent them. However, there are some "absolute certainties" in life. Among them, the certainty that there are **"consequences"** for failing to responsibly confront, and/or for irresponsibly applying knee-jerk fixes to "mental-health," "radical/militant Islam," and our nation's other "tough issues."

For instance:

- **Consequences of** mental-health policies that have, over a period of 50 years or so, led to the release of most of our nation's mentally-ill patients from hospitals and other institutions. Released to the community, and left dependent upon mood-altering psychotropic drugs to provide them with some resemblance of "normal" perception, mental-activity, and behavior.

- **Consequences of** hospitalizing the wrong people and of failure to hospitalize individuals with obvious and very-serious mental problems.

- **Consequences of** neglecting the influence that irresponsibility — on the part of parents, educators, psychiatrists, therapists, political leaders, drug companies, entertainment industry, and social-media, etc. — has on the incidence of mass-murder and other violent acts in our society.

- **Consequences of** putting the "privacy rights" of persons with obvious and very serious mental problems above the safety and welfare of the general public.

- **Consequences of** persons with (known and clearly recognized) serious mental problems, nonetheless having access to guns, ammunition, explosives, automobiles, etc.

- **Consequences of** disregarding our U.S. Constitution, and inhibiting law-abiding and mentally sound citizens from having the option of self-defense through gun ownership and otherwise lawful means.

- **Consequences of** "safe-havens" for mass-murderers, created by "gun-free zones." Ignoring how often mass-murderers take their own lives as soon as they are confronted with armed force and prospects of capture. And that police stations and other known-to-be-armed locations are not often if ever the target of such evil-doers!

- **Consequences of** our government, and politically-biased and agenda-driven media, failing to "responsibly" deal with the "tough issues," such as mental-health, domestic violence, our $18 trillion national debt, and the growing threat of radical/militant Islam.

- **Consequences of** our electing (and leaving in office) political representatives and leaders, that are more focused on keeping their jobs and pursuing self-serving agendas than responsibly tackling our nation's many "tough issues." Those truly threatening our liberty and ultimate survival.

And, for those still committed to resolving our nation's serious threats and other tough issues through irresponsible **"knee-jerk blames and fixes,"** possibly an open-minded and truly serious review of the above generic-list of "consequences" is in order. Followed by some deep thought about what our nation's **"Backup Plan"** might entail after we suffer the devastating consequences of fixes such as: "psychotropic drugs," "legalized marijuana," "gun-free zones," "disarmed law-abiding citizens," "more free-stuff from the public treasury," and "denial that radical/militant Islam has declared unrelenting war against us," "etc." But, before we get to that point, maybe there will be time to, in addition to "all those guns," also get rid of all knives, automobiles, commercial aircraft, and the endless list of other items that can be used as weapons. And then there are always our old reliable **"standby fixes"**: of ignorance, apathy, complacency, denial, greed, and counter-productive fear!

"Every person has free choice. Free to obey or disobey the Natural Laws. Your choice determines the consequences. Nobody ever did, or ever will, escape the consequences of his choices."

–Alfred A. Montapert

"There are historic situations in which refusal to defend the inheritance of a civilization, however imperfect, against tyranny and aggression may result in consequences even worse than war."

–Neinhold Niebuhr

"I hope I'm wrong, but I am afraid that Iraq is going to turn out to be the greatest disaster in American foreign policy – worse than Vietnam, not in the number who died, but in terms of its unintended consequences and its reverberation throughout the region."

–Madeleine Albright

"In nature there are neither rewards nor punishment; there are consequences." –Robert Green

"Everybody, sooner or later, sits down to a banquet of consequences."

–Robert Louis Stevenson

A Wakeup Call

&

"Not to be Wasted Again" Opportunity

> *"Our lives begin to end the day we become silent about things that matter."* – Plato

Our 2014 mid-term elections sent a much needed nationwide wake-up call to the President, Congress, and others! Clearly demonstrating wide-spread repudiation of government arrogance, overreach, intrusiveness, gridlock, overregulation, and of other liberty destroying agendas from the radical left and radical right.

Election results that returned majority control of the U.S. Senate to the Republican Party, along with other upsets nationwide. Overall, a strong "heads-up" that many federal, state, and local government leaders need to better listen to "we the people," change course, exercise their constitutional duties and responsibilities, and more responsibly take care of our nation's business.

A unique chance and special motivation for all parties to set aside personal, self-serving, and ideological agendas. And, instead, focus on a clear and effective strategies for defending our nation from foreign and domestic threats, and for protecting and preserving our borders, economy, English language, culture, and personal liberty.

Yes, the results of our 2014 elections included many loud and clear messages. A few are summarized below.

— National Security/Foreign Policy: Political correctness, false promises, rhetoric, and denial of the dangers around us — including but not limited to radical/militant Islam — will not provide for our national and personal security.

— U.S. Economy: "Entitlement" and "dependency" did not create this great nation of unequaled liberty, freedom, and opportunity. Likewise, no amount of "free" (tax-payer funded) birth control, food stamps, housing, mobile phones, and other government management of our lives, will ever be a sustainable and appropriate substitute for a "good job" — for gainful and otherwise fulfilling employment and opportunity to be self-supporting contributing members of society.

— Immigration: Individually and as a nation we are unable to feed, protect, and otherwise accommodate all of the World's needy — we can however self-destruct by ignoring this reality. Our immigration policies must focus on attracting true "contributors" — as opposed to "takers" and "abusers," and "amnesty" for the illegal.

— <u>Healthcare</u>: Regardless of dreams, wishes, best intentions, and irresponsible government promises — unlimited heath care available to all is not possible. It is also counter to good judgment and common sense for our health care to be in the hands of government bureaucracies historical for corruption, inefficiency, and abuse of power and privilege. The VA and IRS being but two examples of many.

— <u>Transformation</u>: Long ago, in the face of tyranny, lack of religious freedom, taxation without representation, and other oppressions — very wise, uniquely creative, and unquestionably courageous individuals, established what remains today, the first and one-of-its-kind constitutional republic — our United States of America. A nation of unequaled liberty, freedom, and opportunity. A tried and proven envy of the world. And, not needing "transformation" — but instead "protection" and "preservation"-- for present and future generations of Americans!

— <u>Voting</u>: Voting, and not voting, really matter and have consequences — often costly and otherwise serious consequences. Our constitutional right to vote must always — and only — be available to "verifiable" U.S. Citizens.

A fair and balanced review of U.S. history would support that, over the years and through various administrations, the agendas and priorities of our federal government have often been irresponsibly out-of-step with our nation's best interests.

If this were not so, it is unlikely that today we would have, for example: a rapidly growing $18 trillion National Debt (about $154,000 per taxpayer); over 45 million food stamp recipients; about 8.07 million "officially" unemployed; some 47.6 million living in poverty; a disappearing middle-class; only 118.9 million income taxpayers within a population of about 322 million; skyrocketing health care costs; a Veteran's Administration and Internal Revenue Service still plagued with inefficiency and abuse of power; unsecured U.S. borders; uncontrolled immigration; our U.S. English language being diluted and compromised by a foreign language--Spanish; our U.S. Culture threatened by political correctness gone berserk; the growing reality of foreign/domestic terrorism; and our foreign policy in an ongoing state of chaos; etc.

Common sense and our 2014 mid-term election results dictate that issues such as those mentioned above should be among— if not "the"—top priorities of our government. But, unfortunately, such has not been the case. And, much to the contrary, the President, Congress, and Supreme Court have ignored our 2014 mid-term election results, and have just "continued on" with the same old prior-there-to "status-quo."

Blatantly disregarding the strong wake-up call from "we the people," demanding a "change of course." And arrogantly carrying on with unyielding ideological and special interest agendas in conflict with the voting-citizens' expressed will.

And, in a very troubling atmosphere of seemingly endless Presidential arrogance, disregard of the will-of-the-people, and unproductive blame-game rhetoric by all parties . . . "amnesty for millions of illegal immigrants (illegal aliens)" continues to be a "top priority" agenda item. A matter of such urgency that—according to the President—it had to be dealt with before the end of 2014. Even if he had to do an end run around Congress, by way of Presidential Executive Orders. A move considered by many to be an unconstitutional act. Clearly, a presidential agenda that puts "amnesty for illegal behavior" ahead of policies that "encourage law-abiding conduct." Ahead of policies that "address our country's countless other needs." Not only defying common sense, but also a terribly unsettling indicator of questionable motives and grossly irresponsible leadership.

Such conduct should prompt our political leaders' phones, e-mail addresses, and social media websites, and U.S. Mail, etc., being overwhelmed with citizens' protests of the strongest nature. Especially from our younger generations who will, all too soon, assume the income tax burdens and other liberty destroying outcomes from past, present, and future irresponsible and out-of-touch government agendas. Much called for citizen-protest that should even force our biased and profit driven news media to, for a change, provide some fair, balanced, and otherwise responsible coverage of our government's shortfalls. But, for now, it is unlikely there will be much if any social media and news worthy outcry and outrage about anything. That is, until . . . someone is "offended" by someone's inattention to political correctness; another objectionable sports team name is discovered; or the next opportunity to (through ignorance or otherwise) support an effort to paint us as a nation of racists, bigots, and privileged persons having little regard for the less fortunate.

As with all elections, our votes—and lack thereof—are a testament of the true character of "we the people." And of those we in good faith entrust to carry out, on our behalf, our government functions. A trust that should always include constructive "wakeup calls," but never "wasted opportunities." The rapidly approaching 2016 elections represent our next crucial opportunity to set our nation on proper course. Truly, a "critical turning-point" for present and future generations of Americans. We and our political leaders must do better this time around. "All" must "do the right thing!" **A good starting point**—becoming well-informed, responsible, and unfailingly-active . . . **voters**!

A daunting challenge, when looking at our shameful voting record: According to July 2015 U.S. Census Bureau Statistics, there are about 218.9 million "eligible voters" in the U.S., of which only about 146.3 million (66.8%) are "registered," from which only about 126.1 million (57.6%) "voted in 2012."

= = =

"Democracy cannot succeed unless those who express their choice are prepared to choose wisely. The real safeguard of democracy, therefore, is education." — Franklin D. Roosevelt

"Days of Reckoning" — Our 2016 Elections

> *"The future of this republic is in the hands of the American voter."*
> *–Dwight D. Eisenhower*
>
> *"A democracy cannot succeed unless those who express their choice are prepared to choose wisely. The real safeguard of democracy, therefore, is education." –Franklin D. Roosevelt*

"A day of reckoning" is commonly defined as: *"The time when past mistakes or misdeeds must be punished or paid for; a time when the degree of one's success or failure will be revealed."*

In accordance with provisions of each of the individual states, candidates for U.S. President and Vice President will be selected through caucuses and primary elections carried out during the time frame of February 01, 2016 (Iowa's caucuses) through June 28, 2016 (Utah's primaries).

Then on **Tuesday, November 08, 2016**, the date scheduled for the 58th quadrennial U.S. presidential election, U.S. voters will select presidential-electors who will in turn, through the electoral-college, elect a new U.S. President and Vice President. The Twenty-second Amendment to our United States Constitution prevents an incumbent president from seeking a third term.

Be not unaware, unconcerned, or misled! Tuesday, November 08, 2016, and the days prior thereto that state caucuses and primaries determine the president and vice president candidates—are truly **"all days of reckoning"** for our great nation and all Americans! Days when, as a result of voting or not voting; of being informed or uninformed voters; and through responsible sacrifice or self-serving denial, complacency, apathy, greed, and counter-productive fears— we will put in office a new U.S. President and Vice President. Thereafter, we will demonstrate the wisdom and courage (or lack thereof) to—under new presidential leadership— "responsibly" deal with our nation's liberty and survival threatening issues, such as:

- Our $18 trillion and rapidly-growing National Debt;
- Our growing $97.5 trillion debt of Unfunded Liabilities;
- Our unsecured and uncontrolled U.S. borders;
- Irresponsible and Unenforced Immigration Policies;
- Failure to purge the U.S. of illegal aliens & sanctuary cities;
- Failure to protect and preserve our English language;
- Various immigrants' refusal to assimilate into U.S. culture;
- The foreign and domestic threat of radical/militant Islam;
- Politically-biased news media;
- "Gun-free Zones" that ultimately render the citizens within such, to be helpless-targets of armed evil-doers;
- Divide & conquer agendas, that pit one against another;
- Political agendas promoting unsustainable "deserve" and "entitled" mindsets and behaviors;
- An ever-growing and ever-intrusive federal government.

Our nation is at a crucial tipping-point. We have reached the point where about one-half of the current U.S. population was born here; the other half, new immigrants. Where approaching one-half of our population is one way or another "on the take" from the public treasury. Where, over recent years the U.S. has been flooded with legal immigrants and illegal aliens that have no interest in assimilating into our U.S. culture — but, rather, to establish their own separate cultures. And to be takers rather than contributors, abusing our nation's generosity. While countless other immigrants of the past and present have done the right thing, and countless others remain standing in line with intent to gain legal entrance to, and become a contributing member of, our U.S. culture. Where, our government has become overwhelmed with "career politicians" absorbed with self-serving retention of power, influence, and benefits from the public treasury — rather than pursuing the best interests of our nation. Where, too many of "we the people" have for much too long, shirked our citizen-responsibility through our ultimately self-destructive behaviors of voter ignorance, denial, apathy, complacency, greed, and counter-productive fears.

Where "we the people" have this (a no doubt rapidly fleeting) opportunity to put our great nation back on a path of recovery and prosperity. By way of what each of us do — what we **must** responsibly do — as hereafter active, informed, and engaged voters! Wisely and courageously starting anew in YR 2016 — and responsibly following through in all years thereafter. Not only for "our" sake — but for our descendants — for all Americans! This, our inescapable duty! We must not fail!

"Our political leaders will know our priorities only if we tell them, again and again, and if those priorities begin to show up in the polls." –Peggy Noonan

"Do not let what you cannot do; interfere with what you can do."
— John Wooden

"The future belongs to those who believe in the beauty of their dreams." — Eleanor Roosevelt

"One man with courage makes a majority." — Andrew Jackson

"Remember, if you ever need a helping hand, it's at the end of your arm, as you get older, remember you have another hand: The first is to help yourself, the second is to help others." –Audrey Hepburn

"Voters don't decide issues, they decide who will decide issues."
–George F. Will

"The ignorance of one voter in a democracy impairs the security of all." –John F. Kennedy

"Half of the American people never read a newspaper. Half never voted for President. One hopes it is the same half." –Gore Vidal

"Your every voter, as surely as your chief magistrate, exercises a public trust." –Grover Cleveland
"We ourselves feel that what we are doing is just a drop in the ocean. But the ocean would be less because of that missing drop."
–Mother Teresa

"To Vote or Not to Vote": Some Reasons & Excuses

Given that we have "not yet" turned our fate over to the hands of a dictatorship, our Constitutional Republic provides us with the opportunity (and obligation) to vote for or against those campaigning for positions of political power and influence in our government, at all levels.

To ensure the continuity of essential government functions, governing our nation includes a mix of recurring elections, timed, at federal, state, and local levels. Involving the U.S. President and Vice President; positions in the U.S. House of Representatives and U.S. Senate; state and territorial governors; state legislators; and various other state and local positions.

During these many elections, billions of dollars are spent in an effort to retain or gain positions of power, influence, privilege, and responsibility. While millions of lawfully eligible voters (and countless unlawful persons) review, finalize, and carry out their voting plans—and others wrestle with whether "to vote or not to vote."

As an aid to present and future persons looking for some justification for **"not voting"**—for **not** letting their political voice be heard—here are a few time-worn excuses to consider: Forgot to register/vote, bad weather, sick, disabled, inconvenient voting place, ID required, proof of U.S. citizenship required, conflicting schedule, had to work, on travel/vacation, disgusted with politics, no good candidates, all political parties are the same, politics is all about money, corrupt politicians, and all that politicians care about is "getting elected." If none of these do the trick, maybe this old standby will help—"our votes don't really count anyway!"

And, for those who choose to do their best to be informed and active voters, please give yourself a big justified pat-on-the-back! Our country needs many more to take your lead and do the same! Be very proud and grateful that you are not among the growing numbers who, election after election, waste their precious voting privilege—that which so many others have sacrificed so much to provide us.

For those who find themselves still undecided, and seeking some justification for the time and effort involved in trying to be informed and active voters, the following very short and incomplete summary of some serious, real-world reasons may hopefully be of help:

Our liberty, freedom, health, and general wellbeing; personal and national security; jobs; hard-earned money and property; use of tax dollars; children's and grandchildren's education; U.S. culture; U.S. common-language English; U.S. borders; right of self-defense, religious freedom, and responsibility as citizen-custodians of our country's affairs.

If none of these seem to work, how about "our childrens' and grandchildrens' future!" That is, the wellbeing of future generations of Americans, already saddled with an outrageous and rapidly growing $18 Trillion National Debt. The result of many years of greed, corruption, and otherwise irresponsible government, and left unchecked by "we the people." Left unattended by too many eligible voters that have been politically uninformed, unengaged, and otherwise inattentive to our nation's affairs! For much too long.

Regardless of our country's imperfections, our first and one of its kind Constitutional Republic remains the envy of the world. Our "informed" and "responsible" votes are of critical importance to our nation, to our families, to us as individuals, and to our descendants.

Our votes are "also" very important to those who continue to spend billions to influence our support. Including, for example, "special interests" contributing to the overall $7 billion spent on the 2012 elections (a number exceeding the Earth's total population at that time). And to the estimated $3 billion or so spent on the not so long ago 2014 election cycle!

We can do our best to be informed and active voters, or waste our privilege. We have the opportunity to be a part of our country's solutions, or its problems. And we have the option of focusing on the **"reasons"** for voting, or the **"excuses"** not to. The freedom of <u>choice</u> is ours — that is, at least <u>so far it is</u>!

= = =

"A vote is like a rifle; its usefulness depends upon the character of the user." — Theodore Roosevelt

"Elections belong to the people. It's their decision. If they decide to turn their back on the fire and burn their behinds, then they will just have to sit on their blisters." — Abraham Lincoln

"A citizen of America will cross the ocean to fight for democracy, but won't cross the street to vote in a national election." — Bill Vaughan

"The ignorance of one voter in a democracy impairs the security of all." — John F. Kennedy

"Democracy cannot succeed unless those who express their choice are prepared to choose wisely. The real safeguard of democracy, therefore, is education." — Franklin D. Roosevelt

"The best argument against democracy is a five-minute conversation with the average voter." — Winston S. Churchill

"Let us never forget that government is ourselves and not an alien power over us. The ultimate rulers of our democracy are not a President and senators and congressmen and government officials, but the voters of this country." — Martin Luther King Jr.

Our U.S. "Bill of Rights"

*"We hold these truths to be self-Evident, that all men are created equal, that they are endowed by their Creator with certain unalienable Rights, that among these are **Life, Liberty and the pursuit of Happiness**. ---That to secure these rights, Governments are instituted among Men, deriving their just powers from the consent of the governed, ..."*

— The U.S. Declaration of Independence, 1776

The following is a transcription of the first ten amendments to our U.S. Constitution in their original form. These first ten amendments to the Constitution were ratified December 15, 1791, and form what is known as the "Bill of Rights."

Amendment I

Congress shall make no law respecting an establishment of religion, or prohibiting the free exercise thereof; or abridging the freedom of speech, or of the press; or the right of the people peaceably to assemble, and to petition the Government for a redress of grievances.

Amendment II

A well regulated Militia, being necessary to the security of a free State, the right of the people to keep and bear Arms, shall not be infringed.

Amendment III

No Soldier shall, in time of peace be quartered in any house, without the consent of the Owner, nor in time of war, but in a manner to be prescribed by law.

Amendment IV

The right of the people to be secure in their persons, houses, papers, and effects, against unreasonable searches and seizures, shall not be violated, and no Warrants shall issue, but upon probable cause, supported by Oath or affirmation, and particularly describing the place to be searched, and the persons or things to be seized.

Amendment V

No person shall be held to answer for a capital, or otherwise infamous crime, unless on a presentment or indictment of a Grand Jury, except in cases arising in the land or naval forces, or in the Militia, when in actual service in time of War or public danger; nor shall any person be subject for the same offence to be twice put in jeopardy of life or limb; nor shall be compelled in any criminal case to be a witness against himself, nor be deprived of life, liberty, or property, without due process of law; nor shall private property be taken for public use, without just compensation.

Amendment VI

In all criminal prosecutions, the accused shall enjoy the right to a speedy and public trial, by an impartial jury of the State and district wherein the crime shall have been committed, which district shall have been previously ascertained by law, and to be informed of the nature and cause of the accusation; to be confronted with the witnesses against him; to have compulsory process for obtaining witnesses in his favor, and to have the Assistance of Counsel for his defense.

Amendment VII

In Suits at common law, where the value in controversy shall exceed twenty dollars, the right of trial by jury shall be preserved, and no fact tried by a jury, shall be otherwise re-examined in any Court of the United States, than according to the rules of the common law.

Amendment VIII

Excessive bail shall not be required, nor excessive fines imposed, nor cruel and unusual punishments inflicted.

Amendment IX

The enumeration in the Constitution, of certain rights, shall not be construed to deny or disparage others retained by the people.

Amendment X

The powers not delegated to the United States by the Constitution, nor prohibited by it to the States, are reserved to the States respectively, or to the people.

= = =

"Liberty must at all hazards be supported. We have a right to it, derived from our Maker. But if we had not, our fathers have earned it for us, at the expense of their ease, their estates, their pleasure, and their blood." — John Adams, 1765

"A Bill of Rights is what the people are entitled to against every government, and what no just government should refuse, or rest on inference." — Thomas Jefferson

"The Bill of Rights wasn't enacted to give us any rights. It was enacted so the Government could not take away from us any rights that we already had." — Kenneth Eade

"The Framers of the Bill of Rights did not purport to "create" rights. Rather, they designed the Bill of Rights to prohibit our Government from infringing rights and liberties presumed to be preexisting."
— William J. Brennan, Jr.

"Can any of you seriously say the Bill of Rights could get through Congress today? It wouldn't even get out of committee."
— F. Lee Bailey

Our U.S. "Pledge of Allegiance"

Official versions
*(changes in **bold underline**)*

1892 (first version)
"I pledge allegiance to my Flag and the republic for which it stands, one nation indivisible, with liberty and justice for all."
1892 to 1922
"I pledge allegiance to my Flag and **to** the republic for which it stands: one nation indivisible, with liberty and justice for all."
1923
"I pledge allegiance to **the** Flag **of the United States** and to the republic for which it stands; one Nation indivisible with liberty and justice for all."
1924 to 1954
"I pledge allegiance to the Flag of the United States **of America,** and to the republic for which it stands; one Nation indivisible with liberty and justice for all."
1954 (current version)
"I pledge allegiance to the Flag of the United States of America, and to the Republic for which it stands, one Nation **under God,** indivisible, with liberty and justice for all."

Section 4 of the U.S. Flag Code states in part that The Pledge of Allegiance to the Flag should ". . . be rendered by standing at attention facing the flag with the right hand over the heart. When not in uniform men should remove any non-religious headdress with their right hand and hold it at the left shoulder, the hand being over the heart. Persons in uniform should remain silent, face the flag, and render the military salute."

A Brief History of our "Pledge of Allegiance"

As shown on the previous page, the "original" **Pledge of Allegiance** read *"I pledge allegiance to my Flag and the Republic for which it stands- one nation indivisible- with liberty and justice for all."* Words written by Francis Bellamy, for Boston, Massachusetts based magazine, *The Youth's Companion,* and published on September 8, 1892, to provide students something special to repeat on Columbus Day that year. After reprinted on circulars distributed to schools throughout the country, on October 12, 1892, millions of school children repeated this *Pledge of Allegiance,* thereby starting a nation-wide school-day practice. Thereafter, on June 14, 1923, at the first National Flag Conference in Washington D.C., the words "my flag" were replaced with the formally-adopted words "the Flag of the United States." Finally, in 1942, the *Pledge of Allegiance* was officially recognized by our U.S. Congress. Then, in June 1943, the Supreme Court ruled that, as protected by the free-speech clause of the First Amendment to our U.S. Constitution, school children could not be forced to salute the Flag or say the Pledge, nor be punished for not doing so. Years later, in June 1954, the words "under God" were added by an amendment. At that time, President Dwight D. Eisenhower reportedly expressed, *"In this way we are reaffirming the transcendence of religious faith in America's heritage and future; in this way we shall constantly strengthen those spiritual weapons which forever will be our country's most powerful resource in peace and war."*

= = =

And, in our "politically-correctness-gone-mad" world of today, even "suggesting" that our children participate in such patriotic acts as saluting our U.S. Flag or reciting the Pledge of Allegiance, can often result in lawsuits, recrimination, someone being "offended," as well as teachers being suspended or fired! Clearly, our country is in much need of an appropriate measure of **"patriotic-correctness"** to ensure an at least **equal-balance** with the liberty-threatening **"political-correctness"** agenda being imposed upon us.

Our U.S. National Anthem

The Star Spangled Banner

(September 20, 1814 — By Francis Scott Key)

O say can you see, by the dawn's early light,
What so proudly we hail'd at the twilight's last gleaming,
Whose broad stripes and bright stars through the perilous fight
O'er the ramparts we watch'd were so gallantly streaming?
And the rocket's red glare, the bombs bursting in air,
Gave proof through the night that our flag was still there,
O say does that star-spangled banner yet wave
O'er the land of the free and the home of the brave?

On the shore dimly seen through the mists of the deep
Where the foe's haughty host in dread silence reposes,
What is that which the breeze, o'er the towering steep,
As it fitfully blows, half conceals, half discloses?
Now it catches the gleam of the morning's first beam,
In full glory reflected now shines in the stream,
'Tis the star-spangled banner - O long may it wave
O'er the land of the free and the home of the brave!

And where is that band who so vauntingly swore,
That the havoc of war and the battle's confusion
A home and a Country should leave us no more?
Their blood has wash'd out their foul footstep's pollution.
No refuge could save the hireling and slave
From the terror of flight or the gloom of the grave,
And the star-spangled banner in triumph doth wave
O'er the land of the free and the home of the brave.

O thus be it ever when freemen shall stand
Between their lov'd home and the war's desolation!
Blest with vict'ry and peace may the heav'n rescued land
Praise the power that hath made and preserv'd us a nation!
Then conquer we must, when our cause it is just,
And this be our motto - "In God is our trust,"
And the star-spangled banner in triumph shall wave
O'er the land of the free and the home of the brave.

A Brief History of Our U.S. National Anthem
"The Star-Spangled Banner"

The lyrics to "The Star-Spangled Banner" were composed by Francis Scott Key, an American lawyer, on September 14, 1814. After he witnessed the massive overnight British bombardment of Fort McHenry in Maryland during the War of 1812. Key watched the siege while being detained on a British ship, and penned our country's famous anthem after seeing in awe that the Fort McHenry flag had survived the awesome British assault of reportedly 1,800 bombs.

After being circulated as a handbill, the lyrics were eventually published in a Baltimore newspaper on September 20, 1814, and later set to the tune of "To Anacreon in Heaven," a popular English song.

Throughout the 19th century, "The Star-Spangled Banner" was considered the national anthem by most branches of our U.S. armed forces and other groups. However, it was not until 1916, and President Woodrow Wilson's signing of an executive order, that it was officially designated as such. Then, in March 1931, Congress passed an act confirming President Wilson's presidential order, soon followed by President Hoover signing it into law on March 3, 1931.

"Hazel & Lillie" —

A Special Tribute to Our Mothers

"I miss thee, my Mother! Thy image is still the deepest impressed on my heart." — *Eliza Cook*

Hazel, the second of four children in her family, was born in the little shack-of-a-house her family lived in near Bentonville, Arkansas, April 30, 1919. Less than a year later, Lillie, the ninth child of eleven in her family, was born in a small log cabin near Decatur, Arkansas, February 24, 1920. For many years they will live miles apart and not know the other exists — but, their life-circumstances will have many similarities.

Both are born into poverty-stricken conditions. Their childhood will not bask in the "Roaring 20's" — theirs will be a life primarily focused on survival, economically and otherwise. One of scarce food, hand-me-down clothes, hand-made dresses made out of livestock feed sacks, few shoes, often barefoot, outdoor bathrooms (privies) , often no running water or electricity, self-made toys and entertainment, family-administered healthcare, few if any luxuries, and parents struggling to find and maintain employment offering some semblance of life-sustaining income.

In spite of many formidable obstacles, both will grow up to be beautiful young women and marry their "first loves". Much too soon, each will become a young widow, as their husbands (at different times, places, and circumstances) both suffer tragic deaths. And, at those devastating moments—Hazel's and Lillie's many plans, hopes, dreams, and other youthful aspirations will be crushed—and replaced with the harsh realities of the Great Depression. And the many hardships born out of the travesties of World War II. Their so brief opportunity for romance and life's innocence must all too soon be replaced by serious focus on survival—for themselves and their children. During this time of special struggle, these very young and proud widows with small children will have few if any "free rides" available to them. There will be no multitude of tax-payer funded agencies pushing free food, free housing, free clothing, free transportation, free health care, free education, free legal services, free job training, free phones, free entertainment, as well as, no tax-payer provided money for tattoos, cigarettes, alcohol, entertainment, etc. Nor, will either of these very strong and most dignified women ever seek such.

For any special kindnesses and other considerations received along their rough paths in life, they will always truly appreciate, often feel guilty and embarrassed about, but will never "expect", or feel "deserving of" or "entitled to." Throughout their lives they will strive hard to pay any debtors, return any favors, and will always be quick to unselfishly extend aid and assistance to others in need. Both will eventually re-marry—Hazel twice; Lillie once. And, like countless others, they and their families will enjoy "relatively" good times and proud moments, as well as suffer sadness, heartbreak, and tragedy. They will experience, respect, cherish, and appreciate "life" and its mixed blessings.

Hazel will raise three sons. She will experience the indescribable pain of losing a son (age 48) to an automobile accident—father of two of her grandchildren. Later she will endure further helpless suffering as her youngest son (age 58), and father of another two of her grandchildren, begins his battle with oral cancer. While she (his very aging mother) will feel so powerless to prevent or ease his suffering. Lillie will raise four daughters and a son, and likewise suffer the terrible pain and hopelessness of seeing her youngest daughter "fall through the cracks" of our complex society.

Some 46 years after their births they will become joint mother-in-laws, as one of Lillie's daughters and one of Hazel's sons marry one another—and add two more to their growing list of "the most adorable" grandchildren and great-grandchildren.

Although Lillie will genetically have more visible heath issues than Hazel, they both will experience the "mixed blessings" of good health and longevity. Lillie will live 90 years; Hazel, 92. Both of their long lives will be filled with much family love, many fun and exciting times, and lots of proud moments. But, each will also experience the indescribable stress and suffering of living through the deaths of their mothers, fathers, and all of their brothers, sisters, and husbands — of the utter loneliness of being "the last to go." An aspect of life known only to those who experience the same.

Throughout their lives, especially their childhoods, each will endure many challenges that their children will never face, nor ever be able to comprehend. But, neither of these "very special ladies" — these "so precious mothers" — will ever leave their children with the impression that they consider themselves to be "victims." Each will, however, and in their own way, dedicate their lives to the wellbeing of their children. They will sacrifice of themselves as necessary to provide for their children's "needs", as well as some of their "appropriate wants" — when able to do so. As they endure being unable to provide their children with the same or similar level of care, gifts, and other considerations that many other parents can and do. But, each will bless their children with the most valuable gift of all — their "unconditional love." Not "unconditional tolerance" — there is a difference, and we benefited from their awareness and application of such.

Hazel and Lillie will also put long, hard, and serious effort into impressing upon their children the importance of moral values, self-respect, respect and consideration for others, self-confidence, self-sacrifice, strong work-ethic, honesty, the importance of treating others the way you wish to be treated, and many other critical life-values. To what extent their tireless efforts towards these aims are deemed ultimately successful, naturally rests within the choices, responsibilities, and other circumstances, involved in their children's' respective life-journeys. For, our dearest Mothers truly did their part! They stepped up to the plate of life and – through considerable self-sacrifice – gave it their best shot! And, they did unsurpassably great! Truly honorable life-achievements, for which they both deserved to hear and receive much more thanks and appreciation from family and others . . . not via these and other post-passing tributes . . . but, during their cherished time with us.

On Saturday, June 26, 2010, Lillie died, at age 90. At that moment – my wife, Ann, lost her deeply-loved Mother and dearest friend. And, I lost my much loved and respected Mother-in-law and our special friendship. Likewise, when Hazel died, at age 92, a little more than a year later, on Tuesday, September 13, 2011, I lost my deeply-loved Mother, and most cherished friend. And, my wife, Ann, lost a deeply-loving Mother-in-law who so truly adored her.

To us and countless others, our Mothers, Hazel and Lillie, were so special, so very precious. Courageous, proud, and dignified ladies, with a healthy sense of humor and unfailing dedication to family. Both truly loved, lived, and enjoyed life. Always quick to extend a helping hand to deserving others, both spending their lives as givers and contributors – not takers and burdens upon others. Ann and I find much comfort in the many warm memories our Mothers left us with. We also feel much blessed that our Mothers were able and willing (and preferred) to live as proud, "independent" ladies up until shortly before their passing. Or, they at least were able to make us believe that such was their wishes – to live independent in their last days. Hopefully, their true wishes – and not more of their unlimited "self-sacrifice." In hind-sight, I am often inclined to think it was the latter – and that, most regretfully, I may have let a once-in-a-lifetime opportunity to address some truly-special needs and caring of our loving Mothers pass us by. We also realize we were especially blessed to have much more time with our mothers than life affords to so many other families. But, in matters such as these, there is never enough time – and as dictated by nature and circumstance, the loss of our respective Mothers is so very personal. Leaving our lives with an indescribable void – and to never again be the same. In loving gratefulness . . . if there is a Heaven, our Mothers – Hazel and Lillie – have truly "earned" a place there! And, until proven otherwise, we choose to believe that Heaven does exist – and that our Mothers are joyfully residing there. Each, still "proud" and "independent", but now "free" of the many life-challenges handled and burdens carried, by each, so long, so graciously, and so willingly – while unfailingly taking of their gift-of-life to bless us with their unconditional love!

With our deepest love, respect, and appreciation . . . we Thank You, our Mothers, Hazel and Lillie! You are missed so terribly much, and in our hearts you will forever so warmly and preciously be!

– Jim, Bob & Bill . . . Kay, Ann, Jim, Mary & Theresa.

Closing Remarks

Please accept my sincerest thanks and appreciation for any time you have spent with this book. I am most aware that you could have chosen to do otherwise with that portion of your precious "gift of life" — your "time."

Hopefully you chose to read it in its entirety, and found such to be a meaningful experience. That something within these pages truly helped to: **provide** a heightened and positive awareness of the growing number and mix of very real threats facing our great nation; **encourage** more-active and better-informed voter participation; and otherwise **promote** and **support** more effective citizen-custodianship of our nation's affairs.

Our great nation **"is"** at a critical point in history, and our liberty and survival depend upon many things. None the least being that **"we take the time," "put forth the effort,"** and **"do our best,"** to be active, informed, and responsible voters, regarding all levels of government. That jointly and individually we unrelentingly and unfailingly strive to maintain a government respectful and protective of our U.S. Constitution. A government truly focused on protecting and preserving our country's borders, common-language English, and culture.

For, it is ultimately "we" who must ensure and maintain a government that recognizes, acknowledges, and protects its citizens from, our foreign and domestic enemies. A government not seeking to disarm law-abiding citizens, but truly dedicated to ensuring our liberty and sovereignty. We need only to look and listen around our world today to see unsettling "real-world and "real-time" examples of the unthinkable cost to be paid, should we fail to address our undeniable citizen-duties and responsibilities. Our inescapable obligations. "We the people" must "do the right thing!"

For, at stake is nothing less than the—now truly at risk—liberty, freedom, and ultimate survival of all present and future generations of Americans!

—William James Moore

= = =

"*You cannot escape the responsibility of tomorrow by evading it today.*" *— Abraham Lincoln*

"*It was by the sober sense of our citizens that we were safely and steadily conducted **from monarchy** to republicanism, and it is by the same agency alone we can be kept from falling back.*"
— Thomas Jefferson (1723-1826)

"*To sit back hoping that someday, someway, someone will make things right is to go on feeding the crocodile, hoping he will eat you last – but eat you he will.*" *— Ronald Reagan*

"Our safety, our liberty, depends upon preserving the Constitution of the United States as our fathers made it inviolate. The people of the United States are the rightful masters of both the Congress and the courts, not to over through the Constitution, but to over through the men who pervert the Constitution." — Abraham Lincoln

"One's philosophy is not best expressed in words; it is expressed in the choices one makes... and the choices we make are ultimately our responsibility." — Eleanor Roosevelt (1884-1962)

Until he has been a part of a cause larger than himself, no man is truly whole." — Richard M. Nixon (Inaugural Address, Jan. 1969)

"The tyranny of a prince in an oligarchy is not so dangerous to the public welfare as the apathy of a citizen in a democracy."
— Charles de Montesquieu

"Let every nation know, whether it wishes us well or ill, that we shall pay any price, bear any burden, meet any hardship, support any friend, oppose any foe to assure the survival and the success of liberty." — John F. Kennedy

"You may have to fight a battle more than once to win it."
–Margaret Thatcher

"We here highly resolve that these dead shall not have died in vain; that this nation shall have a new birth of freedom; and that this government of the people, by the people, for the people, shall not perish from the earth." –Abraham Lincoln

"It is not necessary to change. Survival is not mandatory."
— Dr. W. Edwards Deming

"We are at war, and our security as a nation depends on winning that war." –Condoleezza Rice

"The survival of liberty in our land increasingly depends on the success of liberty in other lands. The best hope for peace in our world is the expansion of freedom in all the world."
— George Walker Bush

"Good history is a question of survival. Without any past, we will deprive ourselves of the defining impression of our being."
— Ken Burns

"Standing in the middle of the road is very dangerous; you get knocked down by the traffic from both sides." –Margaret Thatcher

The Magic Bank Account

(The author of the following appears to be unknown – it was reportedly found in the billfold of the legendary Alabama University Coach, Paul Bryant, after his death in 1983.)

= = =

Imagine that you had won the following "PRIZE" in a contest: Each morning your bank would deposit $86,400 in your private account for your use.

However, this prize has rules:

1. Everything that you didn't spend during each day would be taken away from you.

2. You may not just simply transfer money into some other account.

3. You may only spend it.

4. Each morning upon awakening, the bank opens your account with another $86,400 for that day.

5. The bank can end the game without warning: at any time it can say, "Game Over!" It can close the account and you will not receive a new one.

What would you personally do? You would buy anything and everything you wanted right? Not only for yourself, but for all the people you love and care for. Even for the people you don't know, because you couldn't possibly spend it all on yourself, right? You would try to spend every penny, and use it because you know it would be replenished in the morning, right?

ACTUALLY, this game is REAL! . . . Shocked??? . . . YES!
Each of us is already a winner of this *PRIZE*. We just can't
seem to see it.

The PRIZE is *TIME*

1. Each morning we awaken to receive 86,400 seconds as a gift
of life.

2. And when we go to sleep at night, any remaining time is
NOT credited to us.

3. What we haven't used up that day is forever lost.

4. Yesterday is forever gone.

5. Each morning the account is refilled, but the bank can
dissolve your account at any time WITHOUT WARNING . . .

So, what will YOU do with your 86,400 seconds?

Those seconds are worth so much more than the same amount
in dollars. Think about it and remember to enjoy every
second of your life because time races by so much quicker
than you think.

So take care of yourself, be happy, love deeply and enjoy life!
**Here's wishing you a wonderful and beautiful day. Start
"spending" . . . .**

= = =

*"The only reason for time is so that everything doesn't happen at
once."* — *Albert Einstein*

"The bad news is time flies. The good news is you're the pilot."
— *Michael Altshuler*

Heroes

"A hero is someone who has given his or her life to something bigger than oneself." — Joseph Campbell

"It's not just children who need heroes." — Tamora Pierce

"A leader is one who knows the way, goes the way and shows the way." — John C. Maxwell

A Ralph Waldo Emerson quotation reads: *"Each man is a hero and an oracle to somebody."*

A "hero" is commonly defined as *"a person who, in the opinion of others, is admired for their achievements, distinguished courage, brave acts, or exceptionally noble qualities."* And, an "oracle" is often considered to be *"a person giving wise or authoritative decisions or opinions."* Given the above Emerson quotation, and these commonly recognized definitions . . . who we consider a "hero" seems to ultimately rest in the "eye of the beholder." That is, in our opinion—and in the opinion of others. As likely it should be.

And, while speaking of "opinions," what follows are a few of mine. About a "once very special" designation—that of "hero." A "should be" especially-unique distinction, that has become so frivolously and commonly used as to often be demeaning and disrespectful of those "exceptional among us" to whom "hero" truly should apply. My "opinion," of course.

"Heroes" give us hope! In a world that includes much despair and countless examples of the dark-side of mankind, heroes are beacons of light. Proof that regardless of how much danger, evil, and suffering may surround us, there also exists exceptionally-honorable people whom will, at unthinkable risk to themselves, defend and carryout the greater-good!

Yes, regardless of our age, sex, race, religion, political persuasion, favorite sport, food preference, chosen social media friends, etc. — we all need heroes in our lives. That is, "real" heroes, who truly measure-up to our individual needs and expectations. And hopefully seen as being such, in keeping with good judgment and common-sense. Including a level of insight that, for example, appropriately distinguishes between "childhood heroes," "adult heroes," and "virtual-reality heroes." Judgement that recognizes our "true heroes."

As a healthy contrast to the many "negatives" being constantly brought to our always media-connected and otherwise information-overwhelmed attention, we need people especially worthy of our respect and admiration. We need competent and trustworthy mentors, positive and constructive role models — and, we need "real heroes."

And while tossing these "opinions" around, I wish to take some respectful exception to Emerson's earlier referenced quotation. For a couple of reasons. One being that as worded (no doubt through oversight) it fails to include "women." Of whom countless have of course been, are, and one day will be — heroes and oracles. Another reason being, it is most unlikely, and certainly defiant of common sense, that "everyone" is a hero and oracle to someone. Yes, I know . . . Emerson is now coming out of his grave, and the "political correctness" squad is hastily plotting my demise!

Nevertheless, we **do not** live in a perfect world — and **not all of us** are heroes! As human beings, we all have our failings. Some among us being seriously flawed by nature; some through exercise of our free-will (our choices). And not all are blessed with mental and physical characteristics and aptitudes that fall within society-defined "normality." Furthermore, due to one or more of a multitude of reasons, many of us live our lives never presented with challenges that test one's ability and willingness to respond "heroically," or in an "oracle" manner. In short, from any sensible perspective, it simply defies all resemblance of sound reasoning and common-sense . . . to seriously consider that the entire human race has in the past responded heroically, and will do likewise in the present and future, when put to the test.

Likewise, with respect to being an oracle, we are awash with evidence all around us that not "all" of us are equipped to offer wise or authoritative decisions or opinions. And, of course, in the opinion of some readers — by way of this book I may well have "personally" demonstrated and affirmed such. If so, hopefully not to large and unrecoverable extent! Nevertheless, no amount of common-sense, reasoning, or evidence that the distinction of "hero" may not apply to "all" of us, will likely ever slow down the growing agenda of "political-correctness gone mad." An agenda insanely-driven to stamp-out "inequality" from the planet Earth. An ill-conceived and liberty-threatening mind-set insisting that everything be "fair" and "equal," that no one be "offended," that no one be "inferior" or "superior." That "everyone receive" a certificate or trophy for just "showing up." An agenda that ultimately leads to having "no heroes"—unless, that is, everyone either is or can be "the same." An agenda where no one is special, unless all are; that no act or behavior be considered special, unless all are. An agenda that ultimately leads to a world where **nothing** is OK—unless, **everything** is!

As we are led down this path of political-correctness absurdity, the "hero designation" continues to be diluted, abused, overused, and inconsistently used. For instance, some among us rubber-stamp "all" police personnel as unspeakable anti-citizen villains, while others declare them "all" heroes—regardless of individual circumstances and records of actual performance. Some treat our military personnel and veterans with disrespect and neglect, while others consider them "all" heroes. Again, regardless of individual circumstances and records of achievement. The outcome—a demeaning and otherwise damaging distraction from appropriate recognition of, and appreciation and respect for, the "true heroes" among us. Those of the past, present, and future.

And, for a little closer-to-home example. One of our local SE Kansas TV stations routinely includes a brief clip in its evening news broadcasts, each day recognizing a U.S. military veteran from the Four-state Area of Kansas, Missouri,

Oklahoma, and Arkansas. An obvious in-good-faith effort to show some much-due recognition and respect for our military personnel in general. But, again, this no doubt well-intended gesture doesn't stop at just appropriately recognizing our "veterans" . . . in keeping with political-correctness absurdity, **each** nominated (submitted) veteran is declared to be a "Four-state Hero." Once again, designated as such regardless of individual circumstances and records of achievement. A dramatic "180 degree" departure from the disrespect and other mistreatment countless Americans extended in years past to our to military personnel of the Vietnam War era. When the designation of "hero" was shamefully little-spoken—regardless of circumstances and sacrifice.

Well, at the risk of being misunderstood, accused of being unpatriotic, and barred from the human race, here's another opinion for consideration—"the job" alone doesn't make one a "hero." The various roles of our military are in fact "jobs", for which our military personnel are compensated by pay and other benefits. As is the case regarding the roles of our police, fire departments, wild-fire combatants, and the countless other "jobs" that peoples worldwide undertake each day.

Furthermore, being injured or killed on the job, or on the way to or from work, does not alone make one a "hero." Most if not "all" jobs involve risk. Think not? Then, for example, spend a few quality moments with the family of a loved one seriously injured or killed in a tragic accident on the way to or from or while at . . . "work." For, a severed-spine, lost limb, or lost life, are non-the-less a tragedy, whether the result of a bullet, bomb, auto-accident, private industry occupation, or otherwise. In likeness to countless others, as it turned out, the jobs I held while in the military involved considerably less risk and hazard than involved in many of the jobs I had in private industry. Of course, such circumstances are certainly not typical of all private-industry roles, or of all roles within our military. Especially regarding combat units and others assigned to areas of conflict.

In 1944, at the age of 37, my father was killed in a tragic mining accident. On a job in a hazardous industry that employed thousands of workers and reportedly furnished some one-third or more of all the lead used by the U.S. in World War II. Nevertheless, my dad's "job" or the "circumstances of his tragic death" did not make him a hero. About 24 years later I became employed at an Army Ammunition Plant in SE Kansas. A facility that, during peak operations, employed thousands of people, many of whom were involved with potentially hazardous operations. In 1988 two of those workers, a man and a woman, lost their lives during an accidental explosion of a weapon being produced for the U.S. war effort. Again, their jobs and the circumstances of their tragic deaths, did not make them heroes. If "tragedy" was the basis of denoting "heroism"—the earth would be covered with the grave-sites and living-presence of "heroes."

And, while digging this bottomless-pit of "opinions," at this point, it seems this section would be grossly incomplete without a few words about "**serving**." No doubt an also potentially emotional and highly controversial subject.

Nevertheless, for starters, I find it bordering on the absurd and repulsive that politicians who are compensated with salaries, healthcare, retirement benefits, and countless other perks—well above that ever to be realized by their average constituents—can with a straight face and good conscience even suggest that their jobs entail "serving" the people.

And, a little closer to home—around the age of 19, I was blessed with the opportunity to enlist in the Air Force. In doing so my reasons had absolutely nothing to do with "serving." To the contrary, my motives had everything to do with a sought-after career-opportunity. A way to better my employment prospects through military-offered training and experience in "electronics." A direction in life sparked at the time by a favorite uncle (an "oracle" to me), engaged at the time in a Navy career. Working in the career field of, yes, you guessed it—"electronics."

During my four years of state-side, non-combat time in the Air Force, I was associated with hundreds of military personnel of various ages, ranks, branches of military, and roles (military jobs). All of whom (including myself) were duly compensated with military pay and other benefits. None of whom (including myself) were considered, by ourselves or known others, as being heroes by virtue of "being in the military." None of whom (including myself) were, during our association with one another, ever confronted with circumstances presenting the opportunity to demonstrate, or fail to demonstrate, acts of heroism. Likewise, I know of none who ever expressed or otherwise evidenced to me that they had joined the military to "serve." Rather, in likeness to my circumstances, I found their motives to also be rooted in employment considerations and the prospects of self-improvement, etc. By way of an opportunity for military training and experience in their respective areas of personal interests and job-related fields of preference.

It is hopefully understood, that the personal experience and opinions shared in this section are in no way meant to say, or imply, that there are no heroes in the ranks of our active military, military reserves, or military veterans. Or that no one — past, present, and future — has been or will be driven to enter the military by an in-good-faith desire and intent to "serve." For, our nation is blessed by the fact that the designation of hero, and/or, the desire to serve, did in the past, do now, and will in the future, truly apply to an untold many. Those "uniquely" committed to the "greater good."

And, of course, known and unknown acts of heroism, past and present, are unquestionably great in number. A few are randomly summarized at the end of this section. Real-world examples showing that various jobs and circumstances — some more or less than others — can at times influence heroic behavior. That is, may involve the potential for being confronted with a challenge to respond, or fail to respond, in a heroic manner. Regardless of whether in the military, private industry, self-employed, or elsewhere. However, these same noteworthy examples also show that being a true hero often has little if anything to do with a "job." But, **always**, everything to do with "behavior." "Unique" human behavior.

Demonstrating exceptional achievement, distinguished courage, brave acts, and/or exceptionally noble qualities. Examples of the nature and quality of human "response" to formidable challenge that distinguishes our "**true heroes**." The exceptional ability and willingness that none of us will ever have "advance certainty" to exist (or not exist) within us. Until faced with our own—unpredictable challenge to sacrifice ourselves for the greater good! And, in the eyes of others—become a true "hero."

= = =

Edith Cavell: An otherwise ordinary nurse who, during World War I, sacrificed her own personal safety and welfare by helping soldiers escape from captivity. Truly heroic behavior for which she was executed by German authorities.

Chris Mintz: A 30 year old army veteran reportedly in stable condition in an Oregon hospital on October 2, 2015. Miraculously recovering from some 7 gunshot wounds received during a mass shooting on October 1, 2015 at the Umpqua Community College in Roseburg, Oregon, which left 10 people dead (including the attacker) and at least 9 seriously wounded. Seven gunshot wounds Chris Mintz received as he—while unarmed himself—tried to protect others in his classroom by selflessly and courageously confronting their heavily-armed, crazed attacker.

[The above being another massacre, by another mentally-deranged individual, at another "Gun-Free Zone," protected by another "unarmed security employee." The solution: Don't focus on mental illness; the untold hundreds of mental-health institutions closed over the past 50 years or so; and the growing and irresponsible sale and use of psychotropic drugs; etc. Instead, disregard our U.S. Constitution and prevent law-abiding citizens from having guns—from the right to defend themselves, their family, schools, churches, neighbors, and others. These intentionally-cynical words are of course aimed at the liberty and survival threatening agendas pushed by President Obama, various members of Congress, the Supreme Court, and others. Many of whom live and work in "gated or otherwise secured" areas, and are otherwise protected by security personnel armed with—"guns." People who— bordering on insanity-thinking themselves, just refuse to accept the indisputable fact that criminals, mentally-ill, terrorists, or otherwise crazed individuals don't give a damn about laws, regulations, the rights of others, or "Gun-Free zones." And, when they choose to do harm to others, they will find a way to do so. If not by "guns," then by knives, axes, poisons, automobiles, aircraft, explosives, fire, etc.]

Marcos Ugarte: A 14 year old young man who, in September 2011, at great risk to his own life, saved a neighbor's 8 year old son who was trapped in a room on the second floor of their burning home.

Anaiah Rucker: A 9 year old girl who, in February 2011, at unthinkable risk to her own life, saved her 5 year old sister from certain death, by pulling her out of the path of an unnoticed truck approaching their school bus stop, bearing the entire impact herself, and as a result, suffering serious injuries, including loss of a leg and a broken neck.

Lt. Brian Murphy & Officer Sam Lenda: Two police officers who received Congressional Badges of Bravery for their response to the deadly 2012 shooting rampage at the Sikh Temple of Oak Creek, Wisconsin. Lt. Murphy, for example, although shot nine times by the gunman while lending aid to an injured shooting victim, when police colleagues arrived he signaled them away from himself, urging them to first help others.

Elderly Fukushima Nuclear Disaster Volunteers: The hundreds of elderly volunteers willing to (in order to save younger men) exposed themselves to high radiation during massive clean-up and containment of hazardous waste from the March 2011 nuclear disaster at Japan's Fukushima Nuclear Power Plant. A nuclear disaster second only to the Soviet Union's Chernobyl disaster of 1986. Critically requiring work, certain to take years off of their lives and include suffering from cancers and other severe illness.

Anthony Omari: Who, as the only adult male on site at the time, and armed with only a hammer, and even after being seriously hacked in his head and face by a machete, nevertheless successfully fought off three armed attackers raiding an orphanage in Kenya operated by Anthony and his mother, home at the time for some 35 abandoned boys and girls.

Captain Steven Logan Bennett (1946-1972): In 1972, while flying on a mission in South Vietnam with his back-seater, Captain Mike Brown, their plane was hit by a SAM missile, damaging an engine, creating a fire, and engaging the left landing gear. After heading the plane to the water of the gulf so they could both eject, it was discovered that Brown's parachute had been damaged by the missile hit. Rather than ejecting to save himself, Bennet ditched the plane, knowing that would give Brown a chance to get out. In doing so, the plane flipped over and began sinking nose first. Captain Brown was picked up by a rescue craft; Captain Bennett's body was recovered the following day.

Sergei Preminin (1965-1986):   An enlisted Seaman in the Soviet Union Navy who, in my view, we in America, and in the rest of the World, owe immeasurable gratitude. A **true hero**, who too much of the World is unaware of. A Soviet Seaman, who at the age of 20, on October 3, 1986, selflessly and courageously sacrificed his life in order to prevent a catastrophic nuclear melt-down and explosion in the ocean waters off the East coast of our United States. An event that—given the Cold-War tensions at the time—most likely would have been (in my view and that of others) misinterpreted to be a nuclear attack on the U.S., leading to a nuclear response against the Soviet Union, which in turn would have set off a full-scale nuclear attack against the U.S., which overall, would have as a minimum killed, injured, and critically sickened countless millions world-wide. And if not a nuclear war, then as a minimum, catastrophic nuclear contamination of America's east coast and elsewhere. Either way, unthinkably changing forever, the nature of life remaining on this earth.

A brief overview of what happened: K-219 was a ballistic missile submarine of the Soviet Navy, capable of carrying 16 liquid-fuel missiles, equipped with an estimated 34 nuclear warheads. On October 3, 1986, while on patrol about 680 miles northeast of Bermuda, K-219 experienced a critical explosion and fire in one of its missile compartments, killing 3 sailors outright. In order to shut down its twin nuclear reactors, the ship was immediately surfaced. And, to get the remaining crew as far as possible away from the explosion site, they were issued gas masks and sent to the bow or stern. All too soon, the nuclear reactors indicated extremely high temperatures, and reactor coolant flow began to slow— meaning that to prevent an imminent nuclear meltdown, reactor emergency shut-down procedures had to be immediately carried out. But, the trigger of reactor control rods had been damaged, and emergency procedures could not be carried out remotely from the ships control station. The only option left was for men to enter the reactor chamber and "manually" lower 4 control rods into the reactor core by use of a hand-crank mechanism. A job exposing anyone carrying out this task to intense heat and deadly radiation from the reactor core, and requiring great physical strength due to control rods damaged by extreme heat. Nevertheless, the Reactor Department Officer, Nikolay Belikov and his subordinate, Seaman Sergei Preminin, opened the chamber hatch, entered, undertook the task, and managed to lower 3 of the 4 rods before Belikov lost consciousness. Seaman Preminin then volunteered to return to the reactor chamber by himself, and managed to complete the emergency shut-down procedure by lowering the fourth rod in place. But, exhausted and overcome by extreme heat and radiation exposure, he could not open the hatch in order to exit the reactor chamber. Nor could the men on the other side, due to the pressure difference built up between the reactor chamber and the control station. Seaman Preminin died alone in the unbearably hot reactor chamber, while, in order to escape rapidly spreading poisonous gases, the remaining crew had to move as far as possible to the rear sections of the ship.

<u>Some Monuments, Honors, and Special Recognition Posthumously-Awarded to Soviet Seaman Sergei Preminin</u>

Monuments honoring Seaman Sergei Preminin have been erected in the cities of Gadzhiyevo and Krasawino. In Gadzhiyevo, a road and two school are also named after him. In his native Skornyakoyo, his heroism is honored by a marble plaque, with an inscription that says: **"To Russian Seaman Sergei Preminin, who has saved the world from a nuclear catastrophe."** Posthumously-awarded honors have included: Order of the Red Star, by decree of Presidium of the Supreme Soviet of the USSR, July 23, 1987; Hero of Russia Medal, August 7, 1997; and Medal of the Order of Service to the Fatherland, October 31, 2003. [While to this day, too many of us in the U.S., and elsewhere in the World, remain unaware of his selfless and tremendously- courageous contribution to humankind. And of the unthinkable consequences had he not so courageously and self-sacrificingly "chosen to" and been "capable of" indisputably being . . . a **"True Hero."**]

= = =

"Heroes are ordinary people who make themselves extraordinary."

–Gerard Way

Old Ammo Plant Buildings—
"More than Just a Hazard"

"To look backward for a while is to refresh the eye, to restore it, and to render it the more fit for its prime function of looking forward."
— *Margaret Fairless Barber*

"We do not remember days; we remember moments."
— *Cesare Pavese*

The June 14-15, 2014 issue of our local newspaper, the Parsons Sun, included a front-page article entitled "Plant buildings still a hazard." A very interesting piece highlighting some of the hidden dangers involved with hazardous waste cleanup at the former ammunition plant east of Parsons.

As an example of such dangers, the article noted that various community members recently had an opportunity to review photos from demolition of Building 706, located in the Plant's 700 Area. A progression of photos—"first showing a dust cloud blowing out the side of the building close to ground level, followed by parts of the building's roof shooting higher into the sky." In emphasizing the risks associated with environmental cleanup efforts at this particular site, the article appropriately included the rhetorical question, "Can you imagine if someone was using a drill or a jackhammer in there?" A non-rhetorical, knowledgeable, and very experienced answer to that question is—"Yes . . . many of us blessed to *yet be above ground* (so-to-speak) certainly can "well-imagine," . . . and, over the many years past, countless others also once could."

For many individuals, the nature of hazards mentioned in the Sun's June 14-15 issue was once "very real, up close, and personal." As, dealing with the inherent dangers involved with production of military ammunition, was once a "routine part" of the daily work experience of many. Over a period of some 68 years, from the plant's construction in 1941 until its final closure.

Explosions involving the loss of certain 700 Area process building roofs, and/or damage to processing equipment, etc., were at times relatively-frequent occurrences. In the not too distant past, a sometimes weekly and often monthly experience. An inherent result of the extremely sensitive nature of the particular "initiating-explosives" involved, and the then available state-of-the-art processes.

All production, test, demolition, etc., areas at the ammunition plant east of Parsons dealt with various types of explosives and their respective dangers (i.e., the 300, 500, 700, 800, 900, 1000, 1100, and 1200, Production Areas; 2000 Area Test Range; and the Demolition and Burning Grounds, etc.). However, 700 Area operations involved "initiating explosives"—those most sensitive to heat, impact, friction, static electricity, etc. Extremely hazardous explosive materials such as, Mercury Fulminate—primarily in use during World War II operations—and Lead Azide, Lead Styphnate, and Tetracene, used during the later Korean War and Vietnam War operations. Explosives entailing unique risks and special safety challenges. And, although (regardless of location) the more hazardous plant operations were done "remotely" and with the use of "protective barricades"—the inherent dangers that any and all explosives/ammunition operations pose, were nonetheless ever-present.

During the Vietnam War era, and while the overall Plant head-count approached 4,000 or so—work in the 700 Area once involved a three-shift operation staffed with well over 300 employees. People drawn from an approximate 50-mile radius of the Parsons area. Their job related efforts and achievements were many. The following examples offer but a very generalized snapshot of a much broader and more meaningful reality.

During the timeframe of 1967 to the latter part of YR2000, the production output of the 700 Area included (but was not limited to) at least 778 million Detonators and 311 million Lead Cup Assemblies. Items used to trigger the larger explosive payloads in various types of military ammunition.

Furthermore, the 700 Area's impressive output was routinely delivered with higher quality and at less cost than that from competing plants. Very noteworthy achievements at the time—not only from the good efforts the 700 Area employees, but also from the likewise competent jobs carried out by the various supporting plant functions. Very challenging accomplishments realized while dealing with some of the more sensitive and hazardous explosives in use at the time.

But the these awesome quantities and quality of 700 Area produced items were not without human cost — serious injury to a relative but nonetheless most significant few, while remarkably with no fatalities. A safety record unfortunately not experienced at all production areas at the Kansas AAP, nor by various other facilities elsewhere in the U.S. For example, in 1989 a devastating explosion occurred during 1100 Area production operations at the Kansas Army Ammunition Plant. Costing two lives and injuring at least 4 others (unnamed herein out of the deepest respect and consideration for those lost and injured, and likewise for their loved ones).

Common-sense alone dictates that working with, in, and around any explosives, and the production of any military ammunition, anywhere, at any time, can involve considerable risk. Nevertheless, military explosives and ammunition operations nation-wide have for years maintained one of the best "safety records" as compared to other industries. Overall, an exceptional record resulting from considerable effort, and of course driven by necessity. "Necessity," in that our military must always have access to uninterrupted and as-required supplies of ammunition. And, obviously . . . damaged or destroyed ammunition production facilities, and facilities that injure or kill the needed work force, can critically disrupt the availability of required ammunition support. Hence, the primary basis of the long-standing "in-our-national-interests" necessity of extra special attention to all aspects of safety at all such military-support facilities.

But, regardless of the level of effort focused on safety— production of military explosives and ammunition has, over the many years, involved the ruined health, serious injuries, and loss of life, for an untold many at various work sites nation-wide. And, at times, the catastrophic damage to, or loss of, various military-support production facilities.

Some Additional History: The Kansas Ordnance Plant (KOP) was a 26.9 square mile, 17,214 acres (later reduced to 13,727 acres) government-owned, contractor-operated (GOCO) facility located east of Parsons, Kansas. Construction of the plant started August 18, 1941; by July 14, 1942 it was in full operation.

The facility consisted of some 745 buildings; 1,922,000 square feet of floor space; 122.6 miles of road; 29.6 miles of railroad; 8 Production Areas (300 Area; 500 Area; 700 Area; 800 Area; 900 Area; 1000 Area; 1100 Area; 1200 Area). Each area spanning, according to the nature of its particular operations, a linear distance of approximately one-fourth to three-fourths of a mile. Also included in the facility—the many likewise essential Production-Support Areas. Such as: an Administrative Area (involving functions such as, Operating Contractor Executive Management, Production/Operations, Safety, Training, Contracts, Human Resources, Purchasing, Plant Security, Engineering, Program Management, Environmental, Information Systems, Quality Assurance,

Technical Services, Quality Systems Audits, Production Control, Payroll, Offices Services, Medical; and various on-site Department of Army Administrative functions). As well as, at various other locations, a Gage (Metrology) Lab; Chemistry Lab; Fire Department; Central Maintenance Area (involving functions such as, Machine Shop, Millwright Shop, Carpenter Shop, Paint Shop, Electrical and Electronic Shops, Pipe/Plumbing Shop); Warehousing & Assets; Roads & Grounds; Stores and Transportation; Ammunition Test Ranges; Demolition and Hazardous Waste Disposal Areas; Water Filtration, Sewage Disposal, and hundreds of above-ground warehouses and storage magazine structures; etc.

The Kansas Ordnance Plant (KOP)—later renamed the Kansas Army Ammunition Plant (KSAAP), or Kansas AAP— being but "one" of the U.S. Army's 35 or more industrial ammunition-related operations facilities once in operation throughout the United States.

From August 1941 to August 1945 the plant supported World War II, during which a total of 25,673 people had been employed (the maximum people in one day peaking at 7,358), and 1,081,027 tons of ammunition were produced (or about 27,000 railcar shipments), valued at the time at $550 million. Consisting of: 575,723 Bombs, 36,089,000 Artillery Shells, and 78,591,000 Artillery Shell Components (Fuzes, Detonators, Boosters, Primers, and Supplementary Charges). The lumber used during this first production period to crate, box and brace ammunition for shipment, was enough to build 16,000 five-room modern houses. The number of nails used on this lumber, if laid end to end, would reach 33,350 miles, or 1 and 1/ times around the earth. In September 1945 the facility was placed in standby status.

From August 1950 through July 1957 the plant was reactivated to support the Korean War. During which, ammunition production included: 30.8 million fuses; 57.1 million Delays; 42.2 million Boosters; 29.4 million Supplementary Charges; 188.7 million Detonators; 71.2 million Delays; 22.3 million Primers; 21.2 million 105mm Shells; 8.4 million Cartridge Cases; and, 400 thousand Bombs (from 100 to 750 pound class). In August 1957 the plant was again placed in standby status.

In 1966 the KOP was reactivated to support the Vietnam War, and re-named the Kansas Army Ammunition Plant (KSAAP). Thereafter, operations continued at a range of different production levels, and under various contractual arrangements, for support of the Gulf War and Global War on Terrorism, etc. With employment ranging from about 200 to more than 4,000. During this time frame, ammunition production items included, as a minimum: 271,276,000 HE Grenades (M42, M46, M77); 7,140 SMAW-D Warheads; 2,315 ESMB Units; 270,041,500 Lead Cup Assemblies; 766, 380,000 M55 Detonators; 8,000,000 Booster Assemblies; 234,220 M864 Projectiles HE; 46,500 BDG155C Projectiles; 2,375,312 M483A1 Projectiles HE; 4,250 C76A1 Projectiles HE; 10,000 M106 Projectiles HE; 7,000 M107 Projectiles HE; 7,000 M549 Projectiles HE; 34,000,000 CTG. 105MM MI HE; 10,000,000CTG. 81MM HE; 296,997 81MM Body Loading

Assy.; 1,481 120MM Body Loading Assy.; 1,920 Payload Module Assy. for Cruise Missiles; 147,500 CBU (CEM); 115,000 CBU 24 A/B; 50,000 CBU 49 A/B; 2,186 CBU (SFW); 30,000,000 BLU 97; 89,879 Warheads/SFW; 201 Rockeye Units; 5,600,000 Primers M28B2; 5,751,044 Expulsion Charge Assemblies (51GM, 54GM, 58GM, 65GM, 70GM, 105GM, 130GM); 6,200,000 XM716 Fuzes; 562,000 XM717 Fuzes; 15,080 MT238 Fuzes; 6,500 Grams KDNBF Explosive; 300 MK71 Detonators; 30 Munition Dispenser Units; etc.

Since its construction in 1941, manufacturing processes evolved over the years from basic artillery rounds and their components, to sophisticated air-dropped weapons using infrared and laser technology target detection and guidance systems. Although an "Army Ammunition Plant—its customers included not only the U.S. Army, but also the Air Force, Marine Corps, and Navy; as well as various U.S. Government-approved foreign countries. And, on March 4, 2009, some 68 years after initial construction, the Kansas Army Ammunition Plant (KSAAP) was deactivated as a part of the Department of Defense (DOD) 2005 Base Realignment and Closure Commission—officially ending the KSAAP's ammunition production mission with the Army.

Yes, to thousands of folks, the many "old buildings" at what was originally named the KOP, and later the KSAAP, were once much more than an environmental hazard to a plant-closure effort. They were a work place, a source of income, the origin of meaningful relationships, experiences, and cherished memories. And, to some, a never to be forgotten place where their loved ones were seriously injured, or lost their health or their lives. As also likely the case with other such facilities nation-wide, such as: Anniston Army Depot; Badger AAP; Blue Grass Army Depot; Charleston/U.S. Army Combat Equipment Group-Asia; Corpus Christi Army Depot; Crane AAA; Hawthorne Army Depot; HQ IOC/Rock Island Arsenal/U.S. Army War Reserve Support Command (Provisional); Holston AAP; Indiana AAP; Iowa AAP, **Kansas AAP**; Lake City AAP; Letterkenny Army Depot; Lone Star AAP; Longhorn AAP; Louisiana AAP; McAlester AAP; Milan AAP; Mississippi AAP; Pine Bluff Arsenal; Radford AAP; Ravenna AAP; Red River Army Depot; Riverbank AAP; Savanna / USADACS; Scranton AAP; Seneca Army Depot Activity; Sierra Army Depot; Sunflower AAP; Tobyhanna Army Depot; Tooele Army Depot; Twin Cities AAP; Volunteer AAP; and Watervliet Arsenal.

Considering the subject, and elaboration on various details, this section may be of limited interest to persons unfamiliar with the military ammunition industry. On the other hand, same info may well be meaningful in some way to countless other folks nation-wide. Those associated (in the past, present, or future) personally, or through family, friends, or other relationships, with one or more of above mentioned military-support facilities. Whether such facilities still exist, or are but a memory—of some *old plant buildings*. Facilities that, to some, may for a while remain much more than *just a present-day environmental hazard*.

A Few Words about The Military-Industrial Complex: Our nation cannot long exist without the protection of a sufficiently-strong military. One respectful of the sovereignty (supreme power and authority) of its citizens. Likewise, no military can long stand, nor be victorious, without sufficient ammunition.   And, military weapons cannot exist without support from the public treasury and other citizens' and social sacrifice.   Truly, nothing in life is "free."   Someone pays, someone sacrifices. Nontheleast, for our national security — without which, it is unlikely much else would long matter.

But, in all things, "balance" is crucial. And, as noted — **and warned** — in the quotation below, "we the people" must be ever-mindful of the potential threat to our nation and our liberty, should we ever lose civilian control over the **"military-industrial complex"** (that "mix" of our military and the many military-arms industries supplying it).   For instance, should we fail to recognize and correct a self-perpetuating, "joint military and arms-supplier" existence — one that is nation-destructively feeding off of the public treasury. And/or one that contributes overtly or covertly to our nation's involvement in unnecessary war or other military conflicts.

= = =

"In the councils of government, we must guard against the acquisition of unwarranted influence, whether sought or unsought, by the military industrial complex. The potential for the disastrous rise of misplaced power exists and will persist." — Dwight D. Eisenhower, 34th U.S. President, January 17, 1961, farewell speech.

Accidents Don't Just Happen—
They are Caused!

"An ounce of prevention is worth a pound of cure."

— Benjamin Franklin

"The only purpose for which power can be rightfully exercised over any member of a civilized community against his will is to prevent harm to others." — John Stuart

According to Occupational Safety & Health Administration (OSHA) records—4,679 U.S. workers died on the job in 2014. Men and women, young and old—suffering fatal "accidents." While "working"—for many reasons. Most often in order to sustain and otherwise benefit themselves, their families, and/or others of special importance in their lives. Some compensated more than others. Some treated differently than others. Some considering their "work" a fulfilling opportunity. Some seeing it as otherwise. While, most—if not all—having the natural mindset that "accidents" are and will typically be the "random" misfortune of "someone else." And, through innocent-ignorance or deliberate-denial, too often inattentive to the fact that "accidents don't just happen—they are caused. By someone. The result of something we or others do, or fail to do. And therefore, from a reasonably logical view—accidents are "preventable." At least those involving much of human activity and behavior.

Of course, someone caught in an unforeseen meteor shower, just might, for instance, feel strongly otherwise.

At the time OSHA was created, some 43 years ago, estimates show that every year about 14,000 workers lost their lives on the job. As opposed to many other countries, a growing number of U.S. workplaces are now considerably safer and healthier. Due to a mix of reasons, no doubt including OSHA regulations, inspections, and related penalties. And today, rather than the approximate 38 fatal injuries a day of the 43 years ago time frame, fatal injuries in the U.S. have reportedly dropped to about 12 daily (or about 4,380 each year).

While a basis for encouragement can be found in the above noted trends, further improvement is often hampered by various factors. Nontheleast being our inattention to, as earlier stressed, sound evidence that "prevention" is a logical and effective defense against "accidents." Furthermore — often slipping our minds — we truly don't have to be in military combat, or an iron-worker constructing a big-city skyscraper, or producing military ammunition, or carrying out an experimental deep-sea dive, etc., etc., etc. — in order to become seriously or fatally injured from an "accident." For, among the **major and on-going causes** of serious injury and death — at home and on the job — are **"slips, trips, and falls!** And, while these "accidents" are often especially-aided by nature's otherwise blessings of rain, snow, and ice. Such can nonetheless still be "prevented" by slowing down, paying more attention, wearing proper footwear, making sure stairs and steps are kept free of clutter, and proper use of ladders and step-stools, etc.

What "accidents" have to do with "threats to our liberty and survival" should call for little thought. The connection between a "fatal accident" and "survival," of course being clear. While, "in advance of" a serious non-fatal accident — it being not so obvious how such can impact our mental and/or physical liberty/freedom. Our liberty/freedom to think and act "by ourselves" — without the mental or physical assistance of others, available handicap equipment, etc.

As long as we are blessed with good health and absence of injury, it becomes easy to overlook that accidental injury and accidental death are among the many ever-present potential threats that surround us. And, as discussed in the earlier section titled, "Survival," — our ability to survive depends upon our how well we "recognize," "acknowledge," and "have effective defenses against," our threats. Including those posed by potential "accidents." Those misfortunes that, again stressed, are often considered as applying to "someone else."

Workplace injuries statistics are countless in terms of available sources and content. The few provided in the following Table are a far from all-inclusive "snap-shot." Nevertheless, a hopefully revealing and otherwise meaningful look at some very real and present threats. Ones we truly need to "recognize," "acknowledge," and "prepare effective defenses against." Yes, again — for the sake of our liberty and survival.

10 Leading Causes and Direct Costs of Workplace Injuries in 2012 (Re: Bureau of Labor Statistics and the National Academy of Social Insurance.)			
Rank	Cause	Direct Cost	Percent
1	Overexertion *	$15.1 Billion	25.3%
2	Falls on same level	$9.19 Billion	15.4%
3	Struck by object or equipment	$5.3 Billion	8.9%
4	Falls to lower level	$5.12 Billion	8.6%
5	Other exertions ** or bodily reactions	$4.27 Billion	7.2%
6	Roadway incidents involving motorized land vehicles	$3.18 Billion	5.3%
7	Slip or trip without fall	$2.17 Billion	3.6%
8	Caught in/compressed by equip. or objects	$2.1 Billion	3.5%
9	Repetitive motions involving micro-tasks	$1.84 Billion	3.1%
10	Struck against object or equipment	$1.76 Billion	2.9%

*Overexertion: Injuries typically related to lifting, pushing, pulling, holding, carrying or throwing. ****Other exertions:** Injuries typically due to bending, crawling, reaching, twisting, climbing, stepping, kneeling, sitting, standing or walking.

Falls: The Accident Fund Insurance Company of America and United Heartland recently reported that about one-third of all Midwestern workers' comp claims with lost time were due to slips and falls on ice and snow.

Most Common Risks: Overall, slips/trips and falls, or damage caused by manual handling/lifting, remain the main culprits of injury in the workplace.

Most Common Causes of Occupational Fatalities: Falls, machine-related incidents, motor vehicle accidents, electrocution, falling objects, homicides, and suicides.

Worker characteristics — Fatal Occupational Injuries

(Re: Bureau of Labor Statistics, Census of Fatal Occupational Injuries Summary, 2014, Reported September 17, 2015.)

Fatal injuries to self-employed workers: Rose 10 percent in 2014 to 1,047, up from 950 in 2013. Although higher than in 2013, the 2014 preliminary total for self-employed workers is about the same as the 10-year average for the series. Fatal injuries among wage and salary workers remained at about the same level as in 2013.

Fatal work injuries involving workers age 45 to 54 years, 55 to 64 years, and 65 years of age and over: All increased in 2014 compared to 2013 totals. The number of workers 55 years and over who were fatally injured in 2014 increased 9 percent to 1,621, the highest annual total since the inception of the fatality census in 1992. [Workers of a wide variety of ages are included in the 2014 counts – 8 workers under the age of 16 are included as well as 8 workers age 90 and over.]

Fatal injuries among women: Rose 13 percent in 2014 to 359 from 319 in 2013. Fatal work injuries among men in 2014 were slightly higher than the previous year. Consistent with previous years, men accounted for 92 percent of all fatal occupational injuries.

Injuries and Death due to Accidents at Home: Reportedly, each year Americans suffer over 13 million injuries and some 18,000 deaths due to injuries from accidents at home. Making fatalities from home accidents second only to those from motor vehicle accidents. And, as the case with workplace injury statistics, those available concerning home injury deaths, for example, are likewise countless in terms of source and content. The table below provides only a glance.

The Top Five Causes of Home Injury Deaths (re: Home Safety Council)		
Rank	Cause	Lives Lost Each Year (Approx.)
1	Falls	6,000
2	Poisoning (Actually, #1 cause of accidental home injury deaths for young adults and the middle-aged.)	5,000
3	Fire and Burns	3,000
4	Airway Obstruction (Includes choking, suffocation, & strangulation.)	1,000
5	Water (A special threat to children.)	800

To supplement common-sense accident prevention practices, the Internet is of course engulfed with sources for **home-safety tips**, detailed information, and other **accident prevention aids**. Information worthy of our responsible attention, in that accidents – whether at home, on the job, or elsewhere – "are caused." By something we do – or fail to do.

= = =

"For safety is not a gadget but a state of mind." – Eleanor Everet

"Better a thousand times careful than once dead." – Proverb Proverb

"Accidents, and particularly street and highway accidents, do not happen – they are caused." – Ernest Greenwood

"Growing-up Risks"
& "Simple Affordable Interventions"

Growing-up: Maturing; coming of age. **Risks**: *Exposures to danger.* **Simple**: *Easily understood and done.* **Affordable**: *Inexpensive; reasonably priced.* **Intervention**: *The action or process of "intervening."* **Intervene**: *To come between so as to prevent or alter a result or course of events.*

According to the National Vital Statistics System, average life expectancy in the United States is about 79 years. A life-span too often cut tragically short for a heart-breaking number of children. For example, the little 3-year old girl who died in June 2014 in a neighboring state, reportedly from a gunshot wound. A terrible loss likely ruled as "accidental" — regardless of the reality that accidents don't just happen — they are caused. The result of something we do or fail to do. No matter how unexpected; how unintentional — accidents are nevertheless "caused."

Young children face countless dangers growing up. Potential injury and death from predators, guns, knives, poisons, burns, electrocution, falls, drowning, suffocation, strangulation, lawn movers, automobiles, and mood-altering psychotropic drugs pushed by drug companies and irresponsible medical practitioners, etc. — to list but a few. And, children are at the mercy of "adults" for protection from such threats. The World Health Organization reports that worldwide about **6.6 million children under age 5 died in 2012** and that <u>more than half</u> of early child deaths are due to conditions that can be prevented by **"simple affordable interventions."** Not letting young children have unsupervised access to guns, knives, medications, poisons, power tools, lawn mowers, ladders, etc., seem to be some **"simple affordable interventions."** According to a relatively new report from the Federal Center for Disease Control and Prevention, for children under age 5, drowning is a leading cause of accidental death, with rates even surpassing those of traffic accident fatalities in recent years. Again, not leaving young children unattended and unsupervised in and around bathtubs, swimming pools, rivers, lakes, streams, etc., seems to be a **"simple affordable intervention."** The World Health Organization also reports that overweight or obese infants and young children (5 years and under) increased worldwide from 32 million in 1990 to 42 million in 2013. And at current trends will be 70 million by 2025. Leading to higher risk of heart disease, Type II diabetes, cancer, and other diseases. As of 2015, it is estimated there are 2.3 billion overweight adults in the world; 700 million being obese. Truly, there are family history, medical, and other exceptions, etc. But for the many potentially-fortunate others, a **"simple affordable intervention"** might rest in caloric restriction (healthier diet) and daily vigorous exercise.

Yet, among the "realities" of the young and old, and childhood and parenting, there are times and circumstances where **"simple"** is **"simply"** nonexistent, or not recognizable.

= = =

"The art of simplicity is a puzzle of complexity." – Douglas Horton

No
"Personal Downtime"
Anymore

2013 statistics reported by the Center for Disease Control and Prevention (CDC) show the 10 leading causes of death in the U.S. to be as follows:

- Heart disease: 611,105
- Cancer: 584,881
- Chronic lower respiratory diseases: 149,205
- Accidents (unintentional injuries): 130,557
- Stroke (cerebrovascular diseases): 128,978
- Alzheimer's disease: 84,767
- Diabetes: 75,578
- Influenza and Pneumonia: 56,979
- Nephritis, nephrotic syndrome, and nephrosis: 47,112
- Intentional self-harm (suicide): 41,149

The National Highway Traffic Safety Administration (NHTSA) has reported that in 2013, 10,076 people died in drunk driving crashes — one every 53 minutes, and another 290,000 injured in such crashes. In 2012, over 29 million people admitted to driving under the influence of alcohol — a number greater than the entire population of Texas! In August 2015 the National Coalition for Safer Roads (NCSR) reported that, since 2004, accidents involving "red-light running" have claimed the lives of some 7,799.

Added to the above unsettling statistics — growing thousands of nationwide auto accidents, injuries, and deaths are in fact being caused by drivers of all ages who are <u>texting-while-driving</u>. Including (but not limited to) more than 3,000 U.S. teens each year. With texting-while-driving now the leading cause of death among teenagers in the U.S. — surpassing those killed in drunk driving accidents.

But, what do the above statistics have to do with *"no personal downtime anymore"*? A short answer: Unquestionably, a lot! A more meaningful explanation is offered by way of the following in-good-faith blend of facts, opinions, observations, and experiences. And, while being mindful of individual circumstances — whether one chooses to, or not to, find an opportunity to read the remainder of this section, just might be further testimony of *"no personal downtime anymore."* On the other hand, such may be nothing more than a conscious decision regarding how to best use one's *"blessing of time."*

"Unlimited-Options" & "Ever-Growing Distractions": The survival of all things important to us—especially life, liberty, and pursuit of happiness—greatly depend upon our responsible attention to some "basics." None the least, being "aware" of our *needs* and of the *threats* around us. And having the "ability and willingness" to effectively deal with both. Aided, of course, by the ability to analyze circumstances and make good choices. These being some survival basics—some essentials—that are being seriously challenged! By the *unlimited-options* and *ever-growing distractions* of our increasingly complex world. A world that more and more seems to also leave us with *"no personal-downtime anymore."* The following are a few examples for consideration:

"Always Connected"
& "Often Oblivious to Our Surroundings"

However, before getting into the following examples concerning "no personal-downtime anymore," here's a few words of explanation about "tech-terms": In trying to avoid the abyss of ever-changing technical terminology, please note that **"new-media"**—as used within this book—refers to: **on-demand user access to, and interactivity with, digital information/content anytime and anywhere.** Such as: voice, text, e-mail, music, still/video pictures, video games, movies, e-commerce, social networks, other internet websites, etc. Using any compatible digital device, such as, mobile/smart phones, e-tablets, video game consoles, MP3 players, PC/laptop computers, wearable e-devices, etc.

"Motorcycle Ride": During the summer of 2014, in a small Southeast Kansas town (population, about 10,500), two people on a motorcycle are traveling west on Main Street. Solely by chance, my wife Ann is following in our auto immediately behind the cycle. The driver of the cycle is a young lady, the passenger a young man. The driver's head is extremely tilted to the left against her shoulder. As the cycle and other vehicles come to a halt at a stoplight, the reason for the cycle driver's oddly positioned head becomes clear. While carrying out the various tasks involved with operating a motorcycle, transporting her passenger, and negotiating traffic, etc., the cycle driver also appears to be conversing through a mobile/smart phone clinched tightly between the top of her left shoulder and her cheek!

"To and From School": We live near a High School and Grade School situated on adjoining grounds. The streets and pedestrian walks surrounding these two school facilities span a total length of a little less than one mile — an exercise walking-route we and others often use. Casually observed at times are students, teachers, and others as they arrive or depart. As well as various parents as they drop off or pick up their children in front of their particular school building. Depending on parking space and drop-off/pick-up spot, the distance from the street to the front door of either school building is about 50 to 75 feet or so. A distance that a few of the young and not so young seem unable to travel without being visually/audio *connected* to their mobile/smart phone. As they walk to or from the front door — seemingly oblivious to their surroundings. Likewise, some adults seem unable to stop their vehicle for a brief moment in front of the grade school—to drop-off or pick-up their children—without being *connected* with their mobile/smart phone. No doubt taking care of some texting, talking, internet search, social-media post, or other **new-media** activity calling for priority above-all-else handling. Possibly interrupting what might otherwise be one of those very-special child and parent moments.

"Riding Horseback": U.S. Highway 59 passes through our hometown from the north and south. Not long ago, while traveling south and only a few miles from our town's city limits, we noticed a young lady riding a beautiful horse—just inside the fence of a field adjoining the west side of the highway we were traveling on. It was a nice summer morning, and from our highway-view the horse and rider portrayed such a beautiful picture and relaxing moment. A special opportunity for the lucky rider and horse to mutually enjoy the peace and tranquility of the great outdoors. A time for some special human and horse bonding. As the horse very slowly ambled along it was noticeable that the reins were not in in the rider's hands, but instead lay draped across the back of the horse's strong neck and beautiful mane. While the *new-media connected* rider had clutched in her hands—not the reins—but a mobile/smart phone that she appeared to be deeply engaged with. Sadly, from our perspective, her mind likely oblivious to much of her surroundings, and the special moment it portrayed from our view. Possibly missing a unique opportunity—an increasingly-difficult-to-find chance for some truly-quality *personal-downtime*.

"Eating Out": Next time you "go out" for breakfast, lunch or dinner, take a good look at what is going on (or not going on) around us. *[Even if putting away one's own personal e-device for a moment is necessary.]* Note the number of adults and children who cannot *just* enjoy a nice meal, that is, without being *new-media-connected* at some point during, or throughout, the meal. Note also the growing numbers of TV's, e-tablets, e-menus, e-tabletops, and other new-media devices, being built into the customer accommodations at more and more restaurants and other public places. Notwithstanding the mix of new-media devices that are now optional/standard equipment in our automobiles and other forms of transportation. Catering to our ever-growing craving to be forever *"connected."* Through technology and distractions that can help "save us" from the unspeakable fate of *just* enjoying a good meal, and from the rapidly disappearing-experience of face-to-face conversation with others. And from the becoming-lost-arts of verbal communications, eye contact, body language, and other human interactions — once unaided and unfiltered by new-media technology.

No Time for "Just" Anything: Whether the result of preventable or uncontrollable circumstances — there now seems to be no time for *just* a motorcycle ride; no time to *just* walk to the front door of a school; no time to *just* drop off or pickup our children at school; no time for *just* a relaxing horse-ride on a beautiful day. And, certainly, no time to *just* focus on responsibly driving a vehicle, regardless of the risks to one's self and others for failing to do so! Regardless of the risk of injury, death, and destruction of property. Texting, tweeting, phone conversations, social-media chatter, and other potentially-deadly distractions can't wait! Yes, no longer is there time for *"just"* anything. And, especially no room for some potentially health-improving, sanity-maintaining, and otherwise life-saving *"personal-downtime."*

Multi-Tasking Gone Mad: To aid us in our unrelenting efforts to cram *two-pounds-of-life* into a *one-pound bag* — coming to our rescue, the double-edged sword of *technology*! A life-saving and otherwise benefit to the human race in countless ways. And, on the other hand, the source of overwhelming distractions and otherwise threats to our wellbeing. Regarding the latter, for example, with the aid of technology we now no longer need be bored by focus on any *"single"* endeavor. Seemingly to most anything we are involved in, we can now add about as many distractions as we (and others around us) can tolerate. At our fingertips — our new-media connection! Potential 24/7 access to social networks, e-mail, blogs, chats, skype, work, shared photographs, videos, tweets, texting, e-shopping, e-games, e-books, news, political propaganda, streaming radio and movies, and countless other competing distractions.

And with our countless "distraction-options" freshly in mind — seriously consider for a moment, what may actually be on the minds of the "drivers." Of those multi-thousand pound vehicles we will "so closely" meet, when next traveling our streets and highways. Such thoughts are unsettling — and they should be! If not, maybe another more serious look at the auto-accident stats at the beginning of this section is called for.

Some special focus on not-so-simple "Downtime":

A very brief and over-simplified definition of "downtime" would be: *A time of inactivity or reduced activity.* However, it involves a subject far from simple. For, "downtime" is found throughout nature, government, business, and even in our human design.

In **government**, our politicians often threaten, create, and use disruptions (downtime) in government operations and services, in order to advance support for certain partisan policies and agendas, etc. And to manipulate our votes and other behavior.

In **business**, downtime is generally viewed as *"time during which some type of business **machine, process, or facility**, is out of action or unavailable for use."* It is commonly understood that machines, processes, and facilities, must from time to time be updated, upgraded, repaired, restored, renovated, and otherwise maintained. Given this reality, if planned downtime is used to carry these critical activities, it can be an important and beneficial part of a successful business plan. However, if unplanned and unprepared for, business downtime can have very costly and otherwise serious consequences. Such as, late or missed deliveries of products, unavailable customer services, disappointed or lost customers, failure to comply with contracts and regulatory requirements. As well as, potential fines, penalties, lost business income and profits, as well as the risk of bankruptcy, etc.

As a result, many businesses dedicate considerable resources for emergency backup and standby capabilities, and sophisticated preventative maintenance programs, in an effort to eliminate, minimize, or otherwise manage and control, any and all unplanned business disruptions—downtime. From the employees' point of view business downtime can also mean lost, delayed, or otherwise disrupted: workdays, salaries, wages, benefits, jobs, lifestyle, health, and general wellbeing.

With respect to **nature** and our **human design**, "downtime" provides our bodies and minds with the opportunity to refresh and rejuvenate. We and other creatures rest, nap, sleep—some also hibernate. Our hearts even take a rest break between beats! In turn, most if not all plant life includes some form of inactivity or reduced activity in its seasonal cycle of growing, flowering, setting seed, etc.

Being *individuals,* our needs of course vary. But, common to "all" of us is our need for some *personal-downtime.* Time for our bodies and minds to get proper rest, relaxation, and sleep. Time to repair, restore, rejuvenate, unwind, step off of the treadmill. Time to reflect and meditate—to see, feel, smell, hear, taste, and otherwise appreciate "life's many roses."

Ignoring or being deprived of these basic needs can have very serious consequences. Such as, to randomly mention but a few: on-the-job and off-the-job accidents and injuries; impaired judgment; poor mental and physical performance; job-related and family-related burn-out; loss of employment;

missed opportunities; damaged or destroyed personal relationships; deteriorating physical and mental health; premature death; etc.

Never Enough "Time": Generally speaking, we are often pretty good at accepting the need, finding the time, and dedicating the money and effort, to take care of our "machines" — our "stuff." Unfortunately, such is too often not the case when it comes to taking care of ourselves. Too easily and too often ignored are the personal-downtime needs of our mind and body. Our typical reason (more often, excuse) — not enough time for such. Not even with the benefit of the ever-growing conveniences and time-savers provided by the Industrial Revolution years ago, later by the Internet, and more recently by the new-media age. Still, it seems there is never enough *time* for everything! Certainly not enough *time* to be informed, active, and responsible voters.

Long, long ago, our ancestors had to spend most if not all of their time in search of food and shelter. And on efforts to survive the countless known and unknown threats they faced. Today, while millions continue to suffer many of life's devastating circumstances and misfortunes, many more-fortunate others have access to countless "time-saving" conveniences. **Such as (to mention but a few):** frozen food, canned food, pre-cooked food, fast-food, drive-thru food, catered-food, home-delivered food, eating-out food, walk-in banking, drive-thru banking, online banking, mobile banking, home-delivered mail, home-printed stamps, UPS/Federal Express deliveries, on-line shopping, mobile shopping,

shopping malls, mini-malls, supermarkets, mini-markets, quick-trips, fast-marts, automatic dishwashers, automatic clothes washers/dryers, home-delivered medications, emergency health care, fast cars, superhighways, interstate highways, slow lanes, fast lanes, round-about intersections, state of the art air travel, countless examples of computer-aided technology at work and at home, universally accessible cloud-based photos/data, fast-drying paints, quick-setting adhesives, fast hair dryers, wrinkle-free clothing, no-wax-needed auto paints, flat-proof auto tires, pre-mixed paints, pre-mixed fuels, no-lube-needed bearings, snow blowers, riding lawnmowers, GPS-guided farm machinery, GPS travel maps/driving instructions, automatic car washes, automobile quick-lube services, auto grammar/spell check, hands-free talk and text, smart cameras, 3D Printing, remote-control functions for about everything that walks, flies, or breathes, as well as the rapidly approaching drone-delivery of consumer products and other items to our doorsteps.

But, we still don't have enough *time!* Certainly not enough that we can afford to set aside a little for our "personal-downtime-deprived" minds and bodies!

Depending on our individual life-circumstances, there can no doubt be many reasons (and excuses) for our ever-growing, real or imagined, *time* shortage. And for failing to provide for our natural need for sufficient personal-downtime. A mountain of research and other detailed material exists on this subject, and those craving in-depth knowledge in this area are encouraged to pursue such.

Otherwise, in keeping with the aims of this book, we will wind-up this section with a few facts-of-life about **"Time."** And, clearly, most of the following info is just plain old common sense. Nevertheless, basic facts-of-life that many of us at some point become detracted from, overlook, or otherwise choose to ignore. Furthermore, the following also highlights at least one aspect about "ourselves" that many of us may have heretofore been little, if any, aware of . . . regarding (according to some research) **what we "actually want."**

(1.) "Time" is NOT an unlimited resource. Regardless of how much we wish, or how well we plan, organize, invent, dream, cut-corners, scheme, advance technologically, or deny this reality. For as long as we are blessed to live, we only have **24** hours in our days, and **7** days in our weeks, etc. This is a not-negotiable fact-of-life.

(2.) "Things to do" always outnumber "Time available." Regardless of who we are, everyone's "things to do" fall into one of two categories—either *essential* or *optional*. What falls into these categories of course varies widely from person to person, depending upon many factors. None the least being, where, when, and into what life-circumstances we are born; the mental and physical attributes we inherit and/or develop; along with the opportunities available or not available to each of us. And of course the choices we have available and make during our gift of life. These things, these individual life-circumstances, determine how much of our (or another's) daily-gift of 24-hours must be used to provide for our *essentials*. That is, for our survival-basics, such as, food, water, shelter, clothing, exercise, sleep, etc. These same personal life-circumstances also determine if—after taking care of the *essentials*—there is any "optional time" left. And if so, how much.

Those blessed with any amount of "optional time" will find there is much competition for it. Including, for instance, friends, family, employers, neighbors, civic/social/charitable organizations, countless marketers, and even *ourselves*. Those less fortunate—those having no "optional time" in their lives—must then, through personal and/or other effort, experience a *change* in their life-circumstances in order for things to ever be different for them.

(3.) We actually want (often crave) "distraction" instead of "personal-downtime." Why we reportedly want (often crave) distraction is covered in-depth by many information sources, which some readers may of course wish to pursue. But, summarized in the most general of terms, it seems that gaps in our activity can leave us "alone with ourselves," and let our minds return to and focus on the fears and uncertainties that we all wrestle with, and try to avoid, one way or another.

And, our strong desire to in some way be "always-connected" to something or someone is thought by many to be a basic aspect of *Maslow's hierarchy of needs*. That is, the psychological theory that attempts to explain our biggest and most basic human needs. According to Maslow, our need to belong ranks right after our need for physical safety. To constantly affirm our existence and relevance we crave relationships—to belong. To great extent, our self-esteem appears to also come from "interaction with others." Hence a basis for today's social-media frenzy? Just a passing thought for consideration.

So, in order to avoid the abyss of our unanswered questions, self-doubt, aloneness, etc., we consciously or subconsciously seek (choose) to fill-the-gaps in our activity with something from our "available options." And, while it seems our down-deep need to be "constantly-connected" has probably been there since the beginning of time, being able to do so has not been possible until lately. But, now, our high-tech, fast-paced, consumption-driven society is filled with endless things to do. Anytime, everywhere, access to ever-growing amounts and types of information—to *"information overload."* At our fingertips a new-media world of mobile audio/visual communications, entertainment, social networking gone-wild, and, for many others, even voluntary/involuntary access to one's *work*—24/7.

Yes, millions of us can now—if we choose—fill any moments of inactivity we might have with one or more of the ever growing number of available "distractions." Furthermore, as shown by *Maslow's hierarchy of needs*, we will naturally be driven to do just that! We will naturally strive to fill our time-alone gaps with something to reassure ourselves—to stay constantly connected. Even if it means giving-up our otherwise also much needed "personal-downtime." Even at the risk of our mental and physical health, wellbeing, and ultimate survival. Many of us will, too often, and to our potential peril, choose *"always connected"* above that of our also-crucial human-need for *"personal downtime."*

Furthermore, it is most likely that *disconnecting-from-it-all* will become even more difficult and challenging as time goes on. Every aspect of our environment is being equipped with technology providing us more and more distraction options. Ways to forever be "media-connected." In any room of our homes; while traveling on foot or by car, truck, bus, plane, boat, or train; while at work, school, play, or shopping, etc. Connected to ever-present distractions. Each being in unrelenting competition for our "life-time blessing" of never more than "24 hours each day."

So what must we do to gain some "personal downtime"?
Given that our individual life-circumstances widely vary, it's most unlikely there will ever be a one-fits-all answer to this question. So, until the *magic-pill* (or *magic-App*) comes along, some say the following may be worthy of our serious consideration:

- We and others are the *chief competitors* for our time. We must not (and cannot) depend on others to *make us* disconnect from available distractions, or *force us* to choose-wisely what to do with our time. Especially regarding any optional-time we may be blessed with.

- We are not only "a *chief competitor*" for our time, we are also "*the owner.*" If we are blessed with optional-time and seriously want to use part of it for personal-downtime, then "we" must *choose* to do so! "We" must be the *successful competitor* for what is truly ours — *"our (limited) blessing of time."*

- Finally, those of us blessed with any opportunity to do so, must be more *proactive* and less *reactive* about how our time is used. Especially regarding any optional-time we may have. To the extent possible and practical, we must take charge of our time and affairs. We must create within our optional-time the as-needed *special spaces* for personal-downtime. And seriously demonstrate the desire, dedication, and willingness to use it for such. The responsibility to do so is ultimately *ours* . . . as long as we have free-will. As long as we are blessed with — and protect, defend, and secure — our precious liberty and freedom of **choice**!

= = =

"To say "too busy" is merely to say "confused priorities."
— *Jonathan Lockwood Huie*

"The bad news is time flies. The good news is you're the pilot."
— *Michael Althsuler*

"We must use time as a tool, not as a crutch." — *John F. Kennedy*

"For time and the world do not stand still. Change is the law of life. And those who look only to the past or the present are certain to miss the future." — *John F. Kennedy*

Tracking & Management of "Time"

> "Footprints in the sands of time . . . Where have you been? Where are you going? Why are you going there?"
>
> — Jonathan Lockwood Huie
>
> "Well arranged time is the surest mark of a well arranged mind."
>
> — Isaac Pitman

The need to track and manage "time" has undoubtedly been with us since "the beginning."

Even for Europe's ice-age hunters some 20,000 years ago or so. Apparently, to keep track of the days between phases of the moon, they scratched lines on and gouged holes in various bones and sticks. Of course, since then, the methods used for tracking and managing *time* have become a bit more complex, accurate, and more widely used.

Our fast-paced, modern-day, industrialized world is now increasingly and critically-dependent upon an accurate and universally recognized means of tracking and managing time. Knowing *when* and *how* things should, must, did, and will happen, are more and more business and life-sustaining matters, as opposed to curiosity, hobby, and convenience.

As aids to our tracking and management of time, many of my *dinosaur-age* generation grew up in homes with **"a"** wind-up clock and **"a"** paper, wall-hanging, calendar. In my particular family setting, most adult men also had **"a"** pocket watch, and the ladies **"a"** wristwatch. Don't recall any of us kids having a watch (at least a workable one) until our teen-years—and don't recall the lack of such being an issue. All schools, businesses, etc., generally had publically displayed clocks and calendars. And, some automobiles even had built-in clocks, although my childhood recall is that few of them actually worked, at least in the cars I had the opportunity, excitement, and joy of occasionally riding in.

But, even with the time-tracking limitations mentioned above, knowing "where" to be, and "when" to be there, never seemed to be a problem for the adults and children.

It is of course noteworthy that the "Dick Tracy Comic Books" of that period, depicted an all-in-one watch and audio/video communication device worn on one's wrist. Few if any adults or children at that time truly imagined that such technology would ever come to pass—but it sure did, and so much more!

Today my wife, Ann, and I live in a relatively mid-sized, three-bedroom, single-level home. During a recent cursory inventory, I easily located at least "twenty-four" time-tracking devices. Not including those in our car, pickup, tool-shop, and garage. Nor, the no longer used clocks and watches stashed away in drawers, boxes, and in various now forgotten places.

And, although surrounded today by state-of-the-art "time" displays, and aided by our personal smartphones equipped with clocks, calendars, reminders, and alert notices, etc. -- we still seem to increasingly struggle to be "where" we need to be, "when" we need to be there. Even though our location-, clock-, calendar-, appointment-, and reminder-enabled "smart-phones" have almost become one of our "body-parts."

Of course, it is fitting and natural that we should on occasion consider that "our" particular time-management challenges might be a bit "age-related." However, an opened-eyes look around us suggests that we are certainly "not alone" in our time-management abyss.

For . . . our streets, sidewalks, highways, shopping malls, businesses, schools, entertainment centers, workplaces, hospitals, doctors and dental offices, etc., all seem to be increasingly filled with too-many people having too-many places to be, in order to do too-much, with too-little time available — "to get it all done!" Given the unchangeable fact of only 24-hours in a day — there nonetheless appears to be a growing denial of the utter futility of trying to fit "two-pounds of daily life into a one-pound bag" — so to speak!

But, all is not hopeless. Once again, "technology to our rescue!" For example, in April 2015, Apple finally began taking orders for the long-awaited Apple Watch! And, those privileged to own one will no doubt eventually have access to specialized "apps." Which, in addition to tracking "time" and one's heart rate, etc., will undoubtedly very soon also be able to wash the car; mow the lawn; do the laundry, dishes, housework, and routine shopping; attend meetings; do one's essential health exercises; carryout routine social media tasks; and maintain one's ever-growing files of contacts and selfie's.

And, in so doing, provide a better opportunity for one to be where they want or need to be, at the time one wishes or is required to be there. Should Ann and I someday take this technological-leap, it could well be the fix for our forgetting or being late to our respective appointments. And, also leave us with a new problem . . . what to do with all the resulting "extra time!"

$$= \quad = \quad =$$

"We must use time creatively." — *Martin Luther King, Jr.*

"We must use time as a tool, not as a couch." — *John F. Kennedy*

"It's not enough to be busy, so are the ants. The question is, what are we busy about?" — *Henry David Thoreau*

"Never let yesterday use up today." — *Richard H. Nelson*

"Whether it's the best of times or the worst of times, it's the only time we've got." — *Art Buchwald*

"I am definitely going to take a course on time management . . . just as soon as I can work it into my schedule." — Louis E. Boone

"You will never find time for anything. If you want time you must make it." — Charles Bruxton

"Time, like life itself, has no inherent meaning. We give our own meaning to time as to life." — Jonathan Lockwood Huie

"So many books, so little time." — Frank Zappa

"Once you have mastered time, you will understand how true it is that most people overestimate what they can accomplish in a year — and underestimate what they can achieve in a decade!"
— Tony Robbins

"If it matters you will find a way. If it doesn't, you will find an excuse." — Unknown

"You will never reach your destination if you stop and throw stones at every dog that barks." – Winston Churchill

"Work is hard. Distractions are plentiful. And time is short."
— *Adam Hochschild*

"Life and time are the two best teachers. Life teaches us to make good use of time and time teaches us the value of life."
— *Anmol Andore*

"Life's tragedy is that we get old too soon and wise too late."
— *Benjamin Franklin*

"Where no plan is laid, where the disposal of time is surrendered merely to the chance of incident, chaos will soon reign."
— *Victor Hugo*

Regrets, Apologies, & Forgiveness

> The Serenity Prayer"
>
> "**God** grant me the . . .
> **Serenity** to accept the things I cannot change;
> **Courage** to change the things I can; and
> **Wisdom** to know the difference."
>
> — Reinhold Niebuhr (1892–1971)

Life is truly a blessing. Often taken for granted. Always coming with a beginning and an end. Much of what happens in between is our-doing; much is not. Nonetheless, we are not only accountable for our-doing, we must also deal with both.

The lasting nature of our *gift-of-life* naturally depends upon many things. Even "where" we are born and live. For instance: worldwide, the average life expectancy over the period 2010-2013 was reportedly 71.0 years (68.5 for males; 73.5 for females); in the United States, 79 (76 for males and 81 for females); in Japan 84 (80 for males; 87 for females); and in the West Africa country of Sierra Leone, 46 (45 for men; 46 for females).   According to the World Health Organization, women on average live longer than men in all countries.

And, of course, how long we get to stick around, and under what circumstances, are influenced greatly by countless other factors. Such as: heredity, mental-attitude, lifestyle, marital-status, war, foreign and domestic terrorism, crime, employment, diet, exercise, education, general healthcare, entertainment, economic-status, religion, spirituality, personal relationships, state and city of residence, water and air quality, police and fire protection, doctors, dental, hospitals, ambulance services, general environment, and most likely even some plain old luck (random chance), etc.

To varying degrees, most if not all of us experience happiness and sadness—and about everything in between. As well as success, failure, gratitude, envy, disappointment, good health, sickness, disease, suffering, healing, good and bad times, prideful moments, embarrassment, shame, and the many other aspects of just being "human." And if truth be known— few if any will escape having or causing "regrets;" owing or being owed "apologies;" and needing to extend or receive "forgiveness." Regarding a range of human shortfalls and failings, from the relatively trivial to the unthinkable. And, most always, in varying degrees, affecting not only the well-being of ourselves, but also that of innocent others.

Some among us handle the challenges of regrets, apologies, and forgiveness very well. Or, at least it appears so. While others, such as I, often stumble, fumble, fall-short, or plainly fail. And, "from the outside looking in," it also appears there are some who are actually "little-or-never" concerned very much about such things. Or, again, at least it appears so. To date, I have never determined to my personal satisfaction whether such apparently "care-free" folks are actually "blessed" or "cursed" by their being so seemingly inclined. However, I am reasonably sure that, when it comes to regrets, apologies, and forgiveness—I have yet to experience "care-free." Whether due to unconscious choice or nature's design. But, before getting too carried away about what I am and am not sure about . . . possibly I need to pause for a moment and reflect upon the following "seemingly fitting" quotations.

= = =

"It is unwise to be too sure of one's own wisdom. It is healthy to be reminded that the strongest might weaken and the wisest might err."
- Mahatma Gandhi

"I am the wisest man alive, for I know one thing, and that is that I know nothing." – Socrates

= = =

And now, with the benefit of the above booster-shot of humbling perspective, I'll now continue with some thoughts, feelings, and circumstances that are nonetheless—at least to me—very much reality. Life has blessed me with many gifts and opportunities, and the responsibilities that come with such. Today, I realize the "most important" among them were and remain that of husband, dad, son, brother, and now also—grandfather (as one of our truly awesome grandson's "papas"). A realization especially clear to me now; one that I so truly wish I had long ago, and much more responsibly, grasped. And although untimely recognized, today a nonetheless most cherished enlightenment, opportunity, responsibility—and, blessing!

It is of course an obviously-biased view that my pass through life so far has included various-attempted, and some-achieved, good things and otherwise worthy deeds. However, beyond any reasonable and knowledgeable dispute is the fact that my life-ledger also includes some truly regretful shortfalls and failings. The most remorseful — those affecting my loved ones, in my role as husband, father, son, and brother. Failings which I truly hope to have, in some meaningful way, demonstrated much due and heartfelt regret and apologies to my family. For any and all pain, suffering, embarrassment, and otherwise harm brought upon them. Truly sincere regrets and apologies, that are in no way diminished by any sense of awareness that I am not alone in my human failings. Personal failings, of which none of my loved ones were ever a source of cause, contributed to, or had the responsibility or capability of preventing.

Shortfalls and failings for which I alone am accountable, and which are not excused by past workaholic tendencies, nor by past abuse of the once chosen-crutch of alcohol. A once thought to be beneficial friend . . . but in reality, when abused, a potential life-destroyer for many among us. One ready and able to assist the abuser in delusional escape from reality. And in unplanned and unwanted pain, suffering, and loss of dignity, for self and our loved ones. Losses not reversible nor delete-able, by even the most sincere and well-intentioned expressions and demonstrations of regrets and apologies. Nor, by receipt of tolerance and forgiveness from others.

For, it is "self-forgiveness" that often remains an unrelenting challenge. A need often seeming beyond-reach, somewhere on a winding, uphill and most rocky path. One softened at times by the prospects of serenity, courage, and wisdom sought through prayer and meditation . . . posed, for example, by the *Serenity Prayer* (Inserted at the beginning of this section, and also on page *IV*).

A very special, life-sustaining prayer that I and countless others have found especially meaningful. As, hopefully, will untold others in all walks of life. Including those struggling now, or in the future, with the human suffering and devastation from the rapidly-spreading use and abuse of "legal" and "illegal" drugs. Such as, alcohol, marijuana, cocaine, and an array of prescription drugs (pain pills, anti-depression pills, etc.). The untold millions, and their loved ones, who are now or soon will be—in addition to a struggle for *survival*—also wrestling with a very upfront and personal relationship with . . . *regrets, apologies,* and *forgiveness.*

However, regardless of our individual life-circumstances . . . at some point we must all find the way and courage to move forward. Playing "life over" is never an option. Our blessing of life does not come equipped with a "reverse gear." We must, each in our own way, do our best to in positive manner use past and present lessons as aids to our "onward journey." And on our way, if and when we open our eyes and minds and look around, we will likely discover that we are not as alone and unique as we much too often think and counter-productively dwell upon.

A best recall from a few holes of golf played in years past, in some settings there applies a rule often called "Ball Played as It Lies." Requiring that—in likeness to "life"—the ball must be played wherever it lands. For, regardless of our individual circumstances, each day that we are blessed to "wake-up," we land somewhere in a "today"—the present. And, it is from that place in "reality" that—each day—we must again start . . . and "choose" to move forward. Not only for the sake of our personal well-being, but also that of our loved ones and affected others.

While **yesterday, today,** and **tomorrow,** naturally occupy our minds, only **"one"** is a reality that can be touched, seen, smelled, heard, and otherwise truly experienced. And it is at great risk that we mentally spend too much time in the **"other two"**—one of which is gone forever, the other not yet arrived. We must play our "ball-of-life" where it lies. Remembering also, that while often unable to control that which is done to us, for us, and around us—rare is the time we are unable to in meaningful manner "choose" how we respond to life's many circumstances. Whether the hand we are dealt be good, bad, or in between.

Today, I especially strive not for the unattainable flawlessness and pleasing-of-people, but to unfailingly be a loving, caring, listening, supportive, and otherwise honorable "papa" to our grandson. With hopes that one day, he and my other loved ones will judge me as being so. And, that, in the end, the "guy in the glass" can likewise—and truthfully--agree.

= = =

The Guy in the Glass

by Dale Wimbrow, 1934

When you get what you want in your struggle for pelf,
And the world makes you King for a day,
Then go to the mirror and look at yourself,
And see what that guy has to say.

For it isn't your Father, or Mother, or Wife,
Who judgement upon you must pass.
The feller whose verdict counts most in your life
Is the guy staring back from the glass.

He's the feller to please, never mind all the rest,
For he's with you clear up to the end,
And you've passed your most dangerous, difficult test
If the guy in the glass is your friend.

You may be like Jack Horner and "chisel" a plum,
And think you're a wonderful guy,
But the man in the glass says you're only a bum
If you can't look him straight in the eye.

You can fool the whole world down the pathway of years,
And get pats on the back as you pass,
But your final reward will be heartaches and tears
If you've cheated the guy in the glass.

= = =

In grateful memory of the author, Dale Wimbrow (1895-1954)

= = =

Definition of "pelf": money; riches.

"Peace comes from within. Do not seek it without."

— *Gautama Buddha*

"Never ruin an apology with an excuse." –Benjamin Franklin

"If you can't forgive and forget, pick one." –Robert Brault

"Many of us crucify ourselves between two thieves — regret for the past and fear of the future." — Fulton Oursler

"One of the greatest regrets in life is being what others would want you to be, rather than being yourself." –Shannon L. Alder

"In this life, when you deny someone an apology, you will remember it at time you beg for forgiveness." — Toba Beta

"Right actions in the future are the best apologies for bad actions in the past." — Tryon Edwards

"To forgive is to set a prisoner free and discover that the prisoner was you." — Lewis B. Smedes

"We must all suffer from one of two pains: the pain of discipline or the pain of regret. The difference is discipline weighs ounces while regret weighs tons." –Jim Rohn

"Forgive yourself for your faults and your mistakes and move on."

— *Les Brown*

"When you forgive, you free your soul. But when you say I'm sorry, you free two souls." –Donald L. Hicks

Recipe for Happiness

> *"This universe is balanced. God made it that way. There is always plenty to be worried and sad about, but there is equally plenty to be happy and at peace with. The choice is yours."* — Steve Maraboli
>
> *"You live longer once you realize that any time spent being unhappy is wasted."* — Ruth E. Renkl

Marlon Brando was an American screen and stage actor, hailed for bringing gripping realism to film acting, and widely considered to be one of the greatest actors of all time. He died at age 80 on July 01, 2004. Reportedly, among Marlon's last spoken words were something to the effect of — *"What the hell was that [his life] all about?"*

The above account may or may not represent what Marlon Brando actually felt or expressed at time of his passing. Nevertheless, whether true, fabricated, or exaggerated, the above account relates to some of the most profound questions the human race has long wrestled with: "Why are we here?" "Where did we come from?" "The meaning of life?" And, "The recipe for happiness?" Questions that, from the beginning, have been the focus of much philosophical, scientific, and theological speculation and debate—and will likely long-remain so.

A number of "answers" have been offered by many different ideological, religious, and cultural sources—and covered extensively in countless books and other historical records. To our individual "personal satisfaction," some among us may have (or profess to have) resolved one or more of these timeless life-puzzles. Most likely, however, many more of us have not. Or, at least not with unquestionable certainty . . . and, therefore, openly or otherwise—continue our "search."

I first met Patsy in 1967, as a co-worker in a quality control organization. A very respectable married lady; blessed with a young son and daughter, and like many parents, proud of them to a fault. At work we occasionally shared some of our self-proclaimed bits of wisdom (or ignorance) about life. Knowing that she was stretched rather thin between employment, family, church, social activities, etc. . . . at times I would jokingly suggest that, in her "spare time," she might try to determine the "meaning of life" and "recipe for happiness." If she ever came up with the "meaning of life," she certainly never shared it with me. However, what she did do one day was hand me a note she had written—a very special little note, which read:

> *The recipe for Happiness:*
> *1. Something to do*
> *2. Someone to love*
> *3. Something to hope for*

(Below is a scanned-copy of the original)

The recipe for Happiness:

1. Something to do
2. Someone to love
3. Something to hope for

In an effort to put this little note into some proper perspective — it was written by a lady whose life-challenges included, but by no means were limited to — the deaths of her husband, and thereafter a most special soul mate; considerable workplace pressures; special child-rearing concerns; and a life-threatening battle with breast cancer. Throughout which she never seemed to lose her faith, hope, sense of humor, work ethic, or desire to pursue her "recipe for happiness."

Early on the morning of November 29, 1998, Patsy died suddenly and unexpectedly, at home, at age 63. We have no way of knowing what flashed through her mind at the moment of her passing. But, if the opportunity was availed to her, I have no doubt that Patsy's parting thoughts were spiritual in nature and about her children's wellbeing. And, much in contrast to that which will (as noted at the beginning of this section) be truthfully or fictitiously said about Marlon Brando's last thoughts . . . about five and one-half years later.

It seems that regardless of the aspects of good or poor health, wealth or poverty, fortune or misfortune, or other life circumstances—some will forever consider their glass to be "half-full," while others will choose to see theirs as being "half-empty." Surrounding us is overwhelming evidence that **"money"** and **"stuff"** can for a while buy entertainment, comfort, convenience, and attention. While in short supply, any evidence that such are a lasting "Recipe for Happiness."

In turn, after all is said and done, or done and said—it is likely that Abraham Lincoln touched upon a universal fact-of-life when he long ago reportedly expressed . . . ***"Most folks are about as happy as they make up their minds to be."***

And, given the merit and wisdom of Abe's words, now comes the often difficult part—"making up our minds"—"making the right choice." But, thanks to our Creator we have been blessed with the tools to do so. It's called, **"free-will."**

= = =

May you find within this section and the following thirty-seven quotations, something of comfort and meaningfully assist to your own personal . . . "Pursuit of Happiness":

"A pessimist sees the difficulty in every opportunity; and optimist sees the opportunity in every difficulty." — Winston Churchill

"Do the best you can, and don't take life too serious." — Will Rogers

"If opportunity doesn't knock, build a door." — Milton Berle

"Failure is simply the opportunity to begin again, this time more intelligently." — Henry Ford

"The worst thing that happens to you may be the best thing for you if you don't let it get the best of you." — Will Rogers

"There is a strange reluctance on the part of most people to admit they enjoy life." — William Lyon Phelps

"Most folks are about as happy as they make up their minds to be."
— Abraham Lincoln

"To understand is to forgive, even oneself." — Alexander Chase

"There is good and there is bad in every human heart, and it is the struggle of life to conquer the bad with the good." — Susan Glaspell

"The happiest people in the world are those who have the most interesting thoughts." — William Lyon Phelps

"Life isn't about waiting for the storm to pass, it's about learning to dance in the rain." — Vivian Greene

"Your fear is 100% dependent on you for its survival."
— Steve Maraboli

"Humor can be one of our best survival tools." — Allen Klein

"We need 4 hugs a day for survival. We need 8 hugs a day for maintenance. We need 12 hugs a day for growth." – Virginia Satir

"Take time to play! Ask for what you want. Laugh. Live loudly. Be avid. Learn a new thing. Be Yourself!" – Mary Ann Radmacher

"Be yourself; everyone else is already taken." – Oscar Wilde

"To make mistakes is human; to stumble is commonplace; to be able to laugh at yourself is maturity." – William Arthur Ward

"No one can make you feel inferior without your consent."
                                                    – Eleanor Roosevelt

"If you tell the truth, you don't have to remember anything."
                                                    – Mark Twain

"Your perspective on life comes from the cage you were held captive in." – Shannon L. Alder

"When dealing with critics always remember this: Critics judge things based on what is outside of their content of understanding."
                                                    – Shannon L. Alder

"We find comfort among those who agree with us – growth among those who don't." – Frank Clark

"You can never make someone like something they don't like, but you can always help them to better understand it." – Criss Jami

"Learn from yesterday, live for today, hope for tomorrow. The important thing is not to stop questioning." – Albert Einstein

"You've got to take the good with the bad, smile with the sad, love what you've got, and remember what you had. Always forgive, but never forget. Learn from mistakes, but never regret." –Unknown

"Attitude is a little thing that makes a big difference."
– Winston Churchill

"Not everything that counts can be counted, and not everything that can be counted counts." – Albert Einstein

"The only disability in life is a bad attitude." – Scott Hamilton

"Happiness can only be found if you can free yourself of all other distractions." – Saul Bellow

"Change the way you look at things and the things you look at change." – Wayne W. Dyer

"The best day of your life is the one on which you decide your life is your own. No apologies or excuses. No one to lean on, rely on, or blame. The gift is yours – it is an amazing journey – and you alone are responsible for the quality of it. This is the day your life really begins." – Bob Moawad

"I have not failed. I've just found 10,000 ways that won't work."
– Thomas A. Edison

"There are two primary choices in life: to accept conditions as they exist, or accept responsibility for changing them." — Denis Waitley

"If your ship doesn't come in, swim out to meet it!"
— Jonathan Winters

"You only live once, but if you do it right, once is enough."
— Mae West

"Being happy doesn't mean that everything is perfect. It means you've decided to look beyond the imperfections." — Gerard Way

"A sense of humor can help you overlook the unattractive, tolerate the unpleasant, cope with the unexpected, and smile through the unbearable." — Mose Waldoks

"Enjoy the Little Things"

"Enjoy the little things, for one day you may look back and realize they were the big things." — Robert Brault

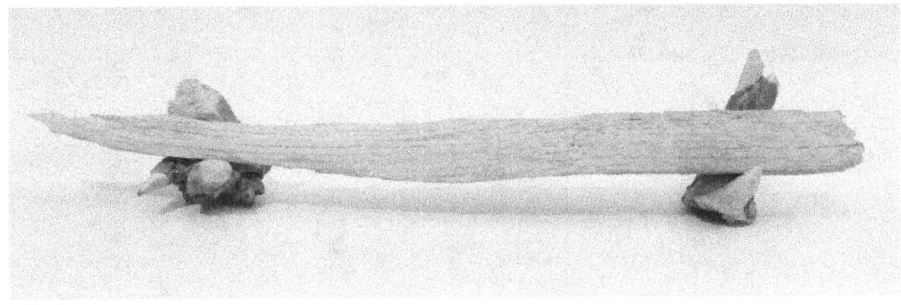

Hand-carvings by Matthew, 2011

"As you admire the wonderful things God has made today, remember you're one of them, wonderful inside and out. You are blessed, you are special, you are loved." –Author Unknown

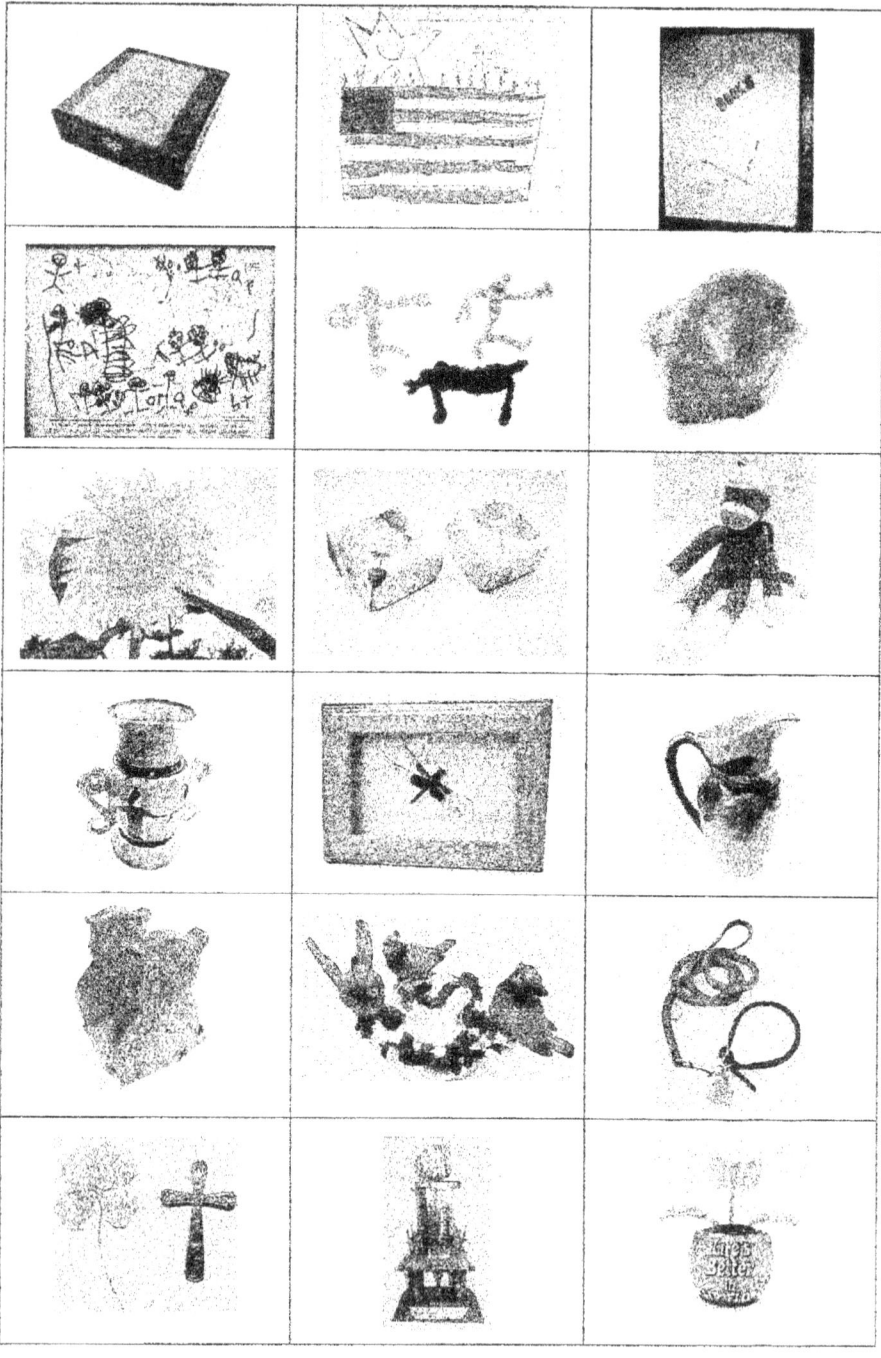

References & Recommended Reading

(Listed Alphabetically by Author's Last Name)

Book Title	Author
The Holy Bible	(Version/Translation supportive of one's Christian faith)
All I Really Need To Know I Learned In Kindergarten	Robert Fulghum
Because They Hate	Brigitte Gabriel
The Haldeman Diaries – Inside The Nixon White House	H. R. Haldeman (Introduction and Afterword by Stephen E. Ambrose)
The Federalist Papers	Alexander Hamilton, James Madison, & John Jay (Introduction by Gary Wills)
Hostile Waters	Peter Huchthausen, Igor Kurdin, & R. Alan White
Who Moved My Cheese?	Spencer Johnson
Two Incomes and Still Broke?	Linda Kelley
The Imitation Of Christ	Thomas A. Kempis
Lights Out	Ted Koppel
• The Liberty Amendments • Plunder and Deceit • Ameritopia • Liberty and Tyranny	Mark R. Levin
The Patriot's Reference	Edited by: Joel J. Miller & Kristen Parrish

References & Recommended Reading – *(Continued)*

(Listed Alphabetically by Author's Last Name)

Book Title	Author
• Killing Jesus • Killing Lincoln • Killing Patton • Killing Kennedy	Bill O'Reilly
I'm Not OK. You're Not OK. But It's OK!	Chris Padgett
Words That Inspired Him— A Lifetime Of Favorite Writings, Poems & Quotations	Norman Vincent Peal
The Most of Andy Rooney *(ESP Article: "Mr. Rooney goes to Washington")*	Andrew A. Rooney
• Liberalism Is A Mental Disorder • Stop The Coming Civil War • Countdown To Mecca • Government Zero	Michael Savage
The Faith Explained	Leo J. Trese
Enemies—A History of the FBI	Tim Weiner
• Mutterings Of An Old Man • I Felt The Floor Shake	Mike Womeldorff
• House Calls • Office Calls • Love Letters from a Marriage • Wisdom for a Woman • Wisdom for a Man	Gary Yarbrough, M.D.

Our tax dollars at work . . .

An "Eight-Page" Listing of 438 Federal Government Agencies!

(In keeping with our Federal Government's ongoing aim of "simplicity" and "efficiency" of operations—its many "agencies" exist under a broad mix of terms and titles, such as: Agencies, Bureaus, Commissions, Departments, Services, Offices, Boards, Corporations, Foundations, Administrations, Councils, Divisions, etc., etc. A practice especially helpful in making it difficult to impossible to track ultimate responsibility; accountability; and outdated or duplicated functions, etc.)

= = =

- Administration Office, Executive Office of the President
  - o National Commission on Fiscal Responsibility and Reform
- Administrative Conference of the United States
- Administrative Office of United States Courts
- Advocacy and Outreach Office
- African Development Foundation
- Agency for Healthcare Research and Quality
- Agency for International Development
  - o International Development Cooperation Agency
- Agency for Toxic Substances and Disease Registry
- Aging Administration
- Agricultural Marketing Service
- Agricultural Research Service
- Agriculture Department
  - o Advocacy and Outreach Office
  - o Agricultural Marketing Service
  - o Agricultural Research Service
  - o Animal and Plant Health Inspection Service
  - o Commodity Credit Corporation
  - o Cooperative State Research, Education, and Extension Service
  - o Economic Analysis Staff
  - o Economic Research Service
  - o Energy Policy and New Uses Office
  - o Farm Service Agency
  - o Federal Crop Insurance Corporation
  - o Food and Consumer Service
  - o Food and Nutrition Service
  - o Food Safety and Inspection Service
  - o Foreign Agricultural Service
  - o Forest Service
  - o Grain Inspection, Packers and Stockyards Administration
  - o Inspector General Office, Agriculture Department
  - o National Agricultural Library
  - o National Agricultural Statistics Service
  - o National Institute of Food and Agriculture
  - o Natural Resources Conservation Service
  - o Operations Office
  - o Procurement and Property Management, Office of
  - o Risk Management Agency
  - o Rural Business-Cooperative Service
  - o Rural Housing and Community Development Service
  - o Rural Housing Service
  - o Rural Telephone Bank
  - o Rural Utilities Service
  - o Transportation Office
- Air Force Department
- Air Quality National Commission
- Air Transportation Stabilization Board
- Alaska Power Administration
- Alcohol and Tobacco Tax and Trade Bureau
- Alcohol, Tobacco, Firearms, and Explosives Bureau
- American Battle Monuments Commission
- Amtrak Reform Council
- Animal and Plant Health Inspection Service
- Antitrust Division

- Antitrust Modernization Commission
- Appalachian Regional Commission
- Appalachian States Low-Level Radioactive Waste Commission
- Architect of the Capitol
- Architectural and Transportation Barriers Compliance Board
- Arctic Research Commission
- Armed Forces Retirement Home
- Arms Control and Disarmament Agency
- Army Department
- Assassination Records Review Board
- Barry M. Goldwater Scholarship and Excellence in Education Foundation
- Bipartisan Commission on Entitlement and Tax Reform
- Board of Directors of the Hope for Homeowners Program
- Bonneville Power Administration
- Broadcasting Board of Governors
- Bureau of the Fiscal Service
- Census Bureau
- Census Monitoring Board
- Centers for Disease Control and Prevention
- Centers for Medicare & Medicaid Services
- Central Intelligence Agency
- Chemical Safety and Hazard Investigation Board
- Child Support Enforcement Office
- Children and Families Administration
- Christopher Columbus Quincentenary Jubilee Commission
- Civil Rights Commission
- Coast Guard
- Commerce Department
  - o Census Bureau
  - o Economic Analysis Bureau
  - o Economic Development Administration
  - o Economics and Statistics Administration
  - o Export Administration Bureau
  - o Foreign-Trade Zones Board
  - o Industry and Security Bureau
  - o International Trade Administration
  - o Minority Business Development Agency
  - o National Institute of Standards and Technology
  - o National Oceanic and Atmospheric Administration
  - o National Shipping Authority
  - o National Technical Information Service
  - o National Telecommunications and Information Administration
  - o Patent and Trademark Office
  - o Technology Administration
  - o Travel and Tourism Administration
- Commercial Space Transportation Office
- Commission of Fine Arts
- Commission on Immigration Reform
- Commission on Protecting and Reducing Government Secrecy
- Commission on Review of Overseas Military Facility Structure of the United States
- Commission on Structural Alternatives for the Federal Courts of Appeals
- Commission on the Advancement of Federal Law Enforcement
- Commission on the Bicentennial of the United States Constitution
- Commission on the Future of the United States Aerospace Industry
- Commission on the Social Security Notch Issue
- Committee for Purchase From People Who Are Blind or Severely Disabled
- Committee for the Implementation of Textile Agreements
- Commodity Credit Corporation
- Commodity Futures Trading Commission
- Community Development Financial Institutions Fund
- Community Living Administration
- Competitiveness Policy Council
- Comptroller of the Currency
- Congressional Budget Office
- Consumer Financial Protection Bureau
- Consumer Product Safety Commission
- Cooperative State Research, Education, and Extension Service
- Coordinating Council on Juvenile Justice and Delinquency Prevention
- Copyright Office, Library of Congress

- Copyright Royalty Board
- Copyright Royalty Judges, Library of Congress
- Corporation for National and Community Service
- Council of the Inspectors General on Integrity and Efficiency
- Council on Environmental Quality
- Counsel to the President
- Court Services and Offender Supervision Agency for the District of Columbia
- Crime and Security in U.S. Seaports, Interagency Commission
- Customs Service
- Defense Acquisition Regulations System
- Defense Base Closure and Realignment Commission
- Defense Contract Audit Agency
- Defense Criminal Investigative Service
- Defense Department
  - o Air Force Department
  - o Army Department
  - o Defense Acquisition Regulations System

- o Defense Contract Audit Agency
- o Defense Criminal Investigative Service
- o Defense Information Systems Agency
- o Defense Intelligence Agency
- o Defense Investigative Service
- o Defense Logistics Agency
- o Defense Mapping Agency
- o Defense Special Weapons Agency
- o Engineers Corps
- o National Geospatial-Intelligence Agency
- o National Security Agency/Central Security Service
- o Navy Department
- o Uniformed Services University of the Health Sciences
- Defense Information Systems Agency
- Defense Intelligence Agency
- Defense Investigative Service
- Defense Logistics Agency
- Defense Mapping Agency
- Defense Nuclear Facilities Safety Board
- Defense Special Weapons Agency
- Delaware River Basin Commission
- Denali Commission
- Disability Employment Policy Office
- Drug Enforcement Administration
- Economic Analysis Bureau
- Economic Analysis Staff
- Economic Development Administration
- Economic Research Service
- Economics and Statistics Administration
- Education Department
- Election Assistance Commission
- Electronic Commerce Advisory Commission
- Emergency Oil and Gas Guaranteed Loan Board
- Emergency Steel Guarantee Loan Board
- Employee Benefits Security Administration
- Employees Compensation Appeals Board
- Employment and Training Administration
- Employment Standards Administration
- Energy Department
- o Alaska Power Administration
- o Bonneville Power Administration
- o Energy Efficiency and Renewable Energy Office
- o Energy Information Administration
- o Energy Research Office
- o Environment Office, Energy Department
- o Federal Energy Regulatory Commission
- o Hearings and Appeals Office, Energy Department
- o Minority Economic Impact Office
- o National Nuclear Security Administration
- o Nuclear Energy Office
- o Southeastern Power Administration
- o Southwestern Power Administration
- o Western Area Power Administration
- Energy Efficiency and Renewable Energy Office
- Energy Information Administration
- Energy Policy and New Uses Office
- Energy Research Office
- Engineers Corps
- Engraving and Printing Bureau
- Environment Office, Energy Department
- Environmental Protection Agency
- Equal Employment Opportunity Commission
- Executive Council on Integrity and Efficiency
- Executive Office for Immigration Review
- Executive Office of the President
- o Administration Office, Executive Office of the President
- o Council on Environmental Quality
- o Counsel to the President
- Export Administration Bureau
- Export-Import Bank
- Family Assistance Office
- Farm Credit Administration
- Farm Credit System Insurance Corporation
- Farm Service Agency
- Federal Accounting Standards Advisory Board
- Federal Acquisition Regulation System
- Federal Aviation Administration
- Federal Bureau of Investigation
- Federal Communications Commission
- Federal Contract Compliance Programs Office
- Federal Crop Insurance Corporation
- Federal Deposit Insurance Corporation
- Federal Election Commission
- Federal Emergency Management Agency
- Federal Energy Regulatory Commission
- Federal Financial Institutions Examination Council
- Federal Highway Administration

- Federal Housing Enterprise Oversight Office
- Federal Housing Finance Agency
- Federal Housing Finance Board
- Federal Labor Relations Authority
  - o Federal Service Impasses Panel
- Federal Law Enforcement Training Center
- Federal Maritime Commission
- Federal Mediation and Conciliation Service
- Federal Mine Safety and Health Review Commission
- Federal Motor Carrier Safety Administration
- Federal Pay, Advisory Committee
- Federal Prison Industries
- Federal Procurement Policy Office
- Federal Railroad Administration
- Federal Register Office
- Federal Register, Administrative Committee
- Federal Reserve System
- Federal Retirement Thrift Investment Board
- Federal Service Impasses Panel
- Federal Trade Commission
- Federal Transit Administration
- Financial Crimes Enforcement Network
- Financial Crisis Inquiry Commission
- Financial Research Office
- Financial Stability Oversight Council
- First Responder Network Authority
- Fiscal Service
- Fish and Wildlife Service
- Food and Consumer Service
- Food and Drug Administration
- Food and Nutrition Service
- Food Safety and Inspection Service
- Foreign Agricultural Service
- Foreign Assets Control Office
- Foreign Claims Settlement Commission
- Foreign Service Grievance Board
- Foreign Service Impasse Disputes Panel
- Foreign Service Labor Relations Board
- Foreign-Trade Zones Board
- Forest Service
- General Services Administration
- Geographic Names Board
- Geological Survey
- Government Accountability Office
- Government Ethics Office
- Government National Mortgage Association
- Government Publishing Office
- Grain Inspection, Packers and Stockyards Administration
- Gulf Coast Ecosystem Restoration Council
- Harry S. Truman Scholarship Foundation
- Health and Human Services Department
  - o Agency for Healthcare Research and Quality
  - o Agency for Toxic Substances and Disease Registry
  - o Aging Administration
  - o Centers for Disease Control and Prevention
  - o Centers for Medicare & Medicaid Services
  - o Child Support Enforcement Office
  - o Children and Families Administration
  - o Community Living Administration
  - o Family Assistance Office
  - o Food and Drug Administration
  - o Health Care Finance Administration
  - o Health Resources and Services Administration
  - o Indian Health Service
  - o Inspector General Office, Health and Human Services Department
  - o National Institutes of Health
  - o National Library of Medicine
  - o Program Support Center
  - o Public Health Service
  - o Refugee Resettlement Office
  - o Substance Abuse and Mental Health Services Administration
- Health Care Finance Administration
- Health Resources and Services Administration
- Hearings and Appeals Office, Energy Department
- Hearings and Appeals Office, Interior Department
- Historic Preservation, Advisory Council
- Homeland Security Department
  - o Coast Guard
  - o Federal Emergency Management Agency
  - o Federal Law Enforcement Training Center
  - o National Communications System
  - o Secret Service
  - o Transportation Security Administration
  - o U.S. Citizenship and Immigration Services
  - o U.S. Customs and Border Protection
  - o U.S. Immigration and Customs Enforcement
- Housing and Urban Development Department

- o Federal Housing Enterprise Oversight Office
- o Government National Mortgage Association
- Immigration and Naturalization Service
- Indian Affairs Bureau
- Indian Arts and Crafts Board
- Indian Health Service
- Indian Trust Transition Office
- Industry and Security Bureau
- Information Security Oversight Office
- Inspector General Office, Agriculture Department
- Inspector General Office, Health and Human Services Department
- Institute of American Indian and Alaska Native Culture and Arts Development
- Institute of Museum and Library Services
- Inter-American Foundation
- Interagency Floodplain Management Review Committee
- Intergovernmental Relations Advisory Commission
- Interior Department
  - o Fish and Wildlife Service
  - o Geological Survey
  - o Hearings and Appeals Office, Interior Department
  - o Indian Affairs Bureau
  - o Indian Trust Transition Office
  - o Land Management Bureau
  - o Minerals Management Service
  - o Mines Bureau
  - o National Biological Service
  - o National Civilian Community Corps
  - o National Indian Gaming Commission
  - o National Park Service
  - o Natural Resources Revenue Office
  - o Ocean Energy Management Bureau
  - o Ocean Energy Management, Regulation, and Enforcement Bureau
  - o Reclamation Bureau
  - o Safety and Environmental Enforcement Bureau
  - o Special Trustee for American Indians Office
  - o Surface Mining Reclamation and Enforcement Office
- Internal Revenue Service
- International Boundary and Water Commission, United States and Mexico
- International Broadcasting Board
- International Development Cooperation Agency
- International Investment Office
- International Joint Commission-United States and Canada
- International Organizations Employees Loyalty Board
- International Trade Administration
- International Trade Commission
- Interstate Commerce Commission
- James Madison Memorial Fellowship Foundation
- Japan-United States Friendship Commission
- Joint Board for Enrollment of Actuaries
- Judicial Conference of the United States
- Judicial Review Commission on Foreign Asset Control
- Justice Department
  - o Alcohol, Tobacco, Firearms, and Explosives Bureau
  - o Antitrust Division
  - o Drug Enforcement Administration
  - o Executive Office for Immigration Review
  - o Federal Bureau of Investigation
  - o Federal Prison Industries
  - o Foreign Claims Settlement Commission
  - o Immigration and Naturalization Service
  - o Justice Programs Office
  - o Juvenile Justice and Delinquency Prevention Office
  - o National Institute of Corrections
  - o National Institute of Justice
  - o Parole Commission
  - o Prisons Bureau
  - o United States Marshals Service
- Justice Programs Office
  - o Victims of Crime Office
- Juvenile Justice and Delinquency Prevention Office
- Labor Department
  - o Disability Employment Policy Office
  - o Employee Benefits Security Administration
  - o Employees Compensation Appeals Board
  - o Employment and Training Administration
  - o Employment Standards Administration
  - o Federal Contract Compliance Programs Office
  - o Labor Statistics Bureau
  - o Labor-Management Standards Office
  - o Mine Safety and Health Administration
  - o Occupational Safety and Health Administration
  - o Pension and Welfare Benefits Administration
  - o Veterans Employment and Training Service
  - o Wage and Hour Division
  - o Workers Compensation Programs Office
- Labor Statistics Bureau
- Labor-Management Standards Office

- Land Management Bureau
- Legal Services Corporation
- Library of Congress
  - o Copyright Office, Library of Congress
  - o Copyright Royalty Board
- Local Television Loan Guarantee Board
- Management and Budget Office
  - o Federal Procurement Policy Office
- Marine Mammal Commission
- Maritime Administration
- Medicare Payment Advisory Commission
- Merit Systems Protection Board
- Military Compensation and Retirement Modernization Commission
- Millennium Challenge Corporation
- Mine Safety and Health Administration
- Minerals Management Service
- Mines Bureau
- Minority Business Development Agency
- Minority Economic Impact Office
- Mississippi River Commission
- Monetary Offices
- Morris K. Udall and Stewart L. Udall Foundation
- National Aeronautics and Space Administration
- National Agricultural Library
- National Agricultural Statistics Service
- National Archives and Records Administration
  - o Federal Register Office
  - o Information Security Oversight Office
  - o National Historical Publications and Records Commission
- National Bankruptcy Review Commission
- National Biological Service
- National Bipartisan Commission on Future of Medicare
- National Capital Planning Commission
- National Civilian Community Corps
- National Commission on Fiscal Responsibility and Reform
- National Commission on Intermodal Transportation
- National Commission on Libraries and Information Science
- National Commission on Manufactured Housing
- National Commission on Terrorist Attacks Upon the United States
- National Commission on the Cost of Higher Education
- National Communications System
- National Consumer Cooperative Bank
- National Council on Disability
- National Counterintelligence Center
- National Credit Union Administration
- National Crime Prevention and Privacy Compact Council
- National Economic Council
- National Education Goals Panel
- National Endowment for the Arts
- National Endowment for the Humanities
- National Foundation on the Arts and the Humanities
  - o Institute of Museum and Library Services
  - o National Endowment for the Arts
  - o National Endowment for the Humanities
- National Gambling Impact Study Commission
- National Geospatial-Intelligence Agency
- National Highway Traffic Safety Administration
- National Historical Publications and Records Commission
- National Indian Gaming Commission
- National Institute for Literacy
- National Institute of Corrections
- National Institute of Food and Agriculture
- National Institute of Justice
- National Institute of Standards and Technology
- National Institutes of Health
- National Intelligence, Office of the National Director
- National Labor Relations Board
- National Library of Medicine
- National Mediation Board
- National Nanotechnology Coordination Office
- National Nuclear Security Administration
- National Oceanic and Atmospheric Administration
- National Park Service
- National Partnership for Reinventing Government
- National Prison Rape Elimination Commission
- National Railroad Passenger Corporation
- National Science Foundation
- National Security Agency/Central Security Service
- National Security Council
- National Shipping Authority
- National Skill Standards Board
- National Technical Information Service
- National Telecommunications and Information Administration
  - o First Responder Network Authority
- National Transportation Safety Board
- National Women's Business Council
- Natural Resources Conservation Service

- Natural Resources Revenue Office
- Navajo and Hopi Indian Relocation Office
- Navy Department
- Neighborhood Reinvestment Corporation
- Northeast Dairy Compact Commission
- Northeast Interstate Low-Level Radioactive Waste Commission
- Nuclear Energy Office
- Nuclear Regulatory Commission
- Nuclear Waste Technical Review Board
- Occupational Safety and Health Administration
- Occupational Safety and Health Review Commission
- Ocean Energy Management Bureau
- Ocean Energy Management, Regulation, and Enforcement Bureau
- Ocean Policy Commission
- Office of Motor Carrier Safety
- Office of National Drug Control Policy
- Office of Policy Development
- Oklahoma City National Memorial Trust
- Operations Office
- Ounce of Prevention Council
- Overseas Private Investment Corporation
- Pacific Northwest Electric Power and Conservation Planning Council
- Panama Canal Commission
- Parole Commission
- Patent and Trademark Office
- Peace Corps
- Pension and Welfare Benefits Administration
- Pension Benefit Guaranty Corporation
- Personnel Management Office
- Physician Payment Review Commission
- Pipeline and Hazardous Materials Safety Administration
- Postal Rate Commission
- Postal Regulatory Commission
- Postal Service
- President's Council on Integrity and Efficiency
- President's Council on Sustainable Development
- President's Critical Infrastructure Protection Board
- President's Economic Policy Advisory Board
- Presidential Advisory Committee on Gulf War Veterans' Illnesses
- Presidential Commission on Assignment of Women in the Armed Forces
- Presidential Documents
- Presidio Trust
- Prisons Bureau
- Privacy and Civil Liberties Oversight Board
- Procurement and Property Management, Office of
- Program Support Center
- Prospective Payment Assessment Commission
- Public Debt Bureau
- Public Health Service
- Railroad Retirement Board
- Reagan-Udall Foundation for the Food and Drug Administration
- Reclamation Bureau
- Recovery Accountability and Transparency Board
- Refugee Resettlement Office
- Regulatory Information Service Center
- Research and Innovative Technology Administration
- Research and Special Programs Administration
- Resolution Trust Corporation
- Risk Management Agency
- Rural Business-Cooperative Service
- Rural Housing and Community Development Service
- Rural Housing Service
- Rural Telephone Bank
- Rural Utilities Service
- Safety and Environmental Enforcement Bureau
- Saint Lawrence Seaway Development Corporation
- Science and Technology Policy Office
- Secret Service
- Securities and Exchange Commission
- Selective Service System
- Small Business Administration
- Smithsonian Institution
- Social Security Administration
- Southeastern Power Administration
- Southwestern Power Administration
- Special Counsel Office
- Special Inspector General for Afghanistan Reconstruction
- Special Inspector General For Iraq Reconstruction
- Special Trustee for American Indians Office
- State Department
- State Justice Institute
- Substance Abuse and Mental Health Services Administration
- Surface Mining Reclamation and Enforcement Office
- Surface Transportation Board
- Susquehanna River Basin Commission
- Technology Administration
- Tennessee Valley Authority

- The White House Office
- Thrift Depositor Protection Oversight Board
- Thrift Supervision Office
- Trade and Development Agency
- Trade Representative, Office of United States
- Transportation Department
  - Commercial Space Transportation Office
  - Federal Aviation Administration
  - Federal Highway Administration
  - Federal Motor Carrier Safety Administration
  - Federal Railroad Administration
  - Federal Transit Administration
  - Maritime Administration
  - National Highway Traffic Safety Administration
  - Office of Motor Carrier Safety
  - Pipeline and Hazardous Materials Safety Administration
  - Research and Innovative Technology Administration
  - Research and Special Programs Administration
  - Saint Lawrence Seaway Development Corporation
  - Surface Transportation Board
  - Transportation Statistics Bureau
- Transportation Office
- Transportation Security Administration
- Transportation Statistics Bureau
- Travel and Tourism Administration
- Treasury Department
  - Alcohol and Tobacco Tax and Trade Bureau
  - Bureau of the Fiscal Service
  - Community Development Financial Institutions Fund
  - Comptroller of the Currency
  - Customs Service
  - Engraving and Printing Bureau
  - Financial Crimes Enforcement Network
  - Financial Research Office
  - Fiscal Service
  - Foreign Assets Control Office
  - Internal Revenue Service
  - International Investment Office
  - Monetary Offices
  - Public Debt Bureau
  - Thrift Supervision Office
  - United States Mint
- Twenty-First Century Workforce Commission
- U.S. Citizenship and Immigration Services
- U.S. Customs and Border Protection
- U.S. House of Representatives
- U.S. Immigration and Customs Enforcement
- U.S. Trade Deficit Review Commission
- U.S.-China Economic and Security Review Commission
- Uniformed Services University of the Health Sciences
- United States Enrichment Corporation
- United States Information Agency
- United States Institute of Peace
- United States Marshals Service
- United States Mint
- United States Sentencing Commission
- Utah Reclamation Mitigation and Conservation Commission
- Valles Caldera Trust
- Veterans Affairs Department
- Veterans Employment and Training Service
- Victims of Crime Office
- Wage and Hour Division
- Western Area Power Administration
- Women's Business Enterprise Interagency Committee
- Women's Progress Commemoration Commission
- Workers Compensation Programs Office

= = =

"As government expands, liberty contracts." —Ronald Reagan

"A government big enough to give you everything you want, is strong enough to take everything you have." – Thomas Jefferson

- 410 -

Immigration Trends (1820 – 2010)

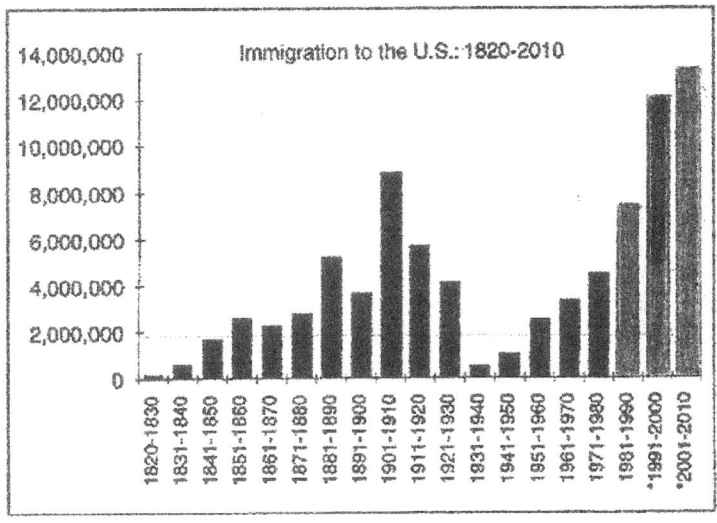

Source: U.S. Census Bureau

= = =

Components of U.S. Population Change

Source: www.census.gov   (As of October 29, 2015)

One birth every **8** seconds;

One death every **12** seconds;

One International Migrant (net) every **33** seconds;

Net gain of one person every **13** seconds.

<u>Top 10 U.S. Ancestry Groups (by number)</u>

Rank	Ancestry group	Number	Percent
1.	German	42,841,569	15.2%
2.	Irish	30,524,799	10.8
3.	African American	24,903,412	8.8
4.	English	24,509,692	8.7
5.	American	20,188,305	7.2
6.	Mexican	18,382,291	6.5
7.	Italian	15,638,348	5.6
8.	Polish	8,977,235	3.2
9.	French	8,309,666	3.0
10.	American Indian	7,876,568	2.8

Source: U.S. Census

= = =

From the beginning of this great nation, untold millions of legal immigrants have did the right thing . . . assimilated American culture, learned and used the U.S. common language English, and become contributors to society. Only to be followed in recent years by an ongoing wave of abusers and takers . . . those legal immigrants and illegal aliens refusing to assimilate American culture, refusing to learn and use our English language, and otherwise posing a burden and threat to our liberty and nation's survival.

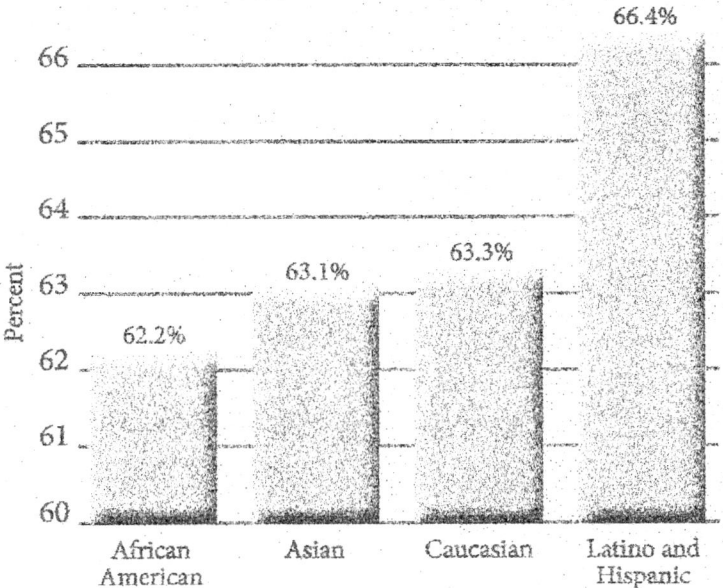

Labor Force Participation By Ethnic Group
Nationwide, July 2015

Source: Bureau of Labor Statistics

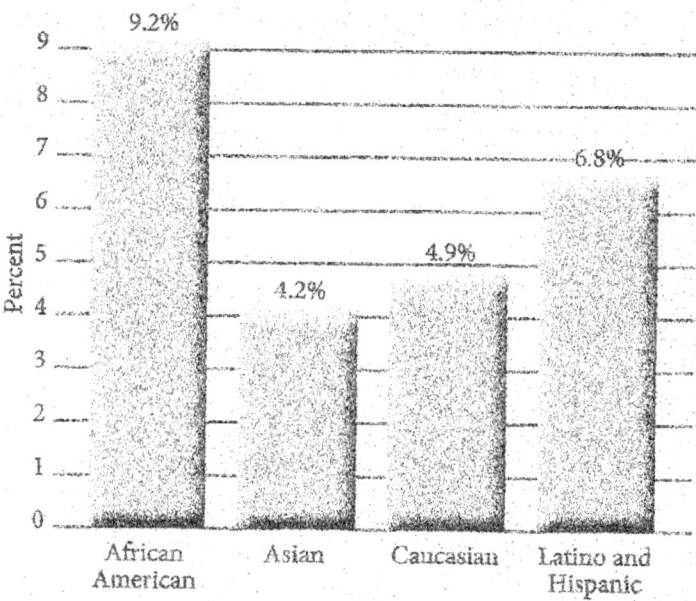

Unemployment By Ethnic Group
Nationwide, July 2015

Source: Bureau of Labor Statistics

Number of Overseas Travelers to the USA by Region of Residence
March 2015

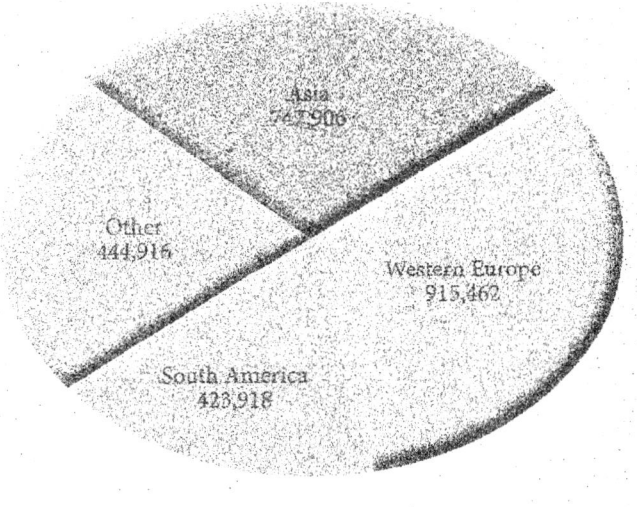

Source: U.S. Department of Commerce, ITA, National Travel and Tourism Office

Where Do Our Tax Dollars Go?

- 51% for Major Entitlements:
  - o 26.3% Medicare, Medicaid, & Other Health Care;
  - o 24.3% Social Security);
- 19% for Income Security & Other Benefits*;
- 17% for National Defense;
- 7% for Net Interest on Debt;
- 3% for Transportation;
- 1% for K-12 Education;
- 3% for All Other.

*Income Security: A range of programs providing cash or near-cash assistance (for instance: housing, nutrition, and energy assistance) to low-income persons, and benefits to certain retirees, persons with disabilities, and the unemployed. Housing assistance programs account for the largest share of discretionary funding in this function. And, major federal entitlement programs such as, unemployment insurance, trade adjustment assistance income support, food stamps, Temporary Assistance to Needy Families, foster care, and Supplemental Security Income. Federal and other retirement and disability programs make up about one third of the funds in this function.

Source: U.S. Office of Management and Budget (2014 Data)

= = =

After looking at the numbers above . . . you have a wild guess where the big cuts will have to come from when the "day of reckoning" on our nation's debt arrives?

How Did We Create an $18 Trillion "National Debt" and $97.5 Trillion of "Unfunded Liabilities"?

The answer to the above question is covered in considerable detail in various sections of this book, such as those titled: *"Our National Debt & Unfunded Liabilities," "The Bottomless Pit of Our Federal Government,"* and *"The Lifespan of our Constitutional Republic,"* etc. Detail that possibly can be put into some common-sense perspective by the following example . . . using a typical median-income U.S. family to demonstrate the irresponsible absurdity of our federal government's borrowing and spending behavior. So, in effect, here is how we got where we now are . . . and where we are headed:

Typical median-income U.S. family Borrowing and Spending Money like our Federal Government ("Example" Based on 2014 Budget)

Although our example-family's typical yearly-income only totals about **$52,000** . . . it spends about **$61,000** every year . . . which means it has to put about **$9,000** on their Credit Cards every year . . . despite already accumulating an unbearable debt of about **$311,000**. And, in likeness to our federal government . . . a sinking ship of unsustainable "debt and spending," taking our nation into a bottomless abyss of liberty and survival threatening disaster!

= = =

Sources: Congressional Budget Office; Treasury Dept.; Census Bureau.

Social Security Deficits are Permanent and Growing!

Despite all the political "BS" to the contrary, in 2010 Social Security started running out of money and began paying out $51 billion more in benefits than received in payroll taxes that year. And, without "reforms" (more taxes and less benefits) Social Security's deficits (spending more than received) will quadruple in less than 20 years. That point in time when its combined trust fund will be depleted!

= = =

Starting in January 2011, more than 10,000 Americans from the "baby boomers" generation began turning 65 "each day" — a pattern that will be continue for the next 19 years. "Boomers" are the 77 million Americans born during time frame of 1946 through 1965.

= = =

Sources: Congressional Budget Office, Office of Management and Budget, and U.S. Census Bureau.

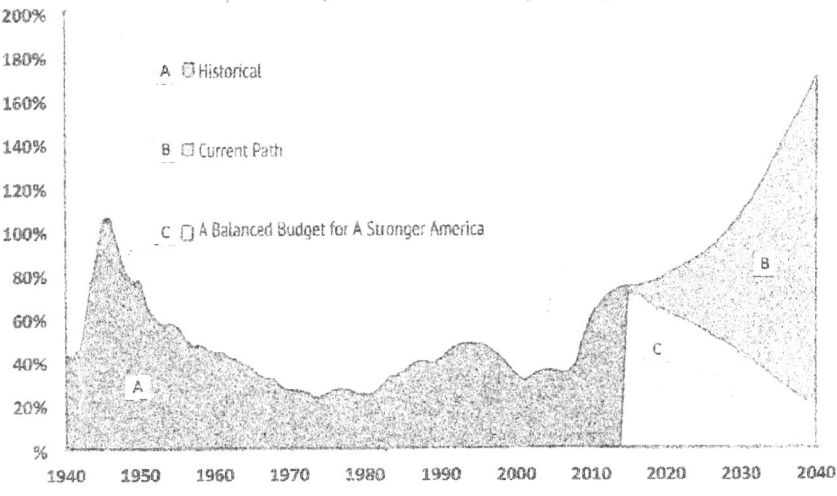

Source: CBO

= = =

In 1970, our U.S. Public Debt per Citizen was $6,783; in 2008, $2,110. A child's share born in 2016 will be about $42,759. At age 18 that share will be about $87,247. And, in 2045, at age 29, same child's share of our public debt will be about $163,452! What a shameful legacy to pass on to our children and future generations of Americans!

= = =

Sources: Congressional Budget Office (CBO);
Treasury Department; Census Bureau.

The Most Recent "Balanced" Federal Budget?
(Source: CBS News; Fox News; U.S. CBO)

Reportedly, the last "balanced" federal budgets were in fiscal years 1998, 1999, 2000, and 2001 — when Democrat Bill Clinton was president, and the Republicans controlled Congress. The Republican-controlled Congress approved the appropriations for each one of those years and Democratic President Bill Clinton signed them. When President Clinton governed with a Democrat-controlled Congress, in fiscal years 1994 and 1995, the federal government reportedly ran deficits of $203.2 billion and $163.9 billion respectively.

However, some have argued that President Clinton and Congress were not totally up-front about the nature of the reported balanced budgets. Critics claiming that, while the official numbers (which included "off-budget" items including the Social Security trust funds) did show surpluses for all four fiscal years of Clinton's second term . . . the "on-budget" totals alone showed a different view. That being, only the 1999 and 2000 fiscal years recorded on-budget surpluses. Therefore, over the years 1998 to 2001 the total surplus may have added up to only about $26 billion. And, furthermore, since most of the surplus was calculated from money flowing into the Social Security trust funds, the National Debt didn't actually get paid-down during the sum of these four years, but instead increased $280 billion or more.

= = =

The bottom line: "fuzzy numbers" are hard to track and determine accountability. No doubt just the way our out of control federal government has planned and wishes it to be!

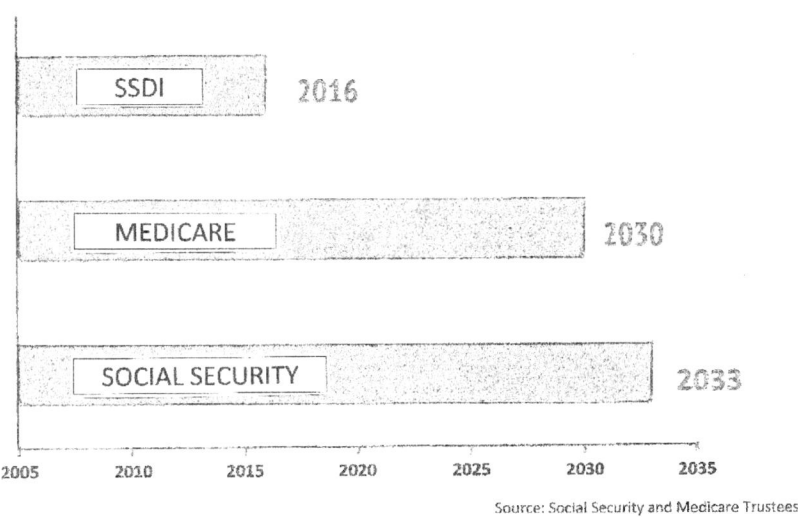

Source: Social Security and Medicare Trustees

= = =

Social Security and Medicare together accounted for 42 percent of Federal program expenditures in fiscal year 2014.

Social Security's Disability Insurance (SSDI) Trust Fund now faces an urgent threat of reserve depletion by 2016.

Medicare Hospital Insurance (HI) Trust Fund is projected to be depleted in 2030.

Trustees say Congress should address the financial challenges facing Social Security and Medicare as soon as possible.

= = =

Source: "A SUMMARY OF THE 2015 ANNUAL REPORTS" -

Social Security and Medicare Boards of Trustees.

"**Risk** more than others think is safe. **Care** more than others think is wise. **Dream** more than others think is practical. **Expect** more than others think is possible." –Claude Bissell

"It's not about time, it's about choices. How are you spending your choices?" –Beverly Adamo

"He who hunts for flowers will find flowers; and he who loves weeds will find weeds." – Henry Ward Beecher

"Never despair, but if you do, work on in despair."
Edmund Burke (1729 – 1797)

"Fear knocked at the door. Faith answered.
And lo, no one was there."
--Anonymous

www.ingramcontent.com/pod-product-compliance
Lightning Source LLC
Chambersburg PA
CBHW071325280526
45787CB00001B/2